Recipes from the Regional Cooks of Mexico

Books by Diana Kennedy

THE CUISINES OF MEXICO
THE TORTILLA BOOK
RECIPES FROM THE REGIONAL COOKS OF MEXICO

Drawings by Sidonie Coryn

NEW YORK, HAGERSTOWN, SAN FRANCISCO, LONDON

Recipes from the Regional Cooks of Mexico

DIANA KENNEDY

HARPER & ROW, PUBLISHERS

Designed by Gloria Adelson

Map by Bernhard H. Wagner

Library of Congress Cataloging in Publication Data

Kennedy, Diana.
   Recipes from the regional cooks of Mexico.
   1. Cookery, Mexican. I. Title.
TX716.M4K47 1978   641.5′972   78–4734
ISBN 0–06–012348–6

  79 80 81 82 10 9 8 7 6 5 4 3 2

I should like to dedicate this book to all the Mexican cooks, my friends, without whom none of my books would have been possible. I should also like it to be considered as a tribute, however modest, to some of the great names in Mexican gastronomy and to some little-known but wonderful cooks who are no longer with us but who taught or inspired me:

Agustin Aragón y Leyva
Salvador Novo
Jaime Saldívar
Josefina Velázquez de Leon
Victoriano, from Tlacotalpan
Chanita, from Pánuco
Fidel Loredo

Contents

Acknowledgments

There are so many people who have been involved with this book that the list seems endless, but I should particularly like to thank my wonderfully patient editor, Frances McCullough; Margery Tippie, my painstaking and equally patient copy editor; Gloria Adelson, the talented and enthusiastic designer who also designed *The Tortilla Book;* and Valerie Marchant, who helped me enormously by test cooking many of the recipes in New York.

I should like to express my thanks to the personnel of the National Mexican Tourist Council, especially Sr. Guillermo Moreno and Sr. Angel Palacio and their efficient helpers, for making my endless journeys throughout Mexico possible; and to Sra. Gloria Duval of the Secretaria de Turismo, whose introductions to cooks in the provinces helped me in my recipe gathering.

And last but not least, my sincere appreciation to my long-suffering hosts in Mexico who let me invade their homes and kitchens over very long periods: Eleanor and Robert Corkery, Deezie and Tom Catron, Lol Sloan, Sally and Armando Ayala, and Gladys and Jean Delmas.

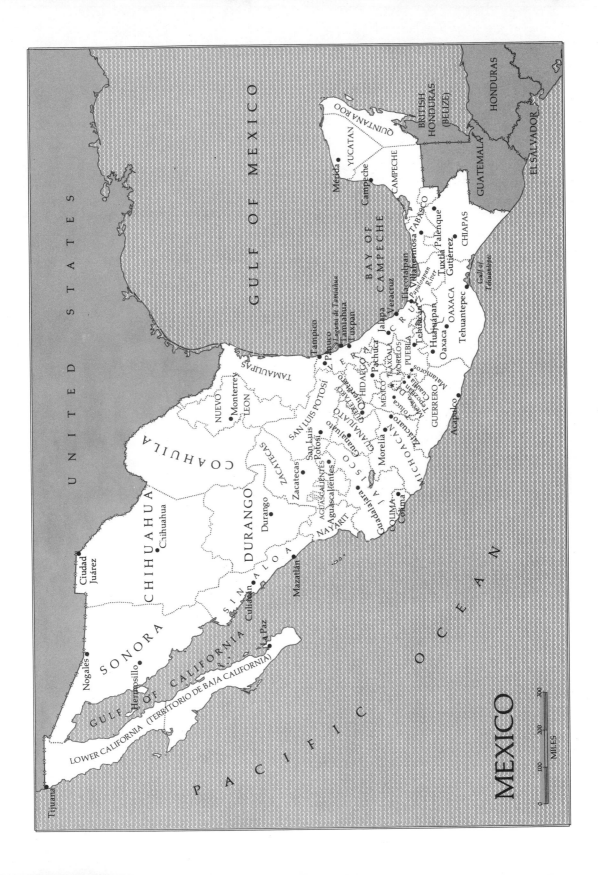

MEXICO

Introduction

While Mexican friends have chided me for not including all their favorite—sometimes obscure—regional recipes in *The Cuisines of Mexico*, when telling people in the United States or England what I am working on, I am almost always met with the astonished rejoinder, "What, more Mexican food? I didn't know there was any more!"

As soon as *The Cuisines of Mexico* was safely in print, I returned to Mexico for my yearly stay. I soon began to hear of cooks I had never met, places I had never visited, and food I had never eaten. And so the chase began all over again, up and down the country, into markets, kitchens, restaurants, and bakeries.

This is therefore—to anticipate the question—a collection of completely new recipes gathered during the past five years of wandering and learning—updating my palate so to speak. But my editor and I thought it only fair to include a few of the basic recipes indispensable to putting together a typical Mexican meal—tortillas, beans, rice, and a few of the more commonly used sauces. As I did in *Cuisines*, I have included sections on ingredients and cooking methods and equipment; these have been substantially revised, as my thoughts on and experiences with them have grown. There is a Guide to Vocabulary and Pronunciation to fit the framework of the new book, and I am happy to say that the Sources for Ingredients section is much larger than the ones in my previous books.

Who are the regional cooks and how do their recipes differ? Mexico is a huge country, stretching for almost two thousand miles along its northern border with the United States and two thousand miles from north to south. It has a fascinating history of many splendid ancient cultures, a rugged topography with breathtaking scenery, and a vastly diverse plant and animal life. It is these cultural and geographical considerations, rather than the more usually employed state divisions (created, of course, for political expediency), that are responsible for the wide differences in cooking methods and ingredients, differences I become increasingly aware of the more I travel.

Food had always played an important role in the ceremonial and ritual life of the pre-Hispanic cultures of Mexico—the Olmec, Maya, and Aztec—whose "great traditions" were either merged among themselves, lost, or took on new syncratic forms with the Spanish conquests. Though transformed and embellished in the convents during the Colonial period, with products and knowledge brought over from the Old World, the age-old culinary traditions, in their purest forms, have lingered on, still to be found among the "little folk traditions" in regional Mexico.

But things in Mexico are changing and changing fast, too fast for the majority of people to fully comprehend and thus conserve what is good and reject what is bad. Too much is being lost through the wild demographic explosion the country is experiencing. Primeval forests are being cut down, to be lost forever; reserves of plants, wildlife, fish, and crustaceans are dwindling rapidly, and along with them traditions, crafts, folklore, indigenous foods—and recipes. For this reason, perhaps presumptuously, I should like to think of my books as contributing toward the recording and preservation of an important aspect of Mexican life and culture.

In this book I have included recipes from some little-known but, to my mind, great regional cooks, whom I write about in the following pages. I am also dedicating it to them, as well as to some of the men and women who are no longer with us but who have contributed so much to keeping the great food traditions alive. Some of them were internationally known and acknowledged, others known to but a few outside their own villages. But they all inspired and helped me to understand their fascinating and complicated craft.

Last year I returned to Mexico to live, work, learn, and teach, and to create what I hope will become a small center that will embody all the ideas to which I am so deeply committed: conservation of land and water, preservation of past traditions, and an experiment in future living with nonpolluting systems, alternate sources of energy . . . my work is only just beginning.

Yes, there will be more books. There is still so much to learn and record about plants, herbs, rare foods—in fact, the wisdom of the past that can guide us into the future.

NOTES TO THE COOK

Those of you who have attended my classes or who are already familiar with my books *The Cuisines of Mexico* and *The Tortilla Book* know that I am always stressing the points that should be observed if you want to cook even the simplest, but authentic, Mexican dish. Don't just open the book for the first time as you light the stove. First read the material in the appendices (pages 217–77), the description of special ingredients and utensils and the places where these can be obtained, and then the section on authentic cooking methods. For this, with its strong peasant roots, is the *haute cuisine* of Mexico, and as much time and trouble should go into its preparation as into that of any intricate French dish. Read the recipes that you want to prepare and shop carefully a few days ahead. Unless substitutions are suggested, don't change the ingredients and expect to come out with the same result—for example, using canned instead of fresh tomatoes; those sweetish yellow onions when the sharp white ones are always called for; watery Florida avocados (all right for slicing and garnishing but not for making rich sauces or guacamole) instead of the creamy ones from California. Don't let me hear wails about not being able to get some of those special ingredients. If you give yourself enough time you can mail-order or ask friends in Texas or California to send you "CARE" packages; you can get together with other *aficionados* and cajole or bully your local supermarket manager into being more imaginative about the produce section. You will find that many of the larger food chains and small specialty stores are becoming more and more aware of the great and growing interest in ethnic foods—and the fact that Mexican food is "in" and here to stay. And if you have a garden or terrace, grow things. Seeds for chilies, though more difficult to grow as their character changes with soil and climate, are available, as are Mexican green tomatoes, *epazote,* and so forth. Don't forget to freeze, hoard, and stock up on the ingredients for some great Mexican food. I have even, in anticipation of Mexican salads, removed the seeds from pomegranates and frozen them; they remain juicy and crisp when defrosted.

Without suggesting that you get down on your hands and knees and grind chilies and corn on the *metate*, I have tried to observe traditional cooking methods. Obviously I can't try cooking the recipes in every type of pot and pan that might be used. Every pot and pan cooks its contents at a different speed and retains a different amount of heat, which will affect cooking time and the amount of liquid used. You will, therefore, have to watch carefully and compensate for differences you observe between the recipe directions and your results. If, for instance, there is more liquid in the pan than the recipe indicates just before the end of the cooking time, remove the lid, raise the flame, and reduce it quickly. If you don't like your food fatty—I have tried to avoid this, but a lot will depend on the meat you buy—then skim the sauce of extra fat. If I say "Fry the chicken with the spices over a high flame" and you find that the spices stick to the pan, lower the flame slightly, add a tablespoon or two of water (no more), scrape the pan well, and continue cooking. The spices have to be cooked at a concentrated point, and they have to season the chicken with a concentrated flavor.

As for heat retention, heavy enamel on metal pans, for example, will retain an enormous amount of heat, so you cannot cook in them with such a high flame as you can in, say, a Mexican *cazuela*. And remember always to calculate the cooking time from the moment the sauce or broth comes to a simmer or boil; that is the starting point.

Stick to the methods I suggest first time around, and then if you want to innovate do what suits you best—without expecting exactly the same result, of course. This reminds me of a recent cooking trip to San Diego. A group of women there had come down to Mexico to cook with me the summer before, and I had given them a few recipes from this book in advance. I found out on that San Diego trip that two of them had not only liked one of the recipes, a chicken dish, and cooked it again, but that the second time the classical French cook had not cooked the dish in a *cazuela* on top of the stove, as directed, but had put the chicken, in its sauce, into an ovenproof casserole, covered it with waxed paper and then foil, Jacques Pepin method, and baked it; the Mexican-Chinese cook, on the other hand, *had* cooked it in a Mexican *cazuela*—but safely and snugly embedded in her wok stove!

I hope that from out of all this we shall get a more discriminating public who will demand better Mexican food (we are not talking about Mexican-American food, which is an entirely different thing). At the moment the public is paying for an awful lot of stomachache and heartburn.

Appetizers

Sikil-P'ak Pumpkin-Seed Dip

According to the eminent Mayan ethnologist, Dr. Alfredo Barrera Vásquez, the correct name for this dish is *ha'-sikil-p'ak: ha'* (water), *sikil* (pumpkin or squash seed), and *p'ak* (tomato). It is a truly Mayan concoction, except for the addition of the coriander, which must have crept in later, and the substitution of chives, which very much resemble in taste and appearance the *cebollina* —a variety of the same plant—used so much in the cooking of Campeche and Yucatán.

    Sikil-p'ak is served in Yucatán today as a dip (horrible word!) with crisp-fried or toasted tortillas—and what a healthy dip it is, compared with those packaged soup and gummy cheese affairs that are guzzled endlessly at American cocktail parties. If you are feeling extravagant with your calories, you can eat it on top of *pimes*, piled with the delicious pork pieces called Lomitos (see page 47).

(continued)

Most cooks will tell you that the tomatoes should be boiled, but some prefer the flavor of them broiled; you may, therefore, do as you like about it. The chili is optional, although, as I have said many times before, the *chile habanero* has an enticing flavor of its own.

In Yucatán the tiniest, unshelled pumpkin seed, locally called *chinchilla,* is used; it is about ½ inch long and ¼ inch wide. However, I have made this dish with practically every squash seed I have come across, and providing you toast them very well indeed and grind them very fine, until they are almost pulverized, they all taste more or less the same.

Sikil-p'ak can be made ahead of time and will keep for a few days, although the fresh coriander taste does suffer a little.

> *1¼ cups raw, unhulled pumpkin seeds*
> *1 chile habanero or any fresh, hot green chili*
> *2 medium tomatoes (about 12 ounces)*
> *1½ teaspoons salt, or to taste*
> *2 heaped tablespoons chopped coriander leaves*
> *2 heaped tablespoons chopped chives*

Heat a thick frying pan or *comal* and toast the seeds, turning them constantly, until the hulls are well browned and crisp (some types of seeds will start to pop open). Set them aside to cool off. Meanwhile, toast the chili, turning it from time to time until it is blistered and black-brown in spots.

Cover the tomatoes with boiling water and simmer until soft—about 15 minutes, depending on size and compactness. Drain, skin, and set aside to cool. (If you wish to broil them instead, see page 262.)

Using an electric coffee/spice grinder, grind the toasted seeds, together with the salt, to a coarse powder. Transfer to a small serving bowl. Stir the tomatoes into the ground pumpkin seeds, together with the coriander, chives, and whole chili (if you prefer a more *picante* dish, blend the chili with the tomatoes before mixing them with the seeds).

Serve it at room temperature, as a dip.

The mixture should have the consistency of mayonnaise. If it is too thick, you may have to add a little water to dilute it.

About 1½ cups

Guacamole Avocado Dip

The word *guacamole* comes from the Nahuatl words for "avocado" *(ahuacatl)* and "mixture," or "concoction" *(molli)*—and what a beautiful "concoction" *guacamole* is, pale green sparked with the coriander's darker green and the red of the tomato. Its beauty is definitely enhanced if it is served in the *molcajete* in which it has been made and where it rightfully belongs. (Never, *never* use a blender to turn it into one of those smooth, homogeneous messes!) *Guacamole* can contain a seemingly infinite variety of ingredients, some of which—garlic, garlic powder, lemon juice, and Tabasco—I consider most inappropriate. I prefer the delightful rustic version below.

Guacamole is usually eaten in Mexico at the beginning of a meal with a pile of hot, freshly made tortillas and other *botanas* (snacks), like crisp pork skins *(chicharrón)* or little pieces of crispy pork *(carnitas)*. It will also often accompany a plate of tacos. It is so delicate that it is best eaten the moment it is prepared. There are many suggestions for keeping it—covering it airtight, leaving the pit in, and so forth—but they will only help for a brief time; almost immediately the delicate green will darken and the fresh, wonderful flavor will be lost.

> ¼ *small onion, finely chopped*
> 2 *chiles serranos or any other fresh, hot green chilies, finely chopped*
> 4 *large sprigs fresh coriander, or to taste, leaves only*
> ¼ *teaspoon salt, or to taste*
> 2 *avocados*
> 1 *large tomato (about ½ pound), peeled and chopped*

THE GARNISH

> ¼ *small onion, finely chopped*
> 6 *sprigs coriander, leaves only, roughly chopped*

In a *molcajete,* or using a regular pestle and mortar, grind the onion, chilies, coriander, and salt together until almost smooth.

Cut the avocados in half. Remove the pit, scoop out the flesh with a wooden spoon, and mash roughly into the ingredients in the *molcajete.* Mix well together to make sure that the ingredients are thoroughly incorporated, then stir in the chopped tomato. Adjust the salt, if necessary. Sprinkle with the onion and coriander, and serve immediately.

About 1¾ to 2 cups

Cacahuates Enchilados Peanuts with Chili Powder

These fiery little snacks invariably turn up on the table in a Mexican bar, providing a great incentive to drink more tequila and then tone it all down by sucking on those half-moon wedges of lime. But if you eat too many of them or make them too *picante,* you may as well forget about eating carefully prepared, delicate foods; your palate can easily be burned out. This is what too often happens in Texan and other southern, so-called Mexican restaurants. Before you even order, they put out, "free" of charge, dreadful little bowls of searing sauces and piles of *"tostada* chips." Perhaps with good reason: you won't be able to taste what follows.

The ordinary commercial chili powder sold in the United States is not sharp enough for this or the following recipe. Use a powder of *chile piquin, chile de árbol,* or cayenne.

> *1 teaspoon peanut or safflower oil*
> *1 cup unsalted peanuts, measured shelled, with*
>   *brown papery skins removed*
> *10 small cloves garlic, peeled*
> *1 to 1½ teaspoons chili powder (see note above), or to taste*
> *1 teaspoon salt, or to taste*

In a frying pan just large enough to accommodate the peanuts in one layer, heat the oil to smoking point. Add the peanuts and garlic cloves and fry for about 2 minutes, turning them over constantly. Lower the flame a little, add the chili powder and salt, and cook for a minute or two longer, stirring constantly; take care that the chili powder does not burn.

Set aside to cool before serving with drinks.

About 1 cup

Mariscos a la Marinera Seafood Cocktail

This cocktail can be prepared with any seafood: raw clams or scallops, abalone, conch, or cooked shrimps. And how much fresher and crunchier a cocktail it is than the usual U.S. restaurant version of rubbery shrimps drowned in a commercially made tomato sauce. It is perhaps best eaten immediately after it is prepared, but if you do want to prepare it ahead, don't let it stand for more than two hours or the ingredients will lose their fresh flavor and crispness. Naturally, it should not be so cold that the flavor is lost and the oil congealed.

I prefer to serve this with hot, freshly made tortillas (see page 246), or with dried tortillas, toasted until crisp on a *comal* or in the oven.

> 3 dozen large raw clams or scallops or medium-sized
>   cooked shrimps
> ½ cup fresh lime juice
> 2 medium tomatoes (about 12 ounces), unpeeled,
>   chopped into small cubes
> 1 small onion, finely chopped
> 1 large avocado, peeled and cut into cubes
> 3 to 4 chiles serranos or any fresh, hot green chilies, finely
>   chopped
> 2 heaped tablespoons finely chopped coriander leaves
> 3 tablespoons olive oil
> Salt and freshly ground pepper to taste

If you are using clams, open them or have them opened for you, saving both the clams and their juice. If you are using scallops, let them marinate in the lime juice for an hour or so first. Combine the clams (and their liquid) or other seafood with the rest of the ingredients, adjust the seasoning, and serve cold.

6 servings

Tostaditas Enchiladas Tortilla Crisps with Chili Powder

> *6 tablespoons peanut or safflower oil*
> *1 cup stale tortilla pieces (each ½-inch square)*
> *1 teaspoon chili powder (see note page 8), or to taste*
> *½ teaspoon salt, or to taste*

Heat the oil to the smoking point, then add the tortilla pieces and fry them, turning them over constantly, until they are quite crisp. Drain off the surplus oil, then lower the flame, add the chili powder and salt, and cook, stirring constantly—take care not to burn the chili powder—for a minute or so longer.

Set aside to cool before serving with drinks.

About 1 cup

Queso Flameado "Flamed" Cheese

This is the Mexican version of the Swiss cheese fondue—not as delicate, of course, but robust and very well complemented by a *picante* tomato sauce and a stack of wheat-flour tortillas.

In and around Guadalajara this is called *queso fundido* (melted cheese), but in the northern states, where it is a favorite first course in restaurants specializing in broiled meats, it is called *queso flameado* or *queso asado* (roasted or broiled cheese); the cheese is melted in a shallow metal dish over the hot embers of the constantly burning wood fire and brought sizzling to the table.

Queso flameado can be served either plain or with cooked and crumbled *chorizo* sprinkled all over it. A *picante* tomato or green tomato sauce is put on the table, along with a stack of wheat-flour tortillas, so that each one can help himself, *al gusto*. The cheese can be served either in individual dishes or one large one. Allow 3 wheat-flour tortillas (page 250) per person; for your tomato sauce, see Salsa Ranchera (page 160), Salsa de Tomate Verde (page 161), or Salsa Mexicana Cruda(page 158).

> *12 to 18 ounces cheese (mild Cheddar or jack)*
> *1½ dozen wheat-flour tortillas (see page 250)*

Slice the cheese fairly thin and place in two layers in a shallow, flameproof dish. Melt the cheese either on top of the stove or in the oven. Heat the tortillas and serve immediately, with the sauce of your choice.

6 servings

Ostiones Pimentados Pepper Oysters

Sr. Angel Delgado (restaurante Las Diligencias, Tampico)

When trying out and writing up a recipe like this, I can hear my own and other voices saying, "What a crime . . . good oysters are best raw . . ." etc. Yes, but this does make an interestingly tasty snack with drinks or served, atypically, as a first course with wafer-thin black bread. Come to think of it, not everyone likes raw oysters, while they will happily consume a can of smoked ones. Enough of excuses . . .

> *4 dozen oysters, removed from shells and liquid reserved*
> *2 teaspoons whole peppercorns*
> *½ teaspoon salt, or to taste*
> *6 cloves garlic*
> *1 tablespoon lime juice, more if desired*
> *2 tablespoons olive oil*
> *1 bay leaf (2 to 3 in Mexico)*

Heat the liquid from the oysters to the simmering point, then add the oysters and poach for 2 to 3 minutes, or until the edges start to curl up. Drain the oysters, reserving the broth.

Pound the peppercorns in a *molcajete* or mortar with the salt until finely ground. Pound in the garlic and gradually add the lime juice. Last of all, add about 3 tablespoons of the reserved oyster broth. Mix well.

Heat the olive oil in a saucepan. Add the bay leaf and the peppercorn mixture and cook over a high flame for about 3 minutes, stirring constantly. Remove the pan from the flame and add the oysters. Adjust the seasoning, then add a squeeze of lime juice and a little of the oyster liquid if desired.

Set aside to cool and serve as suggested above, or leave to season overnight.

6 to 8 servings

Caviar de Chapala

The name speaks for itself. Sometimes it is called *caviar autóctono* ("indigenous" caviar), as it is made from the roe of fish from Lake Chapala. When I
first ate it, it was made from carp roe, but in fact you could substitute cod or
any less expensive roe—but not shad, which costs the earth. It is served as an
appetizer with hot tortillas and little dishes of finely chopped onion, *chile
serrano,* fresh coriander, and green (unripe) tomatoes, so that each person can
make a taco, seasoning it *al gusto.*

> *Salt*
> 1 *pound carp or cod roe*
> ¼ *cup peanut or olive oil*
> 1 *medium tomato (about 6 ounces), chopped*
> ¼ *small onion, finely chopped*
> 1 *clove garlic, peeled and finely chopped*

THE GARNISHES

> ½ *cup finely chopped onion*
> ⅓ *cup finely chopped green, unripe tomatoes*
> ⅓ *cup finely chopped coriander leaves*
> ⅓ *cup finely chopped* chiles serranos *or any other fresh, hot
>   green chilies*

Put a tablespoon of salt and enough water to cover the roe in a shallow pan
and bring to the simmering point. Add the roe and let it simmer for not more
than 10 minutes, then remove and drain. When it is cool enough to handle,
remove the skin and crumble the roe.

Heat the oil in a heavy pan. Add the tomato, onion, and garlic and fry over
a fairly high flame, stirring from time to time and scraping the bottom of the
pan, until the onion is soft and the mixture almost dry. Add the crumbled roe
and 1 teaspoon of salt and continue frying the mixture over a medium flame,
turning it over constantly, until dry and crumbly.

Serve hot, accompanied by the onion and the other finely chopped ingredients, in small separate bowls, and a pile of hot tortillas.

6 servings

Salbutes Puffed Tortillas from Yucatán

Salbutes are one of the favorite *antojitos* (appetizers) of the Yucatán peninsula. Small corn tortillas are fried in lard so that they puff up; then they are
lavishly layered with lettuce, sweet pepper, onion, and tomato, all well seasoned with salt and pepper, and topped, finally, with shredded chicken or
turkey that has been seasoned, according to tradition, with *achiote* and cooked
in a pit barbecue—a *pib,* in Yucatán. A little hot, fresh chili can be added, too,
if you like a bite to it all. Of course, any shredded meat could be substituted.

In the main market of Campeche, the little food stands sell black *salbutes*
called *negritos* (lit., "little black ones"), since the dough has been blackened
with bean paste.

This is pan-to-mouth food that has to be served immediately, or as soon as
it cools down enough to bite into.

> *2 cups Quaker* masa harina *or ½ pound prepared* masa
> *2 tablespoons all-purpose flour*
> *½ teaspoon salt, or to taste*
> *¾ cup water, approximately (optional)*
> *Vegetable oil for frying*

THE GARNISH

> *Shredded lettuce or cabbage*
> *Thinly sliced tomatoes*
> *Sliced onion*
> *Sliced sweet green pepper*
> *Shredded chicken or turkey*

Mix the dry ingredients together (if you are using *masa harina*). Add the
water, all at once, and mix to a soft dough. Set aside for 5 minutes. (If you are
using prepared *masa,* then just work in the all-purpose flour and salt; you
won't need the water.)

Heat a griddle or *comal.* In a small frying pan, heat the oil, which should
be at least ½ inch in depth. While it is heating, take a small ball of the dough,
about 1 inch in diameter, and press it out (see pages 246–49) into a tortilla
3½ to 4 inches in diameter. Cook the tortilla, on the griddle, very lightly on

both sides—until the dough is *just* drying out but does *not* brown. Immediately put it into the hot oil. It should puff up instantaneously, but only if you have cooked it first to the right degree. Leave it for 1 minute, to fry the underside to a golden brown, then turn it carefully, without puncturing it, and fry the second side until golden brown and *just* crisp. Remove from the oil and drain on paper toweling. Top with the garnishes and serve hot.

Repeat until all the tortilla dough is used up, cooking only one tortilla at a time. The frying operation should take 2 minutes or even less. Fill and serve each *salbute* as soon as possible.

6 to 8 servings

Chicharrón en Escabeche Pickled Pork Rind

On a recent visit to Tehuacán in Puebla, I was taken by friends who lived there to visit a grand old lady who had a great reputation as a cook. She lived in a large Porfiriano house in a sad state of disrepair, but the family portraits and faded furniture spoke of a bygone elegance. Most of the dishes she prepared reflected her upbringing in Alvarado by Andalusian parents, so it surprised me that this recipe, Mexican through and through, was one of her favorites.

Chicharrón, or crisp-fried pork skin, is without doubt the great *antojito* of all Mexico. Great, golden-brown sheets of it are to be found in practically every marketplace throughout the Republic. When a pig is killed, the skin is put to dry in the sun for about twelve hours. It is then plunged into a cauldron of boiling lard and fried until it is just beginning to get crisp and brown. It is taken out and immediately put back into another cauldron, into lard that has been heated to an even higher temperature, where it puffs up and acquires its typical honeycomb effect. Small carts parading up and down the parks on a Sunday sell it in enormous quantities, and it is a common sight to see whole families wandering along, munching on huge pieces of *chicharrón* liberally sprinkled with hot chili powder and lime juice.

Chicharrón can be served as a main dish, cooked and softened in green sauce, or ground fine and stuffed into little maize cakes called *tortas.* It is perhaps more often served, broken into small pieces, with a bowl of *guaca-*

mole and some hot tortillas as a hearty forerunner to a large *comida,* the day's main meal.

To my mind, *chicharrón en escabeche* is best served as soon as it has cooled off, but it will keep indefinitely in the refrigerator (although it congeals and must be brought up to room temperature before serving).

When I cooked this recently in California I found that the *chicharrón* tended to be much harder—it had been fried rather a long time, but no doubt for "shelf life" or whatever that horrible expression is. It took at least 10 minutes before it softened and absorbed about 1½ cups vinegar.

> ¼ *cup peanut or safflower oil*
> 2 *medium purple onions, thickly sliced*
> 6 *cloves garlic, peeled and left whole*
> ½ *pound* chicharrón *(see page 223), the thinner the*
>   *better*
> 2 *chiles jalapeños en escabeche*
> 1 to 1½ *cups red wine vinegar*
> ½ *teaspoon oregano*
> ⅛ *teaspoon thyme*
> ½ *teaspoon salt, or to taste*
>   *Freshly ground pepper*
> 1 *avocado, peeled and sliced*

Heat the oil to the smoking point, then lower the flame and gently sauté the onion and garlic without browning for about 2 minutes. Meanwhile, break the *chicharrón* into pieces about 2 inches square and cut the chilies into thin slices. Add the vinegar, oregano, thyme, salt, and pepper to the pan and bring to a boil. Add the *chicharrón* pieces and chilies and cook over a fairly high heat, stirring constantly, until the *chicharrón* has softened and absorbed almost all the vinegar—about 5 minutes. Set aside to cool, then serve, garnished with slices of avocado.

6 servings

Salpicón de Carne Yucatecan Shredded Meat

In Tampico, on the Gulf Coast, one is offered tacos of *salpicón de jaiba*, shredded crabmeat cooked with onion, chilies, and coriander. Further down the coast, along the Lagoon of Tamiahua, the *salpicón* would be a more complicated one, of shredded fish with olives, raisins, and capers, called *saragalla*. But in Yucatán the most common *salpicón* is made of shredded venison that has first been cooked in a pit barbecue called a *pib*. It is then mixed with Seville orange juice and very finely chopped radishes and coriander to make a fresh, crisp filling for tacos on a hot day.

Actually, any meat can be used. It would, in fact, make an interesting way of using up leftover roast.

> *1 cup cooked and shredded meat*
> *½ cup Seville orange juice or substitute (see page 243)*
> *⅔ cup very finely chopped radish*
> *3 tablespoons very finely chopped coriander leaves*
> *2 teaspoons salt, or to taste*

Mix all the ingredients together and let them season for about half an hour before serving.

This *salpicón* is, of course, served cold with a pile of freshly made tortillas (see page 246).

6 servings

Soups

Caldo Michi Fish Soup

Sra. Clara Zabalza de García (Guadalajara)

Two of the largest lakes in Mexico are Pátzcuaro, in the state of Michoacán, and Chapala, in the neighboring state of Jalisco. Both have their own versions of a fish and vegetable soup called *caldo michi* (*caldo* means "broth" and *michi,* "fish," in the language of the Tarascan Indians) and made with fish from the lakes—catfish, carp, or the unique little *pescado blanco* (white fish), with its sharply pointed head and transparent flesh with wide silver stripe down each side.

Usually the whole fish is used because the gelatinous quality of the head adds substance to the broth (leave it out if you can't bear the thought, but do not skin or bone the fish slices). For *caldo michi,* do not first make a broth using the heads, as you would for most fish stews. I have tried it and it doesn't seem to work—perhaps because, with notable exceptions, freshwater fish of this

17

type do not have a particularly fine flavor. Chicken broth is used locally.

Out of many recipes given to me for *caldo michi*, I have chosen that of Señora García. I like the flavor of her soup much better, and in talking to her about the regional food I've found she has a great respect both for traditional cooking methods and for fresh ingredients. Every year she pickles all her own chilies in homemade pineapple vinegar, and she takes great joy in feeding her large family with carefully cooked, almost elaborate Mexican dishes.

As a substitute for *frutas en vinagre*, I suggest you put in a couple of slices of lime and a few sour pickles.

> 2½ *pounds whole catfish or carp*
>   *Salt and freshly ground pepper to taste*
> ¼ *cup peanut or safflower oil*
> 1 *large tomato (about 10 ounces), skinned and sliced*
> 1 *medium white onion, thinly sliced*
> 3 *cloves garlic, peeled and left whole*
> 8 *cups chicken broth*
> 3 *medium carrots (about 4 ounces), scraped and sliced*
> 2 *zucchini (about 6 ounces), trimmed and cut into rounds*
> ¼ *heaped teaspoon oregano*
> 3 chiles jalapeños en escabeche, *roughly chopped*
> ⅔ *cup loosely packed* frutas en vinagre *(see note above) or*
>   *an equivalent amount of sour pickles plus 2 slices*
>   *lime*
> 6 *sprigs fresh coriander, leaves only, roughly chopped*

Rinse and dry the fish well. Cut the body into 1-inch slices and the head, if used, into four pieces. Season with salt and freshly ground pepper.

Heat the oil in a heavy pan and fry the fish pieces very lightly; the flesh should just turn opaque. Remove and set aside.

In the same oil, fry the tomato, onion, and garlic together until the onion is soft and the mixture has a saucelike consistency. Add the broth, carrots, zucchini, oregano, chilies, and *frutas en vinagre* (or substitutes) to the pan and cook until the vegetables are just tender, about 20 minutes. Add the fish pieces and simmer until the flesh flakes easily from the bone—about 10 minutes.

Remove the pan from the flame and add the chopped coriander. Serve the soup accompanied by freshly made tortillas (see page 246).

6 servings

Caldo de Habas Dried Fava Bean Soup

Sra. Maria Elena Lara (restaurante Los Tres Migueles,
Mexico City)

This is quite the most delicious version of dried fava bean soup that I have ever eaten. Even those who say they can't stand coriander leaves will eat them in this soup—providing you don't tell them they are in it. Actually, this is a Lenten dish in Mexico, and a friend of mine there was almost shocked when I served it to her on a cold, rainy summer day.

Cooking time varies enormously, depending, of course, on how old the beans are and their density, which varies between those grown in the United States and those grown in Mexico. Be sure to buy the peeled beans. There are some unpeeled ones on the market that take forever to cook—and then you have the messy business of removing the skins.

This soup keeps very well and freezes successfully, but since it will have thickened up considerably by the day after it is cooked, it will have to be diluted with water.

> ½ *pound dried, peeled yellow fava beans*
> 2 *tablespoons peanut or safflower oil*
> 1 *small onion, roughly chopped*
> 2 *cloves garlic, peeled and chopped*
> 1 *medium tomato (about 6 ounces), peeled and chopped*
> 10 *cups hot water, approximately*
> 6 *sprigs fresh coriander, leaves only, roughly chopped*
> 2 *teaspoons salt, or to taste*

THE GARNISH

> 6 *tablespoons fruity olive oil*
> 2 chiles pasillas, *fried and crumbled (see page 260)*

Rinse the beans well, picking out any loose pieces of skin or fiber.

Heat the oil until smoking and fry the beans, together with the onion and garlic, until they are lightly browned and the onion and garlic are translucent. Add the tomato and fry over a high flame, stirring constantly, until the mixture is almost dry—about 3 minutes. Add the water, coriander, and salt and let the soup cook over a low flame until the beans are mushy and almost disintegrated —about 3½ hours (see note above).

Serve each bowl with a tablespoon of the olive oil and some crumbled *chile pasilla* on top.

6 servings

Consomé de Camarón Seco Dried Shrimp Consommé

Sra. Clara Zabalza de García (Guadalajara)

This is a wonderfully strong-flavored, slightly *picante* soup. Señora García says that she often serves small cups of it just before a meal of Caldo Michi (see page 17). It is great for cold days, to end a long night, or to pep up a dull low-calorie diet.

Try and find the Mexican dried shrimps that have the skin and tail still on. Although they are rather laborious to clean, the soup will have a much better flavor. The quality of these varies enormously, and since they are expensive in any case, choose them carefully. Avoid ones that are very pale in color and powdery, and whose packages include lots of broken pieces at the bottom. Some are packed with the head included—in which case use 12 ounces. If a source for Mexican shrimps is not readily available, then buy the cleaned ones that are sold in Japanese and Chinese groceries—you will need to use 10 ounces of those for this recipe.

If you cannot find the round *cascabel* and *mulato* chilies, then an acceptable substitute would be *guajillos* and *pasillas,* but the flavor will not be as good.

> *8 ounces dried shrimps (see note above)*
> *4 to 5 cups water, approximately*
> *6* **chiles cascabel** *or 4* guajillos *(see note above)*
> *1* **chile mulato** *or 2* pasillas *(see note above)*
> *1* **clove garlic, peeled and left whole**

THE GARNISH

> *Roughly chopped coriander leaves*
> *Finely chopped onion*
> *Lime quarters*

Cover the shrimps, uncleaned, with 2 cups of the water and bring them to a simmer. Cook for 5 minutes, them remove from the flame and set them aside to soak for 5 minutes longer—no more, as the shrimps soon lose their flavor. Drain the shrimps and reserve the cooking water.

Remove the stalks from the chilies and veins and seeds from half of them (if using *guajillos* and *pasillas,* remove veins and seeds from the *guajillos* and leave those of the *pasillas*). Put them into a saucepan, cover with water, and simmer for about 5 minutes, or until soft (time varies, depending on how dry the chilies are). Remove from the flame and set aside to soak for about 5 minutes longer. Drain, discard the water in which they were cooked, and transfer to a blender jar with 1 cup of fresh water and the garlic. Blend until smooth. Pass through a fine sieve or food mill and set aside.

Remove the legs, tails, heads (if present), and as much of the skin of the shrimp as possible and discard. Divide the cleaned shrimp in two equal parts. Roughly break up or chop one-half and reserve, then transfer the other half to the blender jar, together with the water in which they were cooked. Blend as smooth as possible.

Put the chili sauce and the blended shrimps into a heavy saucepan, bring to a simmer, and cook, stirring all the time and scraping the bottom of the pan, for about 3 minutes. Add 1 more cup of the water, bring back to the simmering point, and continue cooking over a low flame for about 5 minutes. Add the shrimp pieces and continue cooking for 5 minutes, no longer. It should be a rather thick soup, but dilute if necessary.

Serve in small cups and pass the garnishes separately.

6 servings

Sopa de Pan Bread Soup

Señora María (Casa Blom, San Cristóbal de las Casas, Chiapas)

There are many versions of this recipe among the old families of Spanish origin. In Chiapas it is always prepared for fiestas, and was probably a Lenten dish until the chicken broth crept in.

French bread in the United States tends to soften very quickly, so if possible use sourdough, which has a tougher crumb. So that it will not absorb too much fat when frying, dry the bread out in the oven first.

> *4 cups stale French-type bread cubes, preferably*
>   *sourdough (see note above)*
> *½ cup peanut or safflower oil, more if necessary*
> *8 tablespoons (1 stick) sweet butter*
> *6 cups chicken broth*
> *4 ounces green beans, trimmed and cut into thirds*
> *4 ounces carrots, scraped and thinly sliced*
> *⅛ teaspoon thyme*
>   *Salt to taste*
> *1 two-inch stick cinnamon*
> *2 whole cloves*
> *10 peppercorns*
> *2 whole allspice*
>   *Large pinch saffron*
> *½ pound potatoes, peeled and cut into ½-inch slices*
> *2 medium plantains (about 1 pound), peeled, quartered,*
>   *and cut into 3-inch lengths*
> *1 pound tomatoes, peeled and thickly sliced*
> *1 large onion, thinly sliced*
> *2 cloves garlic, peeled and thinly sliced*
> *4 hard-cooked eggs, sliced*

Preheat the oven to 300 degrees.

Place the bread cubes on a baking sheet in one layer and bake until they are crisp on the outside but not dried all the way through—20 to 30 minutes.

Heat some of the oil until it smokes, then lower the flame and melt a portion of the butter in it. Fry the bread cubes lightly until golden brown, adding more oil and butter as necessary (if you add it all at once, the bread cubes will absorb it and become soggy). Drain and set aside, reserving the oil in the pan.

Heat the chicken broth, and when it comes to a boil, add the beans and carrots and simmer until just tender—from 10 to 15 minutes. Drain the vegetables and set aside. Add the thyme, salt, and spices to the broth and simmer for about 10 minutes. Strain and reserve the broth—there should be about 5 cups.

Reheat the oil in which the bread was fried, adding about ½ cup more as necessary, and fry the sliced potatoes on both sides until well browned; remove and drain. In the same oil, fry the plantain slices until golden brown; remove and drain. Fry the sliced tomatoes, onion, and garlic together until soft, then remove and set aside.

Preheat the oven to 350 degrees. Grease an ovenproof dish, ideally 8½ × 13½ × 2 inches. Spread alternate layers of the vegetable and tomato mixture in the dish. Cover with the bread cubes and top with the slices of egg. Pour the broth over and bake for about 15 minutes.

Serve hot, in bowls.

6 servings

Sopa Ranchera "Farmhouse" Soup

This is a hearty, filling soup that has all sorts of interesting textures and flavors. Some of the ingredients may not be available; they can be left out or substitutes made with whatever other vegetables or herbs are available. Use it as a guide for a similar soup, using what is fresh in local markets or garden.

> *1½ tablespoons sweet butter*
> *1½ tablespoons peanut or safflower oil*
> *1 small white onion, thinly sliced*
> *2 cloves garlic, peeled and finely chopped*
> *1½ cups fresh corn kernels*
> *¼ teaspoon salt, or to taste*
> *1½ cups finely diced zucchini*
> *1½ cups squash blossoms, cleaned and roughly chopped (optional)*
> *6 cups light chicken broth*
> *2 sprigs epazote*
> *2 chiles poblanos, charred and peeled (see page 260) and cut into small squares, or canned, peeled green chilies*

THE GARNISH

> *3 ounces queso fresco or brick Muenster, cut into cubes*
> *6 tablespoons sour cream*

Melt the butter with the oil in a heavy saucepan, then add the onion, garlic, and corn kernels. Season with the salt, then cover the pan and cook over medium heat, stirring from time to time, for about 5 minutes. Add the squash, chopped flowers, *epazote*, chicken broth, and chili squares and cook over a low flame until all the ingredients are tender—about 20 minutes.

Adjust the seasoning and serve in soup bowls, putting a few cubes of the cheese in first and a spoonful of the cream on top.

6 servings

Sopa de Fideo Aguada Vermicelli in Tomato Broth

This soup turns up predictably four days out of seven on the Mexican dinner table; it is both economical and easy to prepare. Because it is so popular and I am being asked constantly for a recipe, I have included it. But it's not one of my own favorites.

The soup thickens considerably as it stands, so it may have to be thinned down with more stock or water if you make it ahead.

> 3 to 4 *tablespoons chicken fat or peanut or safflower oil*
> 4 *ounces very fine vermicelli*
> ¾ *pound very ripe tomatoes*
> 1 *clove garlic, peeled and roughly chopped*
> ¼ *medium onion, roughly chopped*
> 3 *cups chicken broth plus 4 cups water, or 7 cups water*
>   *and 2 chicken bouillon cubes*
> 2 *sprigs Italian parsley*

Heat the fat until it smokes, add the whole bundles of vermicelli without breaking them up, and fry until a deep golden brown, stirring all the time. Drain off excess fat, leaving about 2 tablespoons in the pan.

Blend the unpeeled tomatoes with the garlic and onion until smooth. Add to the fried vermicelli and continue cooking over a very high flame, stirring and scraping the bottom of the pan, until the mixture is almost dry. Add the broth, water, and/or bouillon cubes and the parsley and bring to a boil. Lower the flame and simmer until the pasta is *soft.* Adjust the seasoning. (It should take about 20 minutes to cook and season well.)

6 servings

Sopa de Lentejas Estilo Querétaro Lentil Soup, Querétaro Style

Obdulia and AnaMaría Vega (Querétaro)

When I rented a house last summer, I was delighted to find that the maids that came with it were from Querétaro. They loved to cook their simple peasant dishes for me, and this is one of them.

If fresh *nopales* are not available, then leave them out, unless you can find them canned in brine and not in vinegar. Cooking time varies depending, of course, on how dry the lentils are, or whether they were grown in the United States or Mexico. The Mexican lentils seem to have a denser consistency and thus thicken the soup more. If you do not use the *nopales*, then increase the amount of lentils to 6 ounces.

Dilute the soup with water or chicken broth if it thickens too much.

> ¼ *pound (½ cup) lentils (see note above)*
> 6 *cups water, approximately*
> ½ *pound* nopales *(about 3 medium-sized cactus paddles) or*
>   1 *cup canned, drained (optional)*
> 2½ *teaspoons salt, or to taste*
>   1 *large green onion, green part included, quartered*
>   *(optional)*
>   1 *large tomato (about ½ pound)*
>   1 *clove garlic, peeled and roughly chopped*
>   2 *tablespoons peanut or safflower oil*
>   ¼ *medium onion, finely chopped*
>   1 *chile jalapeño,* 2 *chiles serranos, or any fresh, hot green*
>   *chili, thinly sliced*
>   1 *cup chicken broth*
>   3 *large sprigs fresh coriander*

Rinse the lentils well in cold water. Put them into a pan with 6 cups of cold water. Bring to a boil, then lower the flame and cook over a low flame until mushy—about 3 hours for Mexican lentils, 2 hours U.S.

Cut the prepared cactus paddles into small squares. Cover with cold water, add ½ teaspoon of the salt and the green onion and simmer until *just* tender —about 20 minutes. Rinse in cold water and drain. (This step is naturally omitted if canned *nopales* are used.)

(continued)

Blend the tomato with the garlic until smooth. Set aside.

Heat the oil and fry the onion and chili gently, without browning, until they are soft. Add the tomato puree and fry for another 3 minutes or so over a high flame, stirring constantly, until the mixture is almost dry. Add the lentils, their broth, the chicken broth, *nopales,* and 2 teaspoons salt to the tomato mixture. Cover the pan and cook over a low flame for about 20 minutes, then add the coriander and cook for 1 minute longer.

6 servings

Sopa Verde de Elote Green Corn Soup

This unusual and delicious soup, with all its wonderfully different flavors, is from *Mi Libro de Cocina,* a book published in San Luis Potosí in 1965. Unless you can get very tender corn, use frozen corn and measure before it defrosts.

This soup can be made ahead and it can be frozen. On defrosting, blend it for a few seconds before heating and serving.

> 4 *tablespoons (½ stick) sweet butter*
> ¼ *medium onion, finely chopped*
> 2 *small cloves garlic, peeled and finely chopped*
> ⅔ *cup* tomates verdes, *cooked (see page 245) or canned*
> 4½ *cups corn kernels (see note above)*
> 5 *cups light chicken broth*
> ⅔ *cup green peas, fresh or frozen*
> 4 *large sprigs fresh coriander*
> 2 *small* chiles poblanos, *charred and peeled (see page 260), or canned, peeled green chilies*
> 3 *large romaine lettuce leaves*
> 1 *teaspoon salt, or to taste*

THE GARNISH

> 6 *tablespoons sour cream*
> *Crisp-fried tortilla pieces (see page 251)*

Melt the butter and fry the onion and garlic, without browning, until soft.

Blend the *tomate verde* until smooth. Add to the onion in the pan and fry over a high flame for about 3 minutes, stirring constantly.

Put the corn kernels into a blender jar (one-third at a time) with 2 cups of the chicken broth and the peas, coriander, chilies, and lettuce leaves and blend until quite smooth. Pass this puree through the medium disk of a food mill, then add to the pan and cook over a fairly high flame for about 3 minutes, stirring and scraping the bottom of the pan constantly, since the mixture tends to stick.

Add the remaining broth and the salt and cook the soup over a low flame until it thickens and is well seasoned—about 20 minutes.

Serve in soup bowls with a large spoonful of the cream and a sprinkling of tortilla pieces for each serving.

6 servings

Sopa de Porros Leek Soup

Sra. Domatila Santiago de Morales (Oaxaca)

This is a very interesting and delicious recipe—Señora Domatila never fails me. I have changed it in only one respect: I sauté the leeks first, whereas she just boils them; I think sautéing improves the flavor.

> *2 tablespoons sweet butter*
> *2 tablespoons peanut or safflower oil*
> *4 cups finely chopped leeks, white and tender green part*
> *only*
> *4 heaped tablespoons finely chopped fresh parsley, leaves*
> *only*
> *6 cups light chicken broth*
> *5 hard-cooked eggs*
> *Salt and freshly ground pepper to taste*

THE GARNISH

> *Fried bread croutons or crisp-fried tortilla pieces (see*
> *page 251)*

Heat the butter with the oil in a large, heavy saucepan and sauté the leeks and parsley until just soft, without browning—about 8 minutes. Add 5 cups of the chicken broth and cook over a medium flame until the leeks are tender—about 8 minutes.

Shell the eggs and separate the whites from the yolks. Chop the whites fine and set aside. Blend the yolks, together with the rest of the broth, until smooth. Add the whites and blended yolks to the broth. Season and continue cooking the soup for another 10 minutes, or until the leeks are completely soft and well seasoned.

Serve the soup with croutons or crisp-fried tortilla pieces.

6 servings

Sopa de Ajo y Migas Garlic and Bread Soup

*Sra. María Elena Lara (restaurante Los Tres Migueles,
Mexico City)*

Prepared as described below, the eggs will form rough strands like egg drop soup. On a recent tour in San Diego, my friend Jerrie Strom taught me a Chinese trick to keep the strands of eggs smoother and more silky: when beating the eggs, add about 1 teaspoon oil.

If you wish to be traditional, you can serve the soup with a garnish of the veins of *chiles pasillas*, toasted, on the side.

> 6 thick slices French-type bread, preferably sourdough (see
>   note page 21–22)
> 6 tablespoons peanut or safflower oil, approximately
> 4 cloves garlic, peeled and sliced
> 6 cups strong chicken broth
> 3 small eggs
> 2 large sprigs epazote
>   Salt to taste, if necessary

Preheat the oven to 300 degrees

Place the bread slices on a baking sheet in one layer and bake until they are crisp on the outside but not dried all the way through—about 30 minutes.

Heat some of the oil in a heavy pan and fry the bread on both sides until very crisp and golden brown, adding more oil as necessary. Drain on paper toweling and set aside to keep warm.

In 1 tablespoon of the remaining oil—add extra or remove as necessary— cook, rather than fry, the garlic over a low flame so that it flavors the oil. Remove the garlic and discard. Pour a little of the broth into the pan, swirl it around, and pour into the rest of the broth.

Heat the broth to simmering. Beat the eggs lightly (see note above) and, stirring constantly in a circular motion, add to the broth. Add the *epazote* and simmer until the eggs are set. Adjust the seasoning, then add the fried bread and simmer for half a minute, no longer.

Serve in deep soup bowls, with a crouton in each bowl.

6 servings

Rice, Pasta, and Beans

In a typical Mexican *comida*, which is eaten about two o'clock in the afternoon, there will always be a *sopa seca*—a "dry soup" course—either of pasta cooked in a Mexican way or rice; it follows the "wet soup" course and precedes the main course. There is also a place for beans in the *comida,* after the main course. Beans have a wide variety of uses as well—as appetizers or as accompaniments to suppertime snacks and even breakfasts.

The red rice cooked with tomatoes (Arroz a la Mexicana, on page 31) is either served alone, with freshly made tortillas and a *picante* sauce to accompany it, or with a fried egg on top—which, incidentally, makes a good brunch dish. The white rice (Arroz Blanco, page 32) is quite often served with a strip of fried plantain.

You can, of course, use a chicken bouillon cube and water for cooking the rice dishes if you don't have any homemade broth handy, and providing it isn't one of those brilliant, mustardy yellow ones, it will not overpower the flavor of the rice and other ingredients. Nowadays in Mexico it is customary for the cooks to use this type of bouillon, but in powdered form, and the trouble is that a little Knorr Suiza or Rosa Blanca has become a habit and is added to everything—vegetables, stews, soups, regardless.

Arroz a la Mexicana Mexican Rice

You can cook rice ahead, then heat it through gently, tightly covered, in a 300-degree oven for about 30 minutes. Leftover rice can be heated through in the same way the next day. (I do not recommend steaming.) Arroz a la Mexicana also freezes successfully. To reheat, make a foil package of it and place, still frozen, in a 350-degree oven. Heat through for about an hour.

> *Hot water to cover*
> *1½ cups long-grain unconverted white rice*
> *⅓ cup peanut or safflower oil*
> *1 large tomato (about ½ pound), chopped*
> *¼ medium onion, roughly chopped*
> *1 clove garlic, peeled and roughly chopped*
> *3½ cups well-salted chicken broth*
> *⅓ carrot, scraped and thinly sliced (optional)*
> *2 tablespoons peas (optional)*
> *1 whole sprig parsley (optional)*
> *Salt to taste*

Pour the hot water over the rice and let it stand for about 20 minutes. Drain the rice and rinse well in cold water, then shake the colander well and leave the rice to drain for about 10 minutes.

Heat the oil in a deep, flameproof dish until it smokes. Give the rice a final shake and stir it into the oil until the grains are well covered, then fry until a light golden color, stirring and turning the rice over so it will cook evenly and will not stick to the pan. This process should take about 10 minutes—depending, of course, on the size of the pan—but it should be done over a high flame or the rice will become mushy in its final stage. Tip the pan to one side and drain off any excess oil (strain and refrigerate and use again).

Blend the tomato, onion, and garlic until smooth—there should be about 1 cup of puree. Add the puree to the fried rice, then, continuing to cook over a high flame, stir and scrape the bottom of the pan until the mixture is dry.

Add the broth, carrot, peas, and parsley. Add salt as necessary, then stir well (do not stir again during the cooking time). Cook over a medium flame, uncovered, until the liquid has been absorbed and small air holes appear in the rice. Remove the dish from the flame, cover tightly with a lid or aluminum foil so that no steam can escape, and set it aside in a warm place for about 20 to 30 minutes, so the rice can continue cooking in its own steam and the grains expand.

Before serving, stir the rice well from the bottom.

6 servings

Arroz Blanco White Rice

>   *Hot water to cover*
> *1½ cups long-grain unconverted white rice*
>   *⅓ cup peanut or safflower oil*
>   *⅓ medium onion, roughly sliced*
>   *1 clove garlic, peeled and roughly chopped*
> *3½ cups well-salted light chicken broth*

Pour the hot water over the rice and let it stand for about 20 minutes. Drain the rice and rinse well in cold water. Shake the colander well and leave the rice to drain for about 10 minutes.

Heat the oil in a deep flameproof dish until it smokes. Give the rice a final shake, add it to the dish, and stir until all the grains are well covered with the oil. Fry until just turning color, then add the onion and garlic and fry a few moments longer until these two ingredients are translucent, stirring and turning almost constantly so that they cook evenly and do not stick to the pan. The entire process should take about 10 minutes—depending, of course, on the size of the pan—and it should be done over a high flame or it will take too long and the rice will become mushy in the final stage.

Tip the pan to one side and drain off any excess oil (strain and refrigerate and use again). Add the broth and cook, uncovered, over a medium flame— do not stir again—until the liquid has been absorbed and small air holes appear in the rice. Cover the dish tightly with a lid or aluminum foil so that none of the steam can escape and set aside in a warm place for about 20 to 30 minutes, so it can continue to cook and the grains expand.

Before serving, stir the rice well from the bottom. Serve, if desired, topped with Rajas de Chile Estilo Oaxaqueño (see page 137) or Rajas de Chiles Jalapeños Frescos (see page 164).

6 servings

Arroz Blanco con Chiles Rellenos de Elote White Rice with Corn-Stuffed Chilies

This is a particularly delicious combination of chilies, rice, and corn, and while it can be made with either *chiles poblanos* or *chiles anchos,* it is particularly good made with *chiles anchos,* prepared as follows:

If the chilies are rather dry, soften them by heating on a warm griddle or *comal.* Make a slit down one side of each chili and carefully remove the seeds and veins. Put them into a saucepan and cover them with water. Simmer them for about 5 minutes, or until the flesh is soft. Drain and stuff with the corn mixture, then follow the recipe below.

A very substantial dish, this makes an excellent vegetarian main course.

> *Arroz Blanco (see page 32), using 2 cups raw rice and 4*
> *   cups broth*
> *Chiles Rellenos de Elote con Crema (see page 136; see*
> *   also note above)*
> *1½ cups homemade sour cream (see page 235) or* crème
> *   fraîche*
> *4 ounces Chihuahua cheese or mild Cheddar, grated*

Preheat the oven to 350 degrees. Butter an ovenproof dish about 4 inches deep.

Spread half of the prepared rice over the bottom of the dish. Place the stuffed chilies in one layer over the rice and top with the remaining rice.

Cover the dish with foil and bake for about 30 minutes, then remove the foil, pour the cream on top, and sprinkle with the cheese. Bake for 15 minutes longer, or until the rice is well heated through and the cheese melted.

6 servings

Arroz Verde Green Rice

Señora María Luisa Camarena de Rodríquez
(Tehuacán, Puebla)

1½ **cups long-grain unconverted white rice**
   Hot water to cover
⅓ **cup peanut or safflower oil**
½ **cup cold water, more if necessary**
1 **small bunch Italian parsley**
3 **sprigs fresh coriander**
3 **large romaine lettuce leaves**
2 **chiles poblanos, *charred, peeled, and cleaned of seeds and**
      *veins (see page 260), or canned, peeled green chilies***
¼ **small onion, roughly chopped**
1 **clove garlic, peeled and roughly chopped**
3 **cups light chicken broth**
   Salt to taste

Cover the rice with hot water and let soak for about 20 minutes. Drain in a strainer, then rinse well in cold water and leave to drain for about 15 minutes.

In a heavy pan, heat the oil until it smokes. Give a final shake to the rice in the strainer and stir it into the oil. Fry over a very high flame, turning the rice thoroughly from time to time, until it is a pale golden color. Tip the pan to one side, holding back the rice with a wide metal spatula, and drain off about 3 tablespoons of the oil.

Pour the ½ cup of water into a blender jar. Add the greens, chilies, onion, and garlic and blend until smooth, adding more water only if absolutely necessary to release the blades of the blender.

Add the blended ingredients to the rice and fry over a high flame, stirring constantly and scraping the bottom of the pan, until the rice is almost dry. Add the broth and salt to taste and cook over a medium flame until all the liquid has been absorbed and small air holes appear in the surface of the rice—about 15 minutes.

Cover the pan with a lid or foil and cook for 5 minutes longer. Turn out the flame and let the rice continue cooking in its own steam for 20 to 30 minutes.

6 servings

Sopa Seca de Fideo Dry Vermicelli "Soup"

As are all dry soups, this is traditionally served alone as a pasta course.

> 6 *tablespoons peanut or safflower oil*
> 8 *ounces fine vermicelli in bundles*
> 1¼ *pound fresh tomatoes or 2½ cups canned, roughly*
> *chopped*
> ¼ *small onion, roughly chopped*
> 1 *clove garlic, peeled and roughly chopped*
> ½ *cup chicken broth or ½ cup water plus 2 chicken*
> *bouillon cubes*
> 2 *whole* chiles chipotles, *dried or canned*
> *Salt to taste*
> ¾ *cup* crème fraîche *or homemade sour cream (see page*
> *235)*
> 2 to 3 *ounces grated Chihuahua cheese or mild Cheddar*

Preheat the oven to 350 degrees. Grease a small casserole or loaf-shaped Pyrex dish.

Heat the oil until it smokes, then lower the flame a little and fry the bundles of vermicelli until they are a deep golden brown. (They brown quickly, so turn them over from time to time; do not break the bundles up.) Remove from the oil.

Blend the tomato with the onion and garlic until smooth. Add to the oil in the pan and fry over high heat, stirring well from time to time, for about 8 minutes. Add the broth, chilies, and salt as necessary, and cook for 3 minutes longer. Add the fried pasta to the tomato sauce. Stir well, then cover the pan and cook over a rather low flame until all the liquid has been absorbed—about 8 to 10 minutes.

Turn the pasta into the prepared dish. Spread the sour cream over the top, sprinkle with the cheese, and cook for 20 to 30 minutes, or until the pasta is just coming away from the sides of the dish and the cheese is well melted.

6 servings

Frijoles de Olla "Pot" Beans

Frijoles de olla are usually served, both beans and broth, after the *comida's* main course. It is traditional to serve them in small earthenware bowls, and they can be scooped up with a tortilla or eaten (less messily) with a spoon. You can dress them up with small pieces of creamy cheese, which will melt most appetizingly, or add a little zest to the taste with a small amount of chili, fresh or *en escabeche*. They are much better a day or so after being cooked.

In Mexico use *frijoles negros* (black beans) or *bayos, canarios, flor de mayo,* etc., etc.; you have a wide choice.

> *1 pound dried beans—black, pink, or pinto*
> *10 to 12 cups cold water, approximately*
> *¼ medium onion, roughly sliced*
> *2 tablespoons pork lard*
> *1 tablespoon salt, or to taste*
> *2 large sprigs epazote, only if black beans are used*

Rinse the beans in cold water and let them run through your hands to make sure that there are no small stones or pieces of earth among them. Put them into a pot and cover with cold water. Add the onion and lard and bring to a boil, then lower the flame and let the beans simmer, covered, until they are just soft and the skins are breaking open—about 2 hours for black beans and 1½ for other varieties, although it is very difficult to be precise. (Much will depend on the age of the beans, how long they have been stored and if they have dried out too much, and on the efficiency of the pot or pan in which you are cooking them.) Add the salt and continue cooking over a low flame for another hour, until the beans are completely soft and the broth thickish and soupy.

For black beans, add the *epazote* just before the end of the cooking time, as it tends to lose flavor if cooked for too long.

10 servings

Frijoles Refritos Well-Fried Beans

Well-fried beans are used for Tortas (page 110) and other recipes in this book, but more commonly they accompany breakfast eggs and suppertime snacks. Pork lard is, of course, best for this recipe, but if you flinch at the quantity cut it down or use peanut or safflower oil. Bacon drippings provide too strong a flavor if you want to cook beans authentically.

Frijoles refritos freeze well, and can always be ready for use just by reheating.

> *6 tablespoons pork lard*
> *¼ medium onion, finely chopped*
> *½ pound beans cooked as for Frijoles de Olla (see page 36),*
>   *approximately 3½ to 4 cups including broth*

In a very heavy frying pan—preferably 10 inches in diameter—heat the lard and fry the onion, without browning, until soft. Add 1 cup of the beans and their broth and mash well as you cook them over a very high flame. Gradually add the rest of the beans, little by little, mashing them all the time until you have a coarse puree.

As the puree begins to dry out and sizzle at the edges, it is ready to be used for the recipes calling for *frijoles refritos.*

6 or more servings

Frijoles a la Huacha "Dirty" Beans

Sra. Berta López de Marrufo (Mérida, Yucatán)

Beans fried with mint is enough to make anyone stop in his tracks, especially the hardened *aficionados* of Mexican food. But it's done in Yucatán. Señora Berta, whose recipe this is, tells me that the word *huacha,* a Mayan word, is used to describe someone from the interior of Mexico, and is usually derogatory, hence the "dirty" in the recipe title.

> *4 to 5 tablespoons pork lard*
> *¼ medium onion, finely chopped*
> *¼ chile habanero or any fresh, hot green chili, finely*
>   *chopped*
> *1 pound black turtle beans cooked as for Frijoles de*
>   *Olla (see page 36)*
> *7 large mint leaves, roughly chopped*

Melt the lard and fry the onion and chili, without browning, until soft.

Blend the beans with 1½ cups of the broth they cooked in until smooth, and add them to the pan. Fry the beans until they reduce to a thick paste (see page 37), adding the chopped mint leaves toward the end of the cooking time. Fry for a few minutes longer and serve.

10 servings

Frijoles Maneados Sonorenses Sonora Bean Puree

Sra. María-Dolores Izabal de Quijano (Mexico City)

Some years ago, an old friend and culinary expert, María-Dolores Quijano, served these beans to me during a late, sumptuous lunch—and I can only say that they are wickedly rich. I had heard that the original recipe was cooked with butter and cream, which is so good in the northwest of Mexico, but María-Dolores assures me that this is how her family, los Izabal, always prepared them when she was growing up in Sonora. The name *maneados* is derived from the continual stirring of the beans to incorporate the rest of the ingredients—before the days of the blender, of course.

> 1 *pound pinto or California pink beans*
> 12 to 14 *cups water, approximately*
> ½ *small onion, roughly sliced*
> 1 *cup plus 3 tablespoons peanut or safflower oil*
> 1 *tablespoon salt, or to taste*
> ⅔ *cup milk*
> 2 **chiles anchos**
> ½ *pound* asadero, *Chihuahua, mild Cheddar, jack, or*
>   *domestic Muenster cheese, cut into ½-inch cubes*

Run the beans through your hands slowly, picking out any small stones or pieces of dirt that might be among them. Rinse in cold water and put into a large flameproof bean pot.

Add 12 cups of the cold water, the onion, and the 3 tablespoons oil and bring to a simmer. Cover the beans and continue simmering until they are just beginning to soften and the skins are splitting open—about 40 minutes (depending on how dry the beans are). Add the salt and continue cooking until the beans are soft and mushy; there should be some broth in the pot. If the broth reduces too much during the cooking time, then add more water. Put the rest of the oil—1 cup—into a casserole. Put the casserole into the oven and set the temperature at 350 degrees.

Meanwhile, put one-third each of the beans and milk into a blender jar with a little of the broth and blend until smooth. Repeat twice to use up the beans and milk.

By the time the beans have been blended, the oil should be very hot; if not, leave in the oven for a few minutes longer. When the oil is ready, stir the bean puree into the casserole and return to the oven to cook, uncovered, until the edges are just drying out and the mixture reduced—about 1 hour 15 minutes.

After you put the bean puree into the oven, slit the chilies open, remove the veins and seeds, and toast lightly on both sides on a warm griddle or *comal.* Tear the chilies into thin strips and add to the bean puree.

At the end of the cooking time, add the pieces of cheese and return the casserole to the oven until the cheese has melted—about 15 minutes. Serve immediately.

10 servings

Frijoles Colados Yucatecos Yucatecan Sieved Beans

Only in southeastern Mexico—Yucatán, Campeche, and Quintana Roo—are beans sieved before they are fried to a smooth paste.

In this book they are used for Pan de Cazón (see page 93); they make a good accompaniment for Yucatecan food.

> 3 tablespoons pork lard
> ¼ medium onion, roughly sliced
> ½ pound black turtle beans, cooked as for frijoles de olla
>   (see page 36) with a lot of epazote
> 1 chile habanero or any fresh, hot green chili, left whole

Melt the lard in a heavy pan and cook the onion, without browning, until translucent.

Pass the beans, together with their broth, through the medium disk of a food mill, then add to the onion, along with the whole chili—it should flavor the beans but not make them *picante*—and cook over a fairly high flame until the beans form a loose paste that plops off the spoon—about 15 minutes (depending, of course, how much liquid there is with the beans in the first place). Be sure to stir and scrape the bottom of the pan from time to time so the beans don't stick.

6 servings

Meats

Cochito al Horno Chiapas Roast Pork

Cochito is the shortened form of *cochinito* ("little pig"), used in Chiapas and Tabasco. Traditionally the rind is left on and the pig cut into large pieces before being seasoned and roasted. The number and amount of spices used, with the predominant flavor of allspice, are characteristic of the food of that area around Tuxtla Gutiérrez, Chiapa de Corzo, and San Cristóbal de las Casas.

In *The Cuisines of Mexico* I wrote about the famous *botanas,* appetizers that are served in bars and small regional restaurants—some hot, some cold—and they often include *cochito* cooked in this way. You won't find it on ordinary menus, but I have seen it served with a pile of hot tortillas as a substantial *almuerzo,* or late breakfast, in the small Tuxtla Gutiérrez airport.

Start one day ahead, preferably.

(continued)

      4 chiles anchos, *cleaned of seeds and veins*
      ¼ teaspoon thyme
      2 bay leaves (4 in Mexico)
     10 peppercorns
      6 whole cloves
     20 whole allspice
 2-inch piece cinnamon bark
      4 cloves garlic, peeled
      ⅔ cup vinegar, approximately
     1½ tablespoons salt
      5 pounds pork roast, with rind, if possible (see note
        above)
      1 cup warm water

THE GARNISH

      2 cups thinly sliced onion
      2 cups shredded romaine lettuce, lightly dressed with oil
        and vinegar

Cover the chilies with boiling water and leave to soak for about 15 minutes, or until soft. Drain and transfer to a blender jar. Crush the herbs and spices, then add, along with the garlic, vinegar and salt to the blender. Blend until smooth, stopping occasionally to release the blades of the blender—you may need to add a little water, but the mixture should have the consistency of a loose paste.

Pierce the meat all over with the point of a sharp knife. Smear the meat liberally with the seasoning paste and set aside for a minimum of 4 hours, but preferably overnight.

Preheat the oven to 350 degrees.

Put the meat into a casserole, cover, and cook for 1 hour. Turn the meat and cook for 1 hour more, still covered. At this point, scrape up the paste that is sticking to the bottom of the pan and dilute it with 1 cup of warm water. Turn the meat again and cook for another 2 hours, or until the meat is very tender, basting from time to time with the pan juices. When the meat is cooked, there should be plenty of sauce in the casserole.

Serve the meat sliced, with some of the sauce from the pan and topped with plenty of onion rings and shredded lettuce. Eat with freshly made tortillas (see page 246).

6 to 8 servings

Puerco en Naranja Pork Cooked in Orange Juice

I know I am always saying how delicious the pork is in Mexico, especially the cut called *lomo* (loin), which would normally be used for this type of recipe and which is actually the round, boneless eye of the loin. I don't recommend it in the United States, however. Due to different feeding methods, American pork has a much more compact texture, and this cut would be too dry. I suggest—as I have elsewhere—the rib or shoulder ends of the loin.

This is one of the many versions of *puerco en naranja*—every cook has her own secret touches—with my method for cooking it. It is often served with *rajas,* strips of *chile poblano* fried together with onions, which complement the meat very well.

> 5 *pounds rib-end pork loin (in two pieces, if necessary, to*
> *make up this weight)*
> 5 *cloves garlic, peeled*
> 1 *tablespoon salt*
> 2 *teaspoons oregano*
> 12 *peppercorns*
> 3 *oranges*

Pierce the meat all over with the point of a sharp knife. Crush the garlic, together with the salt, oregano, and peppercorns, and moisten with the juice of one orange. Rub this mixture into the pork and set aside to season for 1 hour.

Preheat the oven to 350 degrees.

Place the pork in a heavy casserole into which it will just fit comfortably and moisten it with the juice of a second orange. Add the skin of the orange to the casserole, then cover and bake for 2 hours.

Drain off all but about 3 tablespoons of the pan juices and reserve. Turn the meat over and bake for another hour, uncovered, basting the meat from time to time.

Drain off the pan juices again and reserve. Turn the oven up to 400 degrees and brown the top of the meat, then turn it over and brown the other side.

Meanwhile, skim the reserved pan juices of most of their fat. Add the juice of the third orange and reduce quickly over a high flame. Slice the meat and either pass the sauce separately or spoon it over the sliced meat at the moment of serving.

6 to 8 servings

Asado de Puerco a la Veracruzana Veracruz Pork Roast

This recipe was given to me in Huatusco, Veracruz. Preparations should start the day before to improve the flavor. It was originally given for a leg of pork, which I find rather dry and uninteresting, so I have suggested a pork butt or shoulder for this recipe. You can use any small, hot dried chili instead of the *chiles moritas*—that is, *chipotle, japonés, serrano seco.* If banana leaves are not available, then of course omit them.

This is also good the next day, sliced thin and eaten cold.

> 5 *pounds pork roast on the bone, preferably butt or*
>   *shoulder*
> 4 *cloves garlic, peeled*
> 1 *tablespoon salt*
> 1½ *tablespoons lime juice*
> 4 chiles anchos
> 4 chiles moritas *or* 1 chipotle *or* 4 serranos secos
> 4 *whole allspice*
>   *Banana leaves sufficient to wrap the roast in a double*
>   *layer (optional)*

Remove the rind, if any, from the pork. Pierce the meat all over with the point of a sharp knife. Mash the garlic with the salt and moisten with the lime juice. Rub this mixture thoroughly into the roast and set aside to season while you prepare the chili mixture.

Remove the seeds and veins from the *chiles anchos* and toast them lightly (see page 259) on a hot griddle or *comal.* Cover them with hot water, add the whole, untoasted chilies, and simmer for 5 minutes. Turn off the heat and leave the chilies to soak for 5 minutes longer.

Transfer the chilies to a blender jar with ½ cup of the water in which they were soaking. Add the allspice and blend until smooth. Add a little more water only if necessary to release the blades of the blender.

Coat the meat liberally with the chili paste. Hold the banana leaf over a hot flame until it softens and steams and wrap it around the meat. Set the meat aside to season overnight. (If you are not using the banana leaf, simply set the meat aside to season unwrapped.)

Preheat the oven to 325 degrees.

Place the meat in a Dutch oven or casserole with a tightly fitting lid and bake for 2 hours, by the end of which time there should be plenty of juices at the bottom of the casserole. Remove the lid and continue cooking the meat, basting it from time to time, for about 2 hours longer, or until soft and almost falling off the bone.

Serve hot, with freshly made tortillas (see page 246).

6 to 8 servings

Calabaza Guisada con Puerco Pumpkin Cooked with Pork

Sra. Domatila Santiago de Morales (Oaxaca)

This is a very simple Oaxacan stew that is neither *picante* nor heavily spiced. In Oaxaca in the late summer and fall the markets are full of small green pumpkins that are incredibly sweet when picked fresh. We used them for this dish, but you could easily substitute large zucchini squash.

(continued)

THE MEAT

2½ pounds country-style spareribs, cut into 1½-inch cubes
2 teaspoons salt
¼ small onion, roughly chopped
2 cloves garlic, peeled and roughly chopped

THE SAUCE

1½ tablespoons peanut or safflower oil
1 medium tomato (about 6 ounces), peeled, seeded, and
    chopped
¼ small onion, finely chopped
2 small cloves garlic, peeled and finely chopped
1 pound small green pumpkin or zucchini, trimmed and
    cut into ½-inch cubes.
1½ cups fresh corn kernels
1 thick slice fresh pineapple, peeled and cut into small
    pieces
1 chile ancho
⅛ teaspoon cuminseed, crushed
1 medium-sized, very ripe plantain (about ½ pound),
    skinned and cut into ½-inch rounds
    Salt to taste

Put the pork into a saucepan, together with the salt, onion, and garlic, and barely cover with water. Bring to a boil, then lower the flame and simmer until *just* tender—about 45 minutes. Drain the meat, reserving the broth.

Heat the oil in a large, heavy saucepan until smoking, then add the tomato, onion, and garlic and fry over a high flame, stirring constantly, until the mixture is slightly reduced, about 4 minutes. Add the pumpkin, corn kernels, pineapple, and 2 cups of the pork broth. Cover the pan and cook over a medium flame, stirring from time to time, for about 10 minutes—the squash and corn should be *just* tender.

Slit open the *chile ancho*, remove the seeds and veins, cover with hot water, and cook for 5 minutes. Transfer the chili to a blender jar, along with ⅓ cup of the water in which it was cooked and the cuminseed. Blend until smooth.

Add the plantain, the blended chili, and the meat to the sauce, adjust the salt, and simmer for about 15 minutes longer.

Serve with hot tortillas.

6 servings

Lomitos Yucatecan Pork Pieces

Sra. Berta López de Marrufo (Mérida, Yucatán)

This dish rarely appears on the menus of Yucatecan restaurants, but like many of the local specialties, it can be found at its best in the early morning in the marketplaces. I ate it for the first time in the Valladolid market, where it was being served either in tacos or piled onto a *pim* (a round cake made of tortilla dough beaten with lard and salt and cooked on a griddle or *comal;* a *pim* is usually 3 inches in diameter and "one finger" thick.)

Lomitos (lit., "little loins") are also often served on a bed of cooked, sieved *ibis,* small, round white beans grown in the Yucatecan peninsula.

> 1 tablespoon Recado Rojo *(see page 218)*
> 2 tablespoons Seville orange juice *or mild vinegar*
> 2 pounds boneless pork, cut into ½-inch cubes
> 2 tablespoons peanut or safflower oil *or pork lard*
> ¾ pound tomatoes, unpeeled, finely chopped
> ½ green pepper, finely chopped
> ½ medium onion, finely chopped
> 2 teaspoons salt
> 1 small head of garlic, unpeeled
> 1 chile habanero *or any fresh, hot green chili*
> 2 to 2½ cups cold water

Dilute the *recado rojo* with the orange juice and rub it into the pieces of meat. Set aside for about 30 minutes to season.

Heat the oil in a heavy saucepan and fry the tomato, pepper, and onion together over a fairly high flame, stirring well and scraping the bottom of the pan from time to time, for about 10 minutes. Add the salt and set aside.

Toast the whole head of garlic on a griddle or *comal,* turning it from time to time, until it is browned on the outside and the cloves inside are cooked and fairly soft. Toast the *chile habanero.*

Put the meat into a saucepan with the 2 to 2½ cups of water—the water should barely cover. Add the tomato mixture and the toasted garlic and chili and bring to a boil. Lower the flame and simmer the meat, uncovered, until it is tender—about 1 hour. (The sauce should be of a medium consistency; if it appears to be too watery, turn the flame higher and reduce quickly). Serve hot.

6 servings

Ayocotes con Carne de Puerco Estilo Querétaro Ayocote Beans with Pork, Querétaro Style

Obdulia and AnaMaría Vega (Querétaro)

Ayocotes are large dried beans, generally purple in color, that can be found in markets throughout central Mexico. They can be cooked when they are freshly picked, but more often they are dried and stored for the months ahead. The large pods are harvested and dried in the hot October sun, then they are beaten with sticks so they break open and release the beans. *Ayocotes* are cooked and fried like any other type of bean, and are used mostly as an accompaniment to *mole*.

I never really acquired a taste for them until AnaMaría and Obdulia Vega —who had brought a huge bag of them, all tones from pale coffee to deep purple, back from their last visit home—showed me how to cook them as their mother used to at their small Querétaro ranch. The chilies seem to bring out the delicious, earthy flavor of the *ayocotes*—one would think quite the opposite, that they would mask the flavor.

You could quite successfully substitute any large dried beans, such as navy or haricot, in this recipe. It makes a good, hearty dish for a cold day.

THE BEANS

> *3 cups dried* ayocotes, *large navy beans, or haricot beans*
> *8 cups cold water*
> *2 teaspoons salt, or to taste*

THE MEAT

> *1½ pounds country-style spareribs, cut into 1½-inch cubes*
> *(half* carne maciza *and half* costillitas *in Mexico)*
> *1½ teaspoons salt, or to taste*
> *Pork lard, if necessary*

THE SAUCE

> *9* chiles guajillos
> *9* chiles pasillas
> *5 peppercorns*

  ¾ *teaspoon cuminseed*
  3 *whole cloves*
  2 *cloves garlic, peeled*
1½ *cups cold water*
  1 *bay leaf (2 to 3 in Mexico)*

Rinse the beans well, then place in a flameproof bean pot. Cover with the cold water and leave to soak for 30 minutes. In the same water, bring the beans to a boil, lower the flame, and simmer until tender—2 to 3 hours, depending on how dry they are. Add 2 teaspoons salt, or to taste.

In the meantime, cook the pork. Put the cubes into a wide, heavy pan, barely cover with water, add 1½ teaspoons salt, and cook, uncovered, over a medium flame until all the water is consumed and the meat tender. Continue cooking, turning from time to time, so that the fat renders out and the meat browns well in the rendered fat. (If the pork is very lean you may have to add some lard, say ¼ cup.) Remove the meat and all except ¼ cup of the fat.

Remove the stalks from the chilies. Slit them open and take out the seeds and veins. Heat a griddle or *comal* and toast the chilies thoroughly (see page 259), taking care not to burn them or the sauce will have a bitter taste. Cover the chilies with hot water and let them soak for about 5 minutes, then drain them and transfer to a blender jar. Crush the spices, then add to the jar, along with the garlic and 1½ cups cold water. Blend briefly—pieces of chili skin should be visible.

Reheat the lard in the pan, then add the chili sauce and fry over a medium flame, scraping and stirring all the time so it does not stick, for about 8 minutes.

Add the beans with their broth and the bay leaf, adjust the seasoning, and cook over a low flame for another 20 minutes.

6 servings

Mole Verde de Cacahuate Pork in Green Peanut Sauce

Virginia Villalon (Pánuco, Veracruz)

I returned to Pánuco, the small river town in northern Veracruz, in high hopes of visiting Señorita Chanita, who six years before had made a very special, huge *tamal,* called *sacahuil,* for me, only to find that she had died two years before. When I asked around for someone who really knew the local food and was a good cook, I was sent to Virginia Villalon's modest little restaurant in one of the main streets. She was quite young, and had learned from her aunt the simple dishes of the area. She patiently dictated her recipes, stopping now and then to give me tastes from one and then another of the several large *cazuelas* bubbling away on the stove. This *mole* was one of them.

It is curious that in the northern part of Veracruz and in the state of Tabasco, but nowhere else in Mexico, the large-leafed coriander—called *cilantrón* in Veracruz and *perejil* in Tabasco—is used. It is sold in New York in Puerto Rican and Dominican stores. The leaf is long and serrated, and is a darker green and stronger in flavor than the more delicate coriander commonly used.

THE MEAT

> 2¼ *pounds pork, with some fat, cut into 1-inch cubes, or*
>   3½ *pounds country-style spareribs, in small pieces*
> ¼ *onion, roughly chopped*
> 2 *cloves garlic, peeled and roughly chopped*
> 2 *teaspoons salt, or to taste*
> 3 *tablespoons peanut or safflower oil*
> ⅓ *medium onion, sliced*

THE SAUCE

> 1 *tablespoon peanut or safflower oil or pork lard*
> 5 *ounces raw (unroasted, unsalted) peanuts, shelled*
>   *weight*
> 1½ *cups* tomates verdes, *freshly cooked (see page 245), or*
>   *canned, drained*
> 6 *sprigs coriander (see note above)*
> 4 *peppercorns*

3 to 4 chiles serranos, *or any fresh, hot green chili*
2 cloves garlic, peeled

Put the pork, chopped onion, garlic, and salt into a saucepan, cover with water, bring to a simmer, and cook until almost tender—about 40 minutes (much depending on quality and cut of meat). Drain the meat, reserving the broth.

Meantime, heat the 1 tablespoon of oil and fry the peanuts, turning them constantly, until they are a golden brown. Transfer to a blender jar. Add the *tomates verdes,* coriander, peppercorns, chilies, garlic, and ¾ cup of the meat broth and blend until smooth (you may need a little more broth, but be careful not to make the sauce too watery).

Heat the 3 tablespoons of oil and fry the pork and sliced onion together until golden, turning the pieces constantly. Add the blended sauce and cook for a few minutes longer, stirring and scraping the bottom of the pan all the time. Add approximately 2½ cups of the broth, then adjust the seasoning and simmer the stew for about 15 minutes, or until well seasoned. (You may need to dilute the sauce further—it should be of a medium consistency, like thin cream—and it will thicken considerably as it cooks.)

Serve with plenty of the sauce and fresh, hot tortillas (see page 246).

6 servings

Frijol con Puerco Beans with Pork

Sra. Berta López de Marrufo (Mérida, Yucatán)

This is one of those large, composite dishes reminiscent of its popular counterparts around the Caribbean and Brazil. Beans, meat, and rice are black, gaudily and lavishly strewn with finely chopped radishes, coriander leaves, and tomato sauce, and served with lime quarters and slices of avocado—a hearty, crunchy, and filling dish.

I advise you to cook the beans the day before, just up to the point in the recipe where the meat is added. The tomato sauce could be prepared ahead, too, but even then cooking time is about 2½ hours, for not until the meat is cooked can you begin the rice.

(continued)

The Beans

> *1 pound black turtle beans*
> *1 tablespoon pork lard*
> *½ onion, roughly sliced*
> *14 cups cold water, approximately*
> *1 tablespoon salt*
> *1 sprig* epazote

Run the beans through your fingers and pick out any small stones or little pieces of earth that may be among them. Rinse the beans and put into a flameproof bean pot with the lard, onion, and water. Bring to a simmer and continue cooking slowly until the skins start breaking. Add the salt and *epazote* and continue cooking until the beans are just tender but not too soft.

The Pork

> *½ pound boneless stewing pork (*carne maciza *in Mexico),*
> *cut into large cubes*
> *1 pound pork hocks (*chamberete de puerco *in Mexico), cut*
> *into ½-inch slices*
> *1 pound country-style spareribs (*costillitas *in Mexico), cut*
> *into 2-inch cubes*
> *1 pig's ear, cut into small pieces (optional)*
> *1 green pepper, cleaned of seeds and veins and cut into*
> *small squares*
> *2 large sprigs* epazote
> *1 small onion, roughly sliced*
> *1 tablespoon salt, or to taste*

Add the pork and remaining ingredients to the beans, then cover and continue cooking over a low flame, stirring well from time to time. (There should be plenty of broth, bearing in mind that 3 cups of it have to go into the rice. If it seems to have reduced too much, add a cup or so of water.) Cook until the beans are quite soft and the meat tender—about 1 hour 15 minutes, depending on the meat.

During the cooking time, start preparations for the rice.

The Rice

1½ cups long-grain unconverted white rice
6 tablespoons olive oil
¼ small onion, roughly chopped
1 clove garlic, peeled and roughly chopped
3 cups bean broth (see above)
Salt to taste

Cover the rice with hot water and let it stand for about 20 minutes, then rinse in cold water twice and drain well. Heat the oil in a very heavy pan (the bean broth tends to stick rather badly) and stir the rice into it until the grains are evenly coated. Add the onion and garlic and fry the rice, turning it over from time to time so that it becomes an even, pale gold color. Tip the pan and drain off the excess oil.

Add the broth from the beans and salt to taste, then cover the pot and cook the rice gently until all the liquid has been absorbed. Remove from the flame and set aside, tightly covered, for about 25 minutes, to allow the rice to continue cooking and expanding in the steam it generates.

Assembling the Dish

The cooked pork (see above)
The cooked rice (see above)
The cooked beans (see above)
2 cups Salsa de Jitomate Yucateca (see page 159)
1 cup very finely chopped radishes
½ cup very finely chopped coriander leaves
4 small limes, quartered
2 avocados, peeled and sliced

Remove the meat from the beans and serve on a warmed platter. Serve the rice in the casserole in which it was cooked. Serve the beans and their broth in individual small bowls and pass the rest of the ingredients separately so each person can serve himself, *al gusto.*

6 servings

Puerco con Verdolagas Pork with Purslane

Sra. María Elena Lara (restaurante Los Tres Migueles,
Mexico City)

You will always find *verdolagas* (purslane) the year round in the markets of central Mexico. A ground creeper, with small, oval, fleshy leaves that are mid-green in color and fleshy, pinkish-green stems, it grows wild both here and in the United States. I have seen it growing both in California and Maryland, so it must turn up in between the two extremes as well (it should be available soon at Casa Moneo in New York; see Sources for Ingredients, page 273). It has a curiously acid flavor, rather like cactus paddles, and is very much an acquired taste. The preferred way of cooking purslane in Mexico is with pork and *tomates verdes*—a great peasant stew.

I always like to cook country-style spareribs for this type of dish, but typically it is made with *espinazo*—bones of the spine stripped of most of their meat —and the tail.

4½ **pounds country-style spareribs, cut into 2-inch pieces**
   1 **medium onion, roughly sliced**
   8 **cloves garlic, peeled**
   1 **tablespoon plus 1 teaspoon salt, or to taste**
   2 **pounds purslane** (verdolagas)
   2 **cups cold water, approximately**
   1 **teaspoon salt**
   4 **cups tomates verdes, *freshly cooked (see page 245) or***
      canned, drained
4 to 6 **chiles jalapeños *or any fresh, hot green chilies***
   2 **ounces (¼ cup) pork lard**
   1 **large white onion, thinly sliced**
   ½ **teaspoon cuminseed**
   ¼ **teaspoon oregano**

Put the meat into a large saucepan and barely cover with water. Add the roughly sliced onion, 2 cloves of the garlic, and 1 tablespoon salt and bring to a boil. Lower the flame and simmer until the meat is *just* tender—about 40 minutes; do not overcook. Drain the meat, straining and reserving the broth.

Wash the purslane. Remove the roots and very thick stems and chop the leaves and more tender stems up roughly. Put approximately 2 cups of cold water into a pan and add the purslane and 1 teaspoon salt. Cover the pan, bring to a boil over a high flame, and cook the purslane for about 3 minutes, turning it over from time to time. Drain, discarding the cooking water, and set aside.

If you are using fresh *tomates verdes*, cook them as directed on page 245, adding the chilies. If you are using canned *tomates verdes*, just cover the chilies with water and cook for about 10 minutes. Blend the *tomates verdes* and chilies with 1 cup of water in which they were cooked (if using canned *tomates verdes*, simply drain and use 1 cup cold water). Set aside.

In a large flameproof pan, melt the lard and fry the meat and thinly sliced white onion together until the meat is lightly browned and the onion is soft, turning the pieces constantly.

Crush the remaining garlic, cuminseed, and oregano together in a *molcajete* or mortar. Grind until smooth and add to the meat frying in the pan. Take a little of the *tomate verde* puree to "wipe out" the seasoning in the mortar. Add this and the remaining *tomate verde* puree to the pan and fry a few minutes more, stirring constantly.

Add the purslane to the pan with 3 cups of the reserved pork broth and simmer for 10 minutes longer. Adjust the seasoning before serving with freshly made tortillas (see page 246).

6 servings

Caldillo de Puerco Duranguense Durango Pork Stew

Sra. Arcelia Vázquez de Valles (Durango)

The popular dish in the northern states is *caldillo*—really a stew—made with fillet of beef, dried and shredded beef, or pork. It resembles very much the Chihuahua dish Carne de Puerco en Chile Colorado (see page 60).

This recipe was given to me by Sra. Arcelia Vázquez de Valles, a cook of great reputation, particularly renowned for her exquisite marzipan fruits.

> *8 chiles anchos*
> *5½ cups water, approximately*
> *1 cup tomates verdes, freshly cooked (see page 245) or canned, drained*
> *3 tablespoons peanut or safflower oil or pork lard*
> *2¼ pounds boneless pork, with some fat, cut into ½-inch cubes*
> *2 cloves garlic, peeled and finely chopped*
> *½ medium onion, finely chopped*
> *3 teaspoons salt, or to taste*
> *2 teaspoons all-purpose flour*
> *¼ teaspoon oregano*

Remove the stems from the *chiles anchos,* but do not remove the seeds and veins. Cover with water and simmer until soft—about 10 minutes, depending on how dry the chilies are, then drain and transfer to a blender jar. Add 2 cups of the water and the *tomates verdes* and blend until smooth. Set aside.

Heat the oil or lard and fry the meat, together with the garlic, onion, and salt, until golden, stirring constantly—do not let them brown too much. Sprinkle the flour into the pan and fry, stirring until it is lightly browned. Add the blended chilies to the pan and cook for about 10 minutes, scraping the bottom of the pan to prevent sticking.

Add the oregano and approximately 3 cups of the water—the meat should be covered with the sauce—then cover the pan and simmer until the meat is tender—about 30 minutes. (When cooked, the sauce should be quite soupy like a thin gravy; add more water if necessary.)

Serve in bowls, with lots of sauce and wheat-flour tortillas (see page 250).

6 servings

Tinga Poblano Shredded Savory Pork

On every restaurant menu in Puebla you will find *tostadas de tinga*—tortillas fried crisp and topped with this savory pork. It can, of course, be served as a main dish and goes very well, although untypically, with white Mexican rice (see Arroz Blanco, page 32).

The *Diccionario de Aztequismos* translates *tinga* as "vulgar" or "disorder." A very tasty disorder, I must say!

1 pound boneless stewing pork, cut into 1-inch cubes
½ teaspoon salt, or to taste
½ pound chorizos
1 pound tomatoes, peeled and chopped
1 small white onion, roughly sliced
⅛ teaspoon thyme
⅛ teaspoon oregano
1 bay leaf (2 to 3 in Mexico)
3 canned chiles chipotles en vinagre, or en adobo, cut into strips
2 tablespoons liquid or sauce from the canned chilies

THE GARNISH

1 avocado, sliced thinly
1 cup shredded lettuce

Cover the pork cubes with water, add salt, and bring to a boil, then lower the flame and simmer until tender—about 40 minutes. Let the pork cool off in the broth for a short period, then drain, reserving the broth, and shred the meat fine.

Skin the *chorizos*, crumble the meat into a frying pan, and cook over low heat until the fat has rendered out. Remove the *chorizo* pieces from the pan and set aside.

Take out all but 2 tablespoons of the fat in the pan. Add the tomatoes and onion to the pan and fry over a fairly high flame for about 5 minutes, stirring the mixture well and scraping the bottom of the pan from time to time. Add the shredded pork, fried *chorizo*, thyme, oregano, bay leaf, chilies, liquid or sauce from the chili can, and ½ cup of the reserved broth to the tomato sauce.

(continued)

Adjust the seasoning and let the mixture cook and season for about 10 minutes, stirring it well from time to time. It should be moist but not too liquid.

Use as a topping for *tostadas,* garnishing with the avocado and shredded lettuce.

Enough for about 12 tostadas

Albóndigas en Chipotle Quemado Meatballs in "Burnt" Chipotle Sauce

Sra. María Elena Lara (restaurante Los Tres Migueles,
Mexico City)

THE MEATBALLS

    ¼ *teaspoon thyme*
    ¼ *teaspoon marjoram*
    ½ *bay leaf (1 to 1½ in Mexico)*
    ¼ *teaspoon cuminseed*
    8 *peppercorns*
    2 *teaspoons salt*
    ⅓ *cup milk*
    1 *raw egg*
    2 *cloves garlic, peeled*
    1 *slice stale bread*
    ¾ *pound ground beef*
    ¾ *pound ground pork, with some fat*
    ⅓ *cup half-cooked rice*
    1 *egg, hard-cooked and finely chopped*

THE SAUCE

    6 chiles chipotles *(dried, not canned)*
    2 *tablespoons pork lard or peanut or safflower oil*
  1½ *pounds ripe tomatoes, broiled (see page 262)*
    ½ *medium white onion, thinly sliced*

2 *cloves garlic, peeled*
¼ *teaspoon cuminseed*
1 *teaspoon salt, or to taste*
2½ *cups water or meat broth, approximately*

Put the herbs, spices, salt, milk, raw egg, and garlic into a blender jar and blend until smooth. Soak the bread in this mixture until it is mushy, then add it all to the ground meats, along with the rice and chopped egg, and work well with your hands. This quantity will make approximately 24 meatballs about 1½ inches in diameter; form the meatballs and set them aside while you prepare the sauce.

Heat a griddle or *comal* and heat the chilies, turning them from time to time until they become soft and flexible. Slit the chilies open and remove the seeds and veins.

Heat the lard and fry the chilies, flattening them in the fat with a spatula, until they are very dark brown, almost black. Remove from the pan, leaving the lard, and put into a blender jar with the broiled tomatoes. Blend until smooth.

Reheat the lard in the pan and fry the onion gently, without browning, until soft. Crush the garlic, cuminseed, and salt together in a *molcajete* or mortar. Add 2 tablespoons of water—to clean the mortar out—and add the mixture to the onions in the pan. Fry, stirring and scraping, over a high flame until almost dry, then add the blended ingredients and fry over a fairly high flame, stirring and scraping the bottom of the pan constantly, until the sauce has reduced and thickened.

Add the broth and meatballs—the sauce should just cover them—cover the pan, and cook over a gentle heat, turning the meatballs occasionally, until they are cooked through and spongy—about 30 to 45 minutes.

6 servings

Carne de Puerco en Chile Colorado Pork in Red Chili

Sra. Rosa Margarita J. de Mejía (Chihuahua)

When *The Cuisines of Mexico* was published, my northern Mexican friends gently chided me for not taking more notice of their favorite dishes. So for this book, after another extended tour through the northern states, I gathered together a number of recipes from that region, including this one. Admittedly, my taste lies south—with the fascinating herbs, chilies, and vegetables of central Mexico—but I do find these simple dishes extremely good, and very comforting after a lot of more complicated food.

Sra. Rosa Margarita J. de Mejía, a talented cook from Chihuahua who has introduced me to many of her regional dishes, gave me this particular recipe. It is made with the *chile de la tierra,* which has a wide distribution and a variety of names.

> 2¼ *pounds boneless pork, with some fat, cut into*
> ½-inch *cubes*
> 2 *teaspoons salt, or to taste*
> 3½ to 3¾ *cups water, approximately*
> 2 *cloves garlic, peeled*
> ⅛ *teaspoon cuminseed*
> ¼ *teaspoon oregano*
> 8 *chiles de la tierra (see page 228)*
> 2 *tablespoons peanut or safflower oil,*
> *approximately*
> 2 *teaspoons all-purpose flour*

Put the meat, salt, and ¼ cup of the water into a heavy pan, in which the meat will just fit in two layers. Cover the pan and cook over a low flame, shaking the pan from time to time to prevent sticking, until the meat is *just* tender, all the liquid absorbed, and the fat rendering out—about 45 minutes, depending on the cut of meat and how tender it is. If it becomes too dry during the cooking time, then add a little more water.

Crush the garlic, cuminseed, and oregano in a *molcajete* or mortar. Remove the stems from the chilies (leave in the seeds and veins), cover with water, and simmer for about 10 minutes, or until the skin is soft. Drain and transfer to a blender jar, along with 1 cup of the water, the garlic, cuminseed, and oregano, and blend until smooth. Set aside.

Add oil as necessary to the fat in the pan to make up to 3 tablespoons, approximately. Heat the oil and fry the meat lightly, turning it over from time to time. Sprinkle the flour over the meat and keep turning and frying until it browns slightly. Pass the chili sauce through a food mill or strainer into the pan and fry for a few minutes longer, stirring and scraping the bottom of the pan. Add the remaining 2 to 2½ cups of water—the sauce should be rather thin—and cook for 15 to 20 minutes more.

Serve in bowls, with lots of sauce and wheat-flour tortillas (see page 250).

6 servings

Patas de Puerco en Escabeche Soused Pigs' Feet

Sra. Ana María V. de Mackey (Mexico City)

With so much pork eaten in Mexico, you can imagine that there are a lot of pigs' feet around—*patas* ("trotters") or *manitas* ("little hands"), whatever you want to call them. They are very popular cooked and lightly pickled as an appetizer; chopped as a topping for *tostadas;* covered with light batter, then fried and served in a chili or tomato sauce. Indeed, they are very popular however you serve them.

This is an unusual and refreshing way of preparing them that was given to me by a friend's mother who comes from Tampico.

Start the day before you plan to serve these.

> 2½ *pounds pigs' feet (3 large ones cut into four pieces)*
> 2 *tablespoons salt*
> 6 *cups (about 1½ pounds) thinly sliced white onion*
> ½ *cup wine vinegar*
> ⅓ *cup salad or olive oil*
> 2 *teaspoons whole-leaf oregano*
> ¼ *cup juice from a can of* chiles serranos *or* chiles jalapeños en escabeche
> 2 *large tomatoes (1 pound), unpeeled, thinly sliced*
> *Freshly ground pepper*

Scrub the pigs' feet well and singe off any small hairs that still remain, then cover with cold water. Bring to a boil and boil for 1 minute. Drain.

(continued)

Cover the pigs' feet again with cold water, add 1 tablespoon of salt, and simmer until tender—from 1½ to 2 hours, depending on how tough they are. Drain and discard the cooking water.

While the feet are cooking, prepare the onion. Cover with cold water and leave for about 1 hour, then drain and discard the water. Put the onion into a glass or china bowl and add the vinegar, 1½ teaspoons of the salt, the oil, oregano, and the canned chili juice. Mix well and set aside.

If possible, choose twin dishes, with handles or a rim, about 3 inches deep, in one of which the feet will just fit in one layer. Set the second dish aside. Spread the bottom of the other with half of the onion. Spread the tomato slices over the onion, then arrange the pieces of pigs' feet on top. Season with the remaining 1½ teaspoons salt and the pepper and cover the pigs' feet with the rest of the onions. Finally pour the vinegar marinade over the top. Set aside for about 2 hours.

Put the twin dish, upside down, on top of the filled one and transfer the contents with a quick turn so as little of the juice as possible is lost. Leave for another 2 hours, repeat the process, and then leave until the following day.

Serve as an appetizer or buffet dish with hot, freshly made tortillas (see page 246).

Asado Placero Sinaloense Meat and Vegetables in Tomato Sauce Sinaloa

Sra. María Luisa Cárdenas (restaurante La Negra, Mazatlán)

I must say at the outset that this dish does not "send" me. But it is a popular dish in Sinaloa and has a place in any collection of typical Mexican recipes. Nobody, of course, can agree just what vegetables should go into it, and some cooks include carrots, *chayotes,* and green beans.

In Mazatlán it is customary to eat seafood in the middle of the day and at night *asado* or, as in other parts of Mexico, tacos and *antojitos.* If you ask around about the best place to eat *asado,* the unhesitating answer will be La

Negra. I went there, and of course it was closed that week for painting. I found Señora Cárdenas sitting in her kitchen behind the restaurant, and when I explained that I had made a special trip to see her, she generously gave me her recipe.

I suggest that you use chuck or any good stewing beef, or leftover roast beef —in which case you should leave out the first part of the recipe.

THE MEAT AND VEGETABLES

2¼ pounds stewing beef (see note above), in one piece
½ medium white onion, roughly sliced
3 cloves garlic, peeled
Salt
Water or light meat broth to cover
1 pound red bliss or other waxy potatoes
2 cups thinly sliced white onion
½ cup mild vinegar
½ cup cubed, cooked beets (optional)
1 cup finely shredded cabbage
¼ cup peanut or safflower oil
2 cups shredded lettuce

THE SAUCE

1¼ pounds tomatoes
1 clove garlic, peeled
1 chile serrano or any fresh, hot green chili (optional)
½ teaspoon salt, or to taste
½ teaspoon oregano

Put the meat, roughly sliced onion, garlic, and 1 tablespoon salt into a saucepan and cover with water. Bring to the simmering point and cook the beef until tender—time will vary tremendously, depending on the thickness of the piece of meat. Let the meat cool off in the broth. When it is cool enough to handle, cut into ½-inch cubes.

Cover the potatoes with water, add salt to taste, and boil until still slightly crisp. Drain and cool slightly, then peel and cut into ½-inch cubes.

Put the thinly sliced onions into the vinegar with the beets, if used, add salt to taste, and leave to macerate.

Blanch the cabbage in boiling water and drain. Add salt to taste.

(continued)

Prepare the sauce. Cover the tomatoes with boiling water and simmer until soft—about 20 minutes, depending on size. Drain and skin, then blend with the garlic, optional chili, and salt until smooth. Add the oregano and set aside, but keep warm.

Heat the oil and fry the meat and potatoes together until lightly browned, then adjust the seasoning and serve topped with the onion, cabbage, and lettuce. Pass the sauce separately.

6 servings

Bifsteks en Aguacate Steaks in Avocado Sauce

Señora Veronica Cuevas (Zitácuaro)

Zitácuaro will soon be my new home. The countryside is semitropical and lush, and the climate, by local description, "benign." So benign, in fact, that strawberries grow practically the year round and there are two long periods each year when there is a rich harvest of avocados. *Arquitecto* Armando Cuevas is building my ecological house there, and when the subject of food came up in the conversation—as it inevitably does—he told me that his wife took a great deal of interest in the local dishes. And, of course, eventually she invited me to lunch, when she prepared this dish.

Do not try and make it unless you have the rich California avocados. The big, roundish ones with thick skins that come up from Florida will not make a good sauce.

Note that there should be no delay in adding the sauce and serving, as the steaks will lose their juice. If this does happen, then simply heat slowly and stir the sauce.

> *6 shoulder or round steaks, each weighing 4 to 6 ounces*
> *and about ½ inch thick* (diezmillo *in Mexico*)
> *Salt and freshly ground pepper to taste*
> *3 tablespoons oil*
> *1 small white onion, finely chopped*
> *1½ cups freshly cooked* tomates verdes *(see page 245) or*
> *canned, drained*

3 sprigs fresh coriander, leaves only
2 cloves garlic, peeled
*2 avocados (see note above), peeled and pitted at the last
    moment*

Season the steaks with salt and pepper. Heat the oil until smoking and sear the steaks well on both sides. Add the onion and cook for 2 minutes more on each side.

Blend the *tomates verdes* with the coriander, garlic, 1 teaspoon salt, avocados, and 1¼ cups liquid in which the *tomate verdes* were cooked (or water, if canned are used) until completely smooth.

If there is any blood running from the steaks, cook for a little while longer, then pour on the sauce and stir over a low flame for about 5 minutes (the sauce should lightly coat the back of a wooden spoon). Adjust the seasoning and serve immediately, with Raja de Chiles Jalapeños Frescos (see page 164) on the side.

6 servings

Carne con Chile Verde Beef with Green Chili

Sra. Rosa Margarita J. de Mejía (Chihuahua)

*2¼ pounds stewing beef, with some fat, cut into ½-inch
        cubes*
3 cloves garlic, peeled and finely chopped
2 teaspoons salt, or to taste
2 cups water, approximately
2 to 3 tablespoons peanut or safflower oil, approximately
1 medium white onion, finely chopped
1½ tablespoons all-purpose flour
*12 chiles Anaheim, charred and peeled (see page 260)
        and cut into squares, or canned, peeled green
        chilies*
*2 small tomatoes, (about ½ pound), broiled (see page
        262) and chopped*

Put the meat—in two layers, no more—into a heavy pan. Add the salt, garlic, and ½ cup of the water, then cover the pan and cook over a very low flame until the meat is almost tender, the liquid evaporated, and the fat rendering out—about 1 hour, depending very much on the cut and quality of the meat. (It may be necessary to add a little more water to prevent the meat from sticking. On the other hand, if there is too much liquid as the meat approaches the correct point of tenderness, remove the cover, raise the heat, and reduce rapidly.) Shake the pan and turn the meat over from time to time.

Add enough oil to the fat in the pan to make about 3 tablespoons. Turn the heat to medium, then add the onion and brown the meat lightly. Sprinkle the flour into the pan and let it brown lightly, stirring constantly. Add the chilies, tomatoes, and 1½ cups water, then cover the pan and cook over low heat for another 20 minutes. (At the end of the cooking time there should be some liquid in the pan, but it should not be soupy; it may be necessary to add a little more water during the cooking time.)

Adjust the seasoning and serve hot, with wheat-flour tortillas (see page 250).

6 servings

Chamberete de Res en Chile Morita Beef Shin in Chile Morita Sauce

Sra. María Elena Lara (restaurante Los Tres Migueles,
Mexico City)

This is an example of the very earthy country cooking for which Señora Lara is so renowned. The sauce is very hot, so reduce the number of chilies if your palate can't take it. If you cannot find *moritas*—after reading the full description on page 227—substitute *chiles mora,* using about 10 to 12, or use 8 *chipotles.*

> 2½ *pounds beef shin, approximately, cut into 1-inch*
> *slices with bone and marrow*
> ½ *medium onion, roughly chopped*
> 6 *cloves garlic, peeled*
> 1½ *tablespoons salt, or to taste*
> ½ *cup chiles moritas (about ¾ ounces, or 25 chilies; see*
> *note above)*

1½ pounds tomatoes, broiled (see page 262)
¼ heaped teaspoon cuminseed
2 to 3 tablespoons water
3 tablespoons pork lard or peanut or safflower oil
1 medium white onion, thinly sliced
2 large sprigs epazote

Put the beef into a saucepan, together with the onion, 3 cloves of the garlic, and 1 tablespoon salt. Cover well with water and bring to a boil, then lower the flame and cook, covered, until the meat is tender, about 1½ hours (or about 2½ hours in Mexico City, where the meat is not so tender and the altitude affects cooking time). Remove the meat and drain, reserving the broth.

Remove the stalks from the chilies and toast them lightly on a warm griddle or *comal* (see page 259). Transfer to a blender jar, add the broiled tomatoes, and blend until smooth. Set aside.

Crush the remaining 3 cloves of garlic with the cuminseed and remaining ½ tablespoon salt in a *molcajete* or mortar and dilute with 2 or 3 tablespoons of water. Set aside.

Heat the lard and fry the sliced onion, without browning, for a minute or two. Add the meat and continue frying for a minute or so longer. Add the garlic paste and fry for a few minutes more, stirring and turning the mixture constantly. Add the chili sauce and fry over a high flame for another 5 minutes, scraping the bottom and sides of the pan to prevent the sauce from sticking. Add 2½ cups of the reserved meat broth and the *epazote,* adjust the seasoning, and continue cooking over a medium flame for 20 minutes more.

Serve with hot, freshly made tortillas (see page 246).

6 servings

Cebollas Rellenas Estilo Tamiahua Stuffed Onions Tamiahua

Señora Santiago (Tamiahua)

THE ONIONS

> 2 *large white onions*
> ½ *teaspoon salt*

THE STUFFING

> 3 to 4 *tablespoons peanut or safflower oil*
> 3 *cups cooked and shredded beef, roughly chopped*
> ⅓ *medium white onion, finely chopped*
> 1 *clove garlic, peeled and finely chopped*
> 1 *large tomato (about ½ pound), peeled and chopped*
> 2 to 3 *tablespoons broth or water (optional)*
> 1 *teaspoon large capers, finely chopped*
> 4 *green olives, pitted and finely chopped*
> *Salt to taste*

THE SAUCE

> 1½ *pounds tomatoes*
> *Salt to taste*
> 2 *cloves garlic, peeled and roughly chopped*
> 5 *peppercorns*
> 3 *tablespoons olive oil*
> ⅛ *teaspoon thyme*
> ⅛ *teaspoon marjoram*
> 1 *cup water or meat broth*
> 10 *green olives, pitted and halved*
> 2 *teaspoons large capers, roughly chopped*
> 2 *teaspoons vinegar*
> 3 chiles jalapeños en escabeche, *cut into strips*

FOR THE FRYING

> *Vegetable oil for frying*
> 4 *large eggs, separated*

½ teaspoon salt
1 cup all-purpose flour

Trim the onions by cutting off a slice at either end. Remove the dry outer skin.

Put the onions in a pan and cover with cold water. Add the salt, then bring to a boil and simmer until tender but not falling apart; test for doneness after 30 minutes. Set aside to drain and cool.

Heat the oil and fry the meat until it starts to brown. Add the onion, garlic, and tomato and continue frying over a medium flame, scraping the bottom of the pan so the mixture does not stick. If it seems very dry, then sprinkle with the water or broth; at the same time it should not be too wet. Add the capers and olives and adjust the seasoning. Cook until well seasoned and almost dry, then set aside to cool.

Put the tomatoes for the sauce into a saucepan. Cover with water, add salt, and bring to a boil. Lower the flame and simmer until soft but not mushy— about 15 minutes, depending on the size of the tomatoes. Drain and skin and transfer to a blender jar. Add the garlic and peppercorns and blend until smooth.

Heat the olive oil in a heavy pan. Add the blended tomatoes, thyme, and marjoram and cook the sauce over a medium flame for about 8 minutes, stirring and scraping the bottom of the pan from time to time. Add the broth, olives, and capers and cook until the sauce is of a medium consistency—about 8 minutes more. Stir in the vinegar and chili strips and set aside.

When the onions are cool enough to handle, make an incision through to the center of each of them, cutting through the layers from top to bottom. Peel off the layers carefully. Fill each layer with some of the stuffing and roll up, overlapping the edges so the stuffing doesn't fall out.

Pour oil to a depth of ¾ inch into the frying pan. Heat it until it smokes. Meanwhile, beat the egg whites until they are stiff but not dry. Add the salt and the yolks gradually, beating all the time, until they are well incorporated.

Lightly dust the filled onion layers with flour, then dip them into the beaten egg so they are completely covered. Carefully lower them, one at a time, between two spatulas into the hot oil. Fry the stuffed onions, turning or easing them over gradually, until they are puffed and golden all over. Drain on paper toweling. (If you wish, you can make everything ahead of time. Simply heat the stuffed onions at the last moment by placing them on a baking sheet lined with several layers of paper toweling and putting in a 325-degree oven.)

Bring the tomato sauce to a boil, add the stuffed onions, and heat through. Serve the onions with plenty of the sauce and hot, freshly made tortillas (see page 246).

6 servings

Mixiotes Meat Barbecued in Parchment

Sra. María Elena Lara (restaurante Los Tres Migueles,
Mexico City)

Huge century plants, or *maguey,* are a predominating feature of the central
Mexican landscape. The *maguey* has many uses apart from the making of
pulque. The large, pointed, fleshy "leaf" is used to line barbecue pits, and it
gives a very special flavor to the meat. The leaf is covered with a tough,
transparent skin, which is stripped off and used for wrapping meat that is to
be cooked in the barbecue pits. This also, apart from making a waterproof
package, lends a special flavor to the meat. These little packages of chili-
seasoned meat are called *mixiotes.*

Since the chances are that you don't have a barbecue pit lined with *maguey*
leaves, or the *mixiote* skins, use an ordinary steamer and wrap the meat in
parchment or foil. Señora Lara steams hers over a mixture of *pulque* and
water, and some other cooks suggest using beer and water; I myself find that
the latter gives rather too strong a flavor, but it is better than nothing. Although in Central Mexico mutton and rabbit are used most commonly, any
meat is, in fact, very good cooked in this way. I prefer meat on the bone as
a general rule, as it is not as dry and cooks better, and find that ribs of beef
are particularly tender and juicy for this dish.

If you are fortunate enough to be lining your steamer with *maguey* leaves,
sear them first over a hot flame so they soften and become pliable.

Start preparing the dish the day before you plan to serve it.

> *3 pounds meat, approximately, preferably with bone (see*
>   *note above), cut into 2¼-inch squares*
> *4 teaspoons salt, or to taste*
> *8* chiles guajillos
> *7* chiles pasillas
> *1½ cups pulque or beer, or ½ cup vinegar plus 1 cup water*
> *¼ teaspoon cuminseed*
> *½ teaspoon oregano*
> *⅛ teaspoon thyme*
> *¼ teaspoon marjoram*
> *5 whole cloves*
> *1 bay leaf (2 to 3 in Mexico), toasted (see page 258)*
> *3 cloves garlic, peeled*

1 *tablespoon vinegar*
12 *squares (approximately 7 × 7 inches)* mixiotes *(see note above), parchment paper, or foil*
   Liquid for steaming (equal parts pulque *or beer and water)*

The day before, season the meat with 2 teaspoons of the salt and set aside while you prepare the chilies.

Remove the stalks, seeds, and veins from the chilies. Flatten them out and toast them well (see page 259) on a hot griddle or *comal.* (They should be toasted enough so they crumble easily when cool, but care should be taken not to burn them, or the sauce will have a bitter taste.) Put the chilies, crumbled, into a blender jar, add the *pulque,* and leave to soak for about 15 minutes.

Meanwhile, using a *molcajete* or mortar, crush the cuminseed, oregano, thyme, marjoram, cloves, bay leaf, and garlic together with 2 teaspoons salt. Add the vinegar and grind to a paste. Add to the blender jar and blend briefly; there should be some rough pieces of chili in the sauce, so it should not be too smooth.

Cover the meat with the sauce and leave overnight to season.

The next day, if you are using the true *mixiotes,* cover them with hot water and leave to soak for about 5 minutes, or until fairly soft but pliable.

Divide the meat and sauce into twelve portions. Put one portion into the center of each *mixiote* square and gather up the sides to form a small bundle. Tie securely and put into the steamer. Put a coin into the bottom of the steamer (when it stops "dancing," you'll know you need to add more liquid), add the *pulque* (if available) and water, bring to a boil, and let the *mixiotes* cook until the meat is soft—about 2½ hours, depending on type and cut of meat. There should be plenty of juice in the packages.

Serve with hot, freshly made tortillas (see page 246).

6 servings

Carne a la Ranchera "Farmhouse" Meat

*Sra. María Elena Lara (restaurante Los Tres Migueles,
Mexico City)*

Every cook in every region must have her personal method of cooking meat, or using up cooked meat, *a la ranchera*—or, to use that awful expression, "farm style." This is Señora Lara's version. She uses cooked chicken, sliced tongue, pork, or udders, or raw, thinly sliced *filete*. I don't think many people would want to buy *filete* for this, but thinly sliced leftover roast beef would serve very well. In Mexico, where stewing veal on the bone is relatively cheap, I use that with great success.

It is a *picante* dish, but you can, of course, regulate the "heat."

¼ *cup peanut or sesame oil*
½ *medium white onion, roughly sliced*
4 *cloves garlic, peeled and chopped*
1½ *pounds tomatoes, peeled (if you don't like the skin) and chopped*
¼ *cup roughly chopped Italian parsley*
2¼ to 2½ *pounds cooked meat, cut into large cubes or thinly sliced (see note above)*
2 to 3 *teaspoons salt*
1 *cup meat or chicken broth, approximately*
16 *small green olives, pitted but left whole*
6 chiles serranos en escabeche, *left whole*
2 *tablespoons liquid from the chili can*

Heat the oil and gently fry the onion and garlic until soft but not browned. Add the tomatoes and parsley and cook until reduced by about half. Add the meat and salt and cook for about 5 minutes longer. Add the broth, olives, chilies, and juice from the can and cook for about 5 minutes longer, or until well seasoned. (The sauce should neither be too watery nor too dry.)

Serve hot, with hot, freshly made tortillas (see page 246).

6 servings

Mondongo en Kabik Tripe in a Spicy, Picante Broth

Sra. Berta López de Marrufo (Mérida, Yucatan)

Besides being just what its Mayan title says it is, tripe in a *picante* broth, *mondongo en kabik* is a cheap, nutritious dish. I first tried this in a humble little eating place opposite the Mérida railroad station. For ten pesos—after devaluation—I had a large bowl of broth and a plate of tripe and cow's foot, served with French bread—rather soggy, generally, in Yucatán—a slice of lime, chopped chives, and chopped *chile verde* (the *chile verde* of Yucatán— a long, thin, pale-green chili with a smooth surface—has a distinctive flavor, quite unlike those in other parts of the country). It was quite a meal in itself, and very good, even in the heat of the day.

I find myself going back to Doña Berta constantly with any new recipe I may acquire, as there is something very special about her food compared with that of other cooks I have come across. I went back to her with this recipe, and this is her slightly more refined version.

The type of tripe that should be used, according to Yucatecan cooks, is that called *toalla* (towel), since it has the surface texture of a towel. Tripe in the United States is always well scrubbed and deodorized, so the orange juice step could be omitted—but apart from that it does tenderize the tripe, and gives it a pleasant, acidy flavor. If you cannot find the Seville oranges, then use the substitute (see page 243), and for the *chiles verdes* use any fresh, hot green chili.

(continued)

Start the preparation the day before you plan to serve the dish.

THE MEATS

> 1 pound tripe, cut into 1-inch squares
> 2 cups Seville orange juice or substitute (see page 243)
> 1 small calf's foot, cut into pieces
> ½ head garlic, unpeeled and toasted (see page 258)
> 1 teaspoon oregano, toasted (see page 258)
> 1 tablespoon salt

THE TOMATO SEASONING

> 2 tablespoons peanut or safflower oil
> 1 large tomato (about ½ pound), chopped
> ½ small white onion, finely chopped
> 1 small sweet green pepper, cleaned and chopped into
>   small squares
> 4 sprigs epazote, leaves and tops of stems only, roughly
>   chopped
> 3 chiles verdes (see note above), chiles gueros, or any fresh,
>   hot green chilies, toasted (see page 258)
> 1 teaspoon Recado Rojo (see page 218)
>   Salt to taste

THE GARNISH

> 6 chiles verdes or any fresh, hot green chilies, cut into
>   rounds
> ½ cup finely chopped white onion
> ⅓ cup finely chopped chives
>   Lime slices

One day ahead, wash the tripe well, cover with the orange juice, and leave to soak overnight, turning the pieces occasionally. Scrub the pieces of calf's foot. Put into a large saucepan with the garlic, oregano, and salt and cover well with water. Bring to a boil, then lower the flame and let cook gently for about 4 hours, or until the meat is just beginning to get tender. Set aside, in the cooking liquid, in a cool place overnight.

On serving day (horrible expression!), drain the tripe, rinse, and add to the calf's foot, in the calf's foot broth. Bring to a boil and cook slowly until both meats are tender—about 1 hour.

Meanwhile, heat the oil in a heavy pan and add the tomato, onion, sweet green pepper, and chopped *epazote*. Fry, stirring almost constantly, until the onion is soft. Add the chilies and *recado rojo*, along with 2 tablespoons of the broth from the saucepan containing the meats and cook for a few minutes more. Season and set aside.

When the meats are tender, drain, reserving the broth. Remove the bones from the calf's foot and chop the meat, gristle, and skin (all edible) into large pieces. Put the pieces, along with the tripe, onto a warmed serving dish and set aside in a warm place.

If necessary, add water to the reserved broth to make up to 8 cups. Add the tomato seasoning and simmer for about 5 minutes, or until well flavored. (If there is too much fat on top of the broth, skim as necessary.) Serve the broth in large soup bowls; serve the meat separately. Let everyone help themselves to the chilies, onion, chives, and slices of lime *al gusto.* Serve with French bread.

6 servings

Aguayón Estilo Leonor Pot Roast Leonor

This recipe was given to me by a friend's Oaxacan maid, and although I myself don't think it is an outstanding dish, guinea-pig friends of mine love it. It has a pleasant, interesting sauce. I always serve it with fried *chiles pasillas* on top to give it a little extra bite.

> 2½ to 3 *pounds beef pot roast, in one piece*
> 2 *teaspoons salt, or to taste*
> *Freshly ground pepper*
> 3 *tablespoons peanut or safflower oil*
> 3 *chiles pasillas*
> 2½ *cups water, approximately*
> ¾ *pound tomatoes, unpeeled, roughly chopped*
> ¾ *cup sesame seeds, toasted (see page 258)*
> 3 *thick, crisply toasted rounds of French bread*
> 2 *cloves garlic, peeled and roughly chopped*

THE GARNISH

> 4 chiles pasillas, *fried crisp (see page 260)*
> *Small, unskinned waxy potatoes, boiled*

Season the meat with salt and pepper. Heat the oil in a heavy Dutch oven and brown the meat lightly all over. Remove from the oil and set aside.

Remove the stalks, seeds, and veins from the chilies and toast them on a hot griddle or *comal* (see page 259); when they are cool they should be rather crisp, but take care not to burn them or the sauce will have a bitter taste. Put 1 cup of water into the blender and add the tomatoes, the toasted chilies, sesame seeds, bread, and the garlic and blend until smooth. (You may need a little extra water but use only enough to loosen the blades of the blender.)

In the oil in which the meat was browned, fry the blended sauce over a fairly high flame, stirring and scraping the bottom of the Dutch oven, for about 8 minutes. Add the meat, along with 1½ cups of water, and adjust the seasoning, then cover and cook over a slow flame until tender—about 4 hours.

To serve, slice the meat rather thickly, pour the sauce over, garnish with the fried *chiles pasillas,* and surround with the boiled potatoes.

6 servings

Conejo en Chile Rabbit in Chili Sauce

Sra. María Elena Lara (restaurante Los Tres Migueles, Mexico City)

This way of cooking rabbit is great—especially since commercially raised rabbits don't have much flavor. Rabbits are solidly meaty, and a large one (about 2½ to 3 pounds) cuts into six good-sized portions.

THE RABBIT

> 1 rabbit (2½ to 3 pounds), cut into six serving pieces
> 1 tablespoon salt
> ½ cup red wine or wine vinegar
> 1 bay leaf (2 to 3 in Mexico)
> 3 to 4 tablespoons pork lard or peanut or safflower oil
> ⅛ teaspoon thyme
> ⅛ teaspoon marjoram
> 1 medium white onion, thinly sliced
> 2 cups chicken broth or water, more if necessary

THE CHILI SAUCE

> 15 chiles guajillos *(about 2½ ounces)*
> 10 chiles pasillas *(about 2½ ounces)*
> 2 cups water
> 1¼ pounds tomatoes, broiled *(see page 262)*
> 2 teaspoons salt

THE GARLIC SEASONING

> 2 large cloves garlic, peeled
> ¼ teaspoon cuminseed
> ½ teaspoon oregano
> ¼ teaspoon marjoram
> ¼ teaspoon thyme
> 1 bay leaf (2 to 3 in Mexico)
> 2 tablespoons water
> ½ teaspoon salt

Put the rabbit into a saucepan, together with the salt, wine, bay leaf, and herbs. Cover with water and bring to a simmer. Simmer until just tender—about 40 minutes, depending on how tender the rabbit is to begin with. Drain and discard the cooking water.

While the rabbit is cooking, prepare the sauce. Remove the stalks, seeds, and veins from the chilies. Open them up flat and toast them on a hot griddle or *comal* on either side (see page 259), taking care that they do not burn. (When they have cooled off they should be crisp.)

Put the 2 cups of water, tomatoes, and salt into a blender jar and crumble in half of the chilies. Blend until almost smooth. Crumble the remaining chilies into the jar and blend briefly; the sauce should be of a rough consistency, with small pieces of unground chili in it. (You may have to add a little more water to the jar, but be sure it's only enough to release the blades of the blender.) Set aside while you prepare the garlic seasoning.

Crush the garlic in a *molcajete* or mortar, then grind together with the cuminseed, oregano, thyme, marjoram, bay leaf, and salt. Dilute with the water and set aside.

Melt the lard and fry the rabbit pieces lightly, together with the sliced onion. Add the garlic seasoning and fry for a minute more, stirring the mixture constantly. Wash the *molcajete* or mortar out with a little more water if necessary and add to the pan. Add the chili sauce and fry, constantly stirring and scraping the bottom of the pan, for about 2 minutes. Add 2 cups of broth or water and cook over a low flame for about 20 minutes, stirring the sauce from time to time. (The sauce should be of a medium consistency. Add more broth or water if it reduces too much.)

Serve hot, with freshly made tortillas (see page 246).

6 servings

Chicken

Pollo en Salsa de Cacahuate Chicken in Peanut Sauce

I was having tea one afternoon with a Mexican friend who has a great reputation as a cook. During a discussion of the food of Oaxaca, she called in one of her maids who was from Oaxaca and asked her to dictate some of her favorite recipes to us. This she did, without a moment's hesitation and without needing to correct a quantity or an ingredient. Here it is just as she gave it to us—a most interesting and delicious way of preparing chicken. *Pollo enchilado,* which follows, was another of her recipes. (The maid has since left my friend, so now it is I who provides her with those same recipes!)

The sauce is not very *picante*. There should just be a pleasant "afterglow" from the chilies.

(continued)

4½ *pounds chicken parts*
  1 *teaspoon salt, or to taste*
     Freshly ground black pepper
  3 *tablespoons fresh lime juice*
  ¼ *medium white onion, roughly chopped*
  2 *cloves garlic, unpeeled*
1-inch *piece cinnamon bark*
  6 *peppercorns*
  6 *whole cloves*
1¼ *cups raw (unroasted, unsalted) peanuts, measured*
     shelled and papery husks removed
  2 *large tomatoes (about 1 pound), broiled (see page 262)*
  1 *small can (2½ ounces)* chiles chipotles en vinagre *or*
     adobado *(there should be about 3 or 4 to the can)*
  3 *tablespoons peanut or safflower oil*
  2 *cups water*

Sprinkle the chicken with salt, pepper, and the lime juice and set aside to season while you prepare the sauce.

Heat a small, ungreased frying pan or *comal* and toast the onion and garlic until soft (see page 258). Peel the garlic. Toss the spices in the hot pan to toast them lightly, then toast the peanuts until they are lightly colored.

Put the tomatoes, chilies, and the toasted ingredients into a blender jar and blend until quite smooth. Add a little water only if necessary to release the blades of the blender.

Heat the oil in a heavy pan and sauté the chicken pieces, a few at a time, until golden brown. Remove the chicken from the pan and set aside. In the same oil, fry the blended ingredients over a medium flame for 3 minutes, constantly stirring and scraping the bottom of the pan. Lower the flame and let the sauce cook for about 30 minutes longer, continuing to scrape the bottom of the pan.

Add the sautéed chicken pieces and 2 cups of water. Adjust the seasoning and cook over a low flame until the chicken is tender—about 35 to 40 minutes.

Serve the chicken with plenty of the sauce, accompanied by small boiled potatoes.

6 servings

Manchamantel Chicken and Pork Stewed with Fruit

Sra. María Cortes Chávez (Mexico City)

Of the many versions that exist of this recipe, with its fascinating name that translates as "tablecloth stainer," I think this is the most interesting and delicious. It was a prize-winning recipe that appeared in a column of the Mexican newspaper *Excelsior.*

The *jícama* is a potato/radishlike tuber native to Mexico and South America. It can be found in Mexican markets on the West Coast and in Chinese markets all over.

> ¾ *pound boneless stewing pork, cut into 1½-inch*
> *cubes*
> 1 *tablespoon salt, or to taste*
> ¼ *cup peanut or safflower oil or pork lard*
> 1 *large chicken (about 3½ pounds), cut into serving*
> *pieces*
> 25 *almonds, unskinned*
> 1½-inch *piece cinnamon bark*
> 1½ *tablespoons sesame seeds*
> 5 chiles anchos, *cleaned of veins and seeds*
> 2 *medium tomatoes (about ¾ pound), broiled (see*
> *page 262)*
> 1½ *thick slices fresh pineapple, peeled and cut into ½*
> *-inch cubes*
> 1 *small plantain (about ½ pound), peeled and cut*
> *into thick rounds*
> 1 *small* jícama *(about ½ pound), peeled and cut into*
> *¼-inch slices*

Put the pork cubes into a saucepan, add water to cover and 1 teaspoon of the salt, and bring to a simmer. Cover and cook for 25 minutes only, then drain, reserving the broth. Strain the broth, adding enough water to make 4 cups, and set aside.

In a heavy, flameproof casserole, heat the oil and sauté the chicken pieces lightly, a few at a time. Remove and set aside. In the same oil, fry the almonds, cinnamon bark, and sesame seeds separately, adding each to the blender jar, after draining. Drain and transfer to the blender jar.

(continued)

In the same oil, fry the chilies lightly on both sides, then drain and transfer to the blender jar. Add the broiled tomatoes and 1 to 1½ cups of the broth to the blender jar and blend until smooth. (Be careful to add only enough broth to release the blades of the blender; the sauce must not be too watery.)

Reheat the oil remaining in the casserole and fry the chili sauce for about 4 minutes, stirring and scraping the bottom constantly. Add 3 cups of the reserved broth and bring to a simmer. Add the chicken pieces, pork cubes, fruit, and 2 teaspoons salt, then cover and cook over a low flame for 1 to 1¼ hours, or until the meat and fruit are tender, stirring from time to time.

Serve hot, with freshly made tortillas (see page 246).

6 servings

Tapado de Pollo Chicken and Fruit Casserole

This is one of those fruity stews, not too sweet but pleasantly acidy, that one finds in Oaxaca, Veracruz, San Luis Potosí, and throughout the central part of Mexico. It is served very simply, just with hot tortillas and pickled chilies on the side for those who like a bite to their food.

> 4½ *pounds chicken parts*
>   *Salt*
> 6 *peppercorns*
> 1 *whole clove*
> ½-inch *piece cinnamon bark*
> 1 *tablespoon granulated sugar*
> ¼ *cup dry sherry*
> 3 *cloves garlic, peeled and finely chopped*
> ¼ *cup vinegar*
> 1 *large white onion, thinly sliced*
> 2 *medium tomatoes (¾ pound), peeled and sliced*
> 1 *small apple, peeled and cored and cut into thick slices*
> 1 *small pear, peeled and cored and cut into thick slices*
> 1 *bay leaf (2 to 3 in Mexico)*
> ⅛ *teaspoon thyme*
> ⅛ *teaspoon oregano*

THE GARNISH

> ¼ *cup peanut or safflower oil*
> 1 *large, very ripe plantain (about ¾ pound), peeled and*
>   *cut into lengthwise slices*
> 2 *tablespoons large capers, drained*
> 15 *green olives, pitted and halved*

Preheat the oven to 375 degrees. Sprinkle the chicken pieces with salt. Grind the peppercorns, clove, and cinnamon together in a spice grinder and mix with the sugar, sherry, garlic, vinegar, and about 1½ teaspoons salt.

Spread a layer of the onion—about one-third of it—on the bottom of a deep casserole; cover with one-third each of the tomato slices and the fruits. Add the bay leaf and sprinkle with a little of the herbs, then put half of the chicken pieces on top of the fruits and vegetables and pour on half the vinegar/spice mixture. Repeat the layers, finishing up with a topping of onion, tomatoes, and fruit.

Cover the casserole and bake for about 1 hour, then uncover the casserole for 30 minutes longer, or until the chicken is tender and some of the juices have been reduced.

Meanwhile, heat the oil until smoking and fry the plantain pieces until a deep golden brown. Remove and drain. To serve, cover the top of the stew with the capers, olives, and fried plantain.

6 servings

Pollo Enchilado Chilied Chicken

This is a very mild dish. You may serve strips of *chiles jalapeños en escabeche* in a separate dish for those who simply can't do without a *picante* chili of some kind.

(continued)

> 6 *large* chiles anchos
> 4 *ounces lean bacon strips, diced*
> 4 *almonds, unpeeled*
> 5 *large prunes, pitted*
> 1-inch *piece cinnamon bark*
> 4 *whole cloves*
> 4 *peppercorns*
> ⅛ *teaspoon oregano*
> ⅛ *teaspoon thyme*
> ⅛ *teaspoon marjoram*
> 2¾ *cups fresh orange juice (juice of about 6 large oranges)*
> 2 *teaspoons salt, or to taste*
> 1 *cup water*
> 4½ *pounds chicken parts*
> 5 *medium carrots (about ¾ pound), scraped and cut into fours lengthwise*

Remove the seeds and veins from the chilies. Flatten them out and toast them lightly on a hot griddle or *comal* (see page 259). Cook the bacon gently until the fat has rendered out, then drain and transfer to a blender jar.

Fry the chilies briefly in the bacon fat left in the pan. Drain and add to the blender jar. Fry the almonds, prunes, spices, and herbs together in the same fat. Drain and add to the ingredients in the blender jar. Add the orange juice, salt, and water and then blend until quite smooth. The sauce should be rather thick.

Preheat the oven to 375 degrees.

Add oil or lard if necessary to the remaining bacon fat and sauté the chicken, a few pieces at a time, until golden brown. Remove from the pan and place in one layer in an ovenproof dish. (Make sure the pieces fit snugly, so the sauce will not dry up too much during the cooking period.)

Place the carrot pieces around the chicken and pour the sauce over—it should cover everything. Cover the dish with foil and bake until the chicken is tender—1½ to 2 hours.

Serve with plenty of the sauce, accompanied by fresh, hot tortillas (see page 246).

6 servings

Pollo Almendrado Almond Chicken

Sra. Leticia Castro (Coahuila)

Chicken cooked in almond sauce is one of the milder, more elegant dishes of the Mexican cuisine, and there are many versions of it. This one, a more unusual version, was given to me by an enthusiastic and wonderful cook, Sra. Leticia Castro, who comes from Coahuila in the north of Mexico. She generously let me take recipes from the family cookbook that have been handed down for several generations. The original recipe was for a "young and tender chicken" that was thickly covered, inside and out, with the almond "paste." However, the crust falls off when you serve the chicken, so I think this version is more practical.

> 4½ *pounds chicken parts*
> 2½ *teaspoons salt, or to taste*
>   *Freshly ground black pepper*
> 3 *tablespoons lime juice*
> 2 *large, very ripe tomatoes (about 1 pound), broiled*
>   *(see page 262)*
> 6 *peppercorns*
> 2 *whole cloves*
> 1 *bay leaf (2 to 3 in Mexico)*
> ¼ *cup cold water, approximately*
> 2 to 3 *ounces (4 to 6 tablespoons) pork lard*
> 1 *cup peeled almonds*
> 2 *thick rounds stale French bread or hard roll*

Season the chicken with 2 teaspoons of the salt, some pepper, and the lime juice and set aside for at least 1 hour.

Preheat the oven to 350 degrees.

Put the tomatoes, peppercorns, cloves, bay leaf, water, and ½ teaspoon salt into a blender jar. Melt the lard in a small frying pan and fry the almonds to a deep golden color. Transfer to the blender jar. In the same lard fry the bread and add to the blender, then blend all the ingredients to a fairly smooth paste, adding a little more water only if necessary to release the blades. (Note: this is hard work for the blender, so you may wish to roughly chop the almonds and bread, or crush them in a mortar, before adding to the blender.)

(continued)

Choose a shallow, ovenproof dish into which the pieces of chicken will just fit in one layer. Pour a little of the melted lard from the frying pan into the dish and spread the bottom of it with a little more than one-third of the almond sauce. Cover with the chicken pieces and cover them in turn with the remaining sauce. Bake, uncovered, basting from time to time with the rest of the lard until the chicken is tender and the sauce slightly crusty on top—about 45 minutes.

I suggest you serve this with small, boiled new potatoes and a lightly dressed salad. Strips of *chiles jalapeños en escabeche* can be passed separately.

6 servings

Pollo Estilo Guanajuato Chicken Guanajuato

Sra. María Luisa de Martínez (Mexico City)

Oranges are grown on a very large scale in many parts of the Republic, and they are used in a great many regional dishes. Here is one from Guanajuato.

> 1½ *whole chicken (4½ pounds)*
>   *Salt and freshly ground pepper*
> 3 *tablespoons peanut or safflower oil*
> 1 *large onion, thickly sliced*
> 3 *cloves garlic, peeled and finely chopped*
> 3 *medium tomatoes, broiled (see page 262)*
> ¼ *heaped teaspoon thyme*
> ¼ *heaped teaspoon marjoram*
> ¾-inch *piece cinnamon bark*
> 1¼ *cups fresh orange juice*
>   *Rind of ½ orange*
> 12 *small new potatoes, unpeeled*
> 5 *medium carrots (about ¾ pound), scraped and cut*
>   *into fours lengthwise*

Preheat the oven to 350 degrees. Season the cavity of the chicken with salt and pepper.

Heat the oil in a flameproof casserole in which the chicken will just fit snugly and brown the chicken all over. Remove from the casserole and sprinkle with more salt and pepper, then set aside.

Take out all but 2 tablespoons of the oil from the casserole. Fry the onion and garlic gently, without browning, until translucent.

Blend the tomatoes until smooth. Add the puree to the pan, together with the thyme, marjoram, and cinnamon bark and fry over a high flame for about 3 minutes, stirring and scraping the bottom of the pan constantly. Add the chicken, orange juice, orange rind, potatoes, and carrots. Cover the casserole and bake for about 30 minutes, then turn the chicken over and bake until tender—another 20 to 25 minutes, approximately.

Cut the chicken into serving pieces and serve with plenty of the sauce and vegetables.

6 servings

Pollo en Ajo-Comino Chicken in Garlic and Cumin

Sra. María Sánchez (Tamuin, San Luis Potosí)

This is one of those very simple stews served in the marketplaces of little towns in the eastern part of the state of San Luis Potosí, which forms part of the Huastec country. It is one of the dishes that is served at the *fonda típica* in San Luis Potosí; the first of its kind, and sponsored by the state government, the *fonda* was organized by a group of very efficient, public-spirited women who wanted to make sure that visitors had a chance to try the many dishes from different parts of the state. And no wonder, for because of geographical differences within the state, there are three distinct areas—the hot coastal lowlands, the more lush mountainous areas, and the bare, semiarid lands—and each has its own distinctive cuisine.

(continued)

> 4 chiles anchos, *cleaned of veins and seeds*
> 1 teaspoon cuminseed
> 12 peppercorns
> 1 tablespoon salt, or to taste
> 1 whole clove
> 4 cloves garlic, peeled
> 3½ cups water, approximately
> 3 tablespoons peanut or safflower oil
> 4½ pounds chicken parts

Cover the cleaned chilies with water and simmer for about 5 minutes, then leave to soak for 5 minutes. Drain. In a *mòlcajete* or mortar, grind the cuminseed, peppercorns, salt, and clove, then mash in the garlic gradually, adding ¼ cup of the water to dilute the mixture. Set aside.

Transfer the drained *chiles anchos* to a blender jar with ¾ cup of the water. Blend until smooth and set aside.

Heat the oil and fry the chicken pieces (a few at a time so they will brown properly) to a pale gold. Add the spice mixture and fry over medium heat for about 3 minutes, stirring constantly. Add the blended chilies and fry for another 3 minutes, scraping the bottom of the pan constantly. Add about 2½ cups of the water, then adjust the seasoning and cook slowly, uncovered, until the chicken is tender—about 50 minutes, turning the pieces over from time to time. (The sauce should not be thick; add more water if necessary.)

Serve hot, with freshly made tortillas (see page 246).

6 servings

Pollo Tepehuano Chicken Tepehuan

Sr. Gilberto Nuñez (Durango)

For my taste, chicken and rice dishes are generally nice and comforting but rather dull. But there is something about this one, perhaps the coriander and cumin, that gives it quite a fascinating flavor. Even if you do not calculate the time of cooking the chicken and rice quite perfectly and the latter turns out to be rather mushy, it is still good.

The recipe comes from a little town in Durango, and was given to me by Gilberto Nuñez, who for some time was a chef in Mexico City and then returned to his native Durango to open his own restaurant.

> 12 *green onions* (3 cebollas de rabo *in Mexico; see page 241*)
> 4½ *pounds chicken parts*
> 8 *cups strong chicken broth*
> 1½ *cups long-grain unconverted white rice*
> *Salt to taste*
> 2 *tablespoons peanut or safflower oil*
> 1 *large tomato (about 10 ounces), chopped*
> 2 chiles serranos *or any fresh, hot green chilies, finely chopped (optional)*
> 10 *sprigs coriander, leaves only, roughly chopped*
> ¼ *teaspoon cuminseed*

Cut four of the green onions into quarters lengthwise, using the tender part of the green, and put, along with the chicken pieces and broth, into a large saucepan. Bring slowly to a simmer and continue to simmer for about 10 minutes.

Meanwhile, rinse the rice twice in cold water and leave to drain in a strainer. After it has drained sufficiently, stir it gradually into the simmering broth, then add salt to taste. Continue cooking until the chicken and rice are just tender —anywhere from 25 to 40 minutes; the time varies tremendously with the type of cookware used, the type of rice, and the quality of the chicken.

Meanwhile, chop the remaining green onions fine. Heat the oil and fry the onion for about 2 minutes, without browning, then add the tomato, chilies, and coriander and continue cooking for about 5 minutes (the ingredients should have some texture and should have been reduced to a sauce). Add the tomato mixture, along with the cuminseed, to the pan with the chicken and rice and continue cooking for 5 minutes longer. The dish should have a soupy consistency.

Serve hot, with freshly made tortillas (see page 246).

6 servings

Pollo Tekantó Tekantó Chicken

Sra. Berta López de Marrufo (Mérida, Yucatán)

Pollo Tekantó has become the celebration dish of the Marrufo family in Mérida. The recipe was handed down to Señora Berta by her husband's grandmother, who was half Spanish and half Mayan. She lived most of her life in the Hacienda of Tekantó and was renowned for her cooking.

While this is a delicate dish, it has a curiously lingering flavor from the almonds and even more from the onions and garlic, which are charred on the outside while the inside is only partially cooked—a characteristic of Yucatecan cooking. I have altered the recipe in only one respect. It calls for the seasoning paste *recado para bifstek;* I have simply substituted the separate ingredients —oregano, peppercorns, garlic, and salt. (I mentioned in *The Cuisines of Mexico* how the Yucatecan housewife usually buys her *recados* already prepared. In the markets throughout the southeastern peninsula you will see various-sized balls or cakes of them, brown, black, or red.)

This dish is particularly good cooked, as it was originally, with turkey.

If you think of it in time, season the poultry and leave it to sit overnight.

> 2 medium white onions (about ¾ pound)
> 3 chiles x-cat-ik, chiles güeros, or fresh, hot Italian peppers
> 1 head garlic, unpeeled, plus 2 cloves garlic, peeled
> ¾ cup almonds, unskinned
> 1 tablespoon salt, or to taste
> ½ teaspoon oregano
> ½ teaspoon peppercorns
> 2 tablespoons vinegar
> 3½ cups water, approximately
> 4½ pounds chicken or turkey parts
> 4 to 5 tablespoons peanut or safflower oil
> 1½ tablespoons all-purpose flour

THE GARNISH

> ½ cup peanut or safflower oil, approximately
> 12 thick rounds stale French bread

1 large plantain (about ¾ pound), peeled and cut into
    ½-inch rounds slantwise
Lettuce leaves, preferably green leaf or romaine
6 radish flowers

Put the whole onions, chilies, and the unpeeled head of garlic straight onto the flame of a gas stove or charcoal (with an electric stove use a very hot griddle or *comal*) and let them char all over. The chilies should be lightly charred; the onion and garlic should have well-charred crusts and the inside flesh should be transparent but not too soft. Cut the outside crust off the onion and roughly chop the flesh. Set the head of garlic aside; do not peel. Leave the chilies whole; do not peel.

Meanwhile, cover the almonds with hot water, bring to a boil, and simmer for 5 minutes. Set aside to cool off in the water. When the almonds are cool enough to handle, slip off the skins and transfer to a blender jar (the object of boiling them is to soften them for the sauce). Add the salt, oregano, the two peeled (uncooked) cloves of garlic, the cooked onion, peppercorns, ½ teaspoon of the vinegar, and about ½ cup water and blend until smooth. (You may need to add a little more water to release the blades of the blender, but do not add too much, as the consistency should be that of a loose paste.)

Spread one-quarter of the almond mixture over the chicken pieces—it will be a *very* light coating—and set aside to season for a minimum of 2 hours or overnight.

In a heavy pan, heat 3 tablespoons of the oil until it smokes, then lower the flame and let the oil cool off a little before adding the chicken pieces—the almond paste burns readily. Add the chicken, a few pieces at a time, and sauté very lightly, until the pieces are just changing color—you may have to add a little more of the oil.

Drain any remaining oil from the pan. Break up the head of cooked garlic and place the garlic cloves at the bottom of the pan, along with the chilies. Put the chicken pieces on top. Add 3 cups of water—it should almost cover the chicken—cover the pan, and simmer until the chicken is *just* tender—anywhere from 25 to 40 minutes. Change the position of the pieces from time to time so they cook evenly.

Meanwhile, prepare the garnishes. Heat the oil until smoking and fry the bread until crisp and golden, then remove and drain. Fry the plantain rounds in the same oil until golden. Remove and drain.

When the chicken is almost tender, stir in the rest of the almond paste and vinegar and simmer, uncovered, for about 10 minutes.

(continued)

Put the flour into a small bowl. Add a little of the hot sauce and stir until smooth. Add to the chicken, stirring it in well, and cook for a few minutes longer, or until the sauce thickens.

Line the edges of a serving platter with the lettuce leaves. Arrange the chicken pieces, coated with some of the sauce, on the lettuce and decorate with the radish flowers and rounds of plantain. Arrange the fried bread around the edges of the platter and scatter the burnt chilies and garlic over.

Serve the chicken hot, passing the rest of the sauce separately.

6 servings

Seafood

Pan de Cazón Tortillas Layered with Fish and Beans

Pan de cazón, which means, literally, "bread of small shark," is considered to be one of the very special dishes of Campeche on the Gulf Coast of Mexico. The shark is cooked, shredded, and used as a filling, sandwiched between layers of tortillas, black bean puree, and smothered in tomato sauce. It is delicious if each component part is cooked with care—all too rare in restaurants today, even in Campeche, which used to be able to boast two of the most serious regional restaurants in Mexico.

It was explained to me by an enthusiast of the dish in the Campeche fish market that the small, black-finned shark, locally named *jaqueton,* should be used; the flesh of the baby sharks about twelve inches long is too slimy, and that of the much larger sharks too dry and stringy. Shark meat is available in New York (try La Marqueta on Park Avenue at 116th Street or the fish stores on Ninth Avenue), although my fish man thought himself a little too superior to carry it. He did, however, condescend to order me one—a five-pound sand shark, head, tail, and all. I demurred and settled for sierra (kingfish), which makes an unauthentic but adequate substitution, since the flesh is nonfatty and firm enough to shred. All expensive fish should be avoided if you are going to disguise it in this way.

In the southeastern peninsula of Mexico, this is served as a first course, but I find it makes a satisfying meal in itself accompanied by a salad and some sliced avocado.

Everything can be prepared ahead of time and then assembled at the last minute before serving so it does not become soggy.

> 1½ pounds shark, sierra, or mahi-mahi, cut into 1-inch
>   slices with skin and bone
>   1 tablespoon salt
>   1 small bunch epazote (about 8 sprigs)
> 12 six-inch freshly made tortillas (see page 246)
> 1½ cups Frijoles Colados Yucatecos (see page 40)
>   4 cups Salsa de Jitomate Yucateca (see page 159)

Add the salt to enough water to cover the fish and bring to a boil, then lower the flame, add the fish slices and half of the *epazote*, and simmer until the flesh flakes easily away from the bone—about 5 minutes. Remove the fish and drain.

When the fish is cool enough to handle, remove the skin and bone and discard. Squeeze the flesh lightly to get rid of any excess moisture and shred roughly. Remove the leaves from the remaining *epazote* and chop roughly. Add this to the shredded fish, season, and set aside in a warm place. Put an ovenproof dish (one just large enough to hold two of the tortillas side by side) into the oven, then preheat the oven to 300 degrees. Have all the ingredients ready and hot; heat the tortillas one by one as you use them on a hot *comal* or griddle.

Dip two of the tortillas into the hot tomato sauce and lay side by side at the bottom of the warmed dish. Spread each one with some of the black bean puree and one-third of the prepared, shredded fish. Put another tortilla, moistened in the tomato sauce, on top of each one to form a sandwich. Pour over 1 cup of the tomato sauce. Repeat the sandwich layers twice more, put the last two tortillas on top, and pour over the rest of the sauce. Return to the oven to heat through for about 5 minutes and serve immediately, cutting through the stacks of tortillas as you would a cake, in wedges.

6 servings

Camarones en Pipián Shrimps in Pumpkin-Seed Sauce

Sr. Angel Delgado (restaurante Las Diligencias, Tampico)

Hulled pumpkin seeds have become almost a luxury—the price has quadrupled in recent years—as they become more and more in demand as a recognized and valuable source of Vitamin E.

For the most part in Mexico, the unhulled, toasted seeds of certain varieties of pumpkins are ground as a base for the popular dish called *pipián* (although this is sometimes made with a mixture of nuts or sesame seeds). But there are some notable exceptions where hulled pumpkin seeds are called for: the *papa-dzules* of Yucatán (see *The Cuisines of Mexico,* page 70) and the *pipiáns* of that specific area that encompasses the northern part of the state of Veracruz and the southern coast of Tamaulipas. In these areas a pumpkin is cultivated that bears the largest seed of them all, about 1 inch long and with a pretty green border around it to match the color of the very oily seed inside.

This is an elegant and unusual dish, enough, because it is rich, for six portions as a main dish and eight as a first course. The recipe was prepared for me by Sr. Angel Delgado, the owner of Las Diligencias in Tampico, which for many years has had the reputation of being one of *the* serious eating places outside of Mexico City—perhaps the best thing one can say of any restaurant. I have altered Señor Delgado's recipe slightly by reducing the amount of butter considerably—the sour cream is quite rich enough—and by using shrimp broth rather than milk to blend the sauce. (For those who can't get uncleaned shrimps, use some canned clam juice or fish broth for the sauce.)

The shrimps of Tampico also deserve mention. I would go out of my way any day to have a plateful of *camarones al natural* in Tampico—served, as they should be, unskinned with head and tail still on. But you should specify whether you want those from the lagoons along the coastal area or from the sea. I'd take those from the sea every time.

(continued)

1½ pounds medium-sized shrimps, unshelled
1½ cups cold water
  1 teaspoon salt, or to taste
    Freshly ground pepper
  1 cup (about 4 ounces) hulled, unroasted, unsalted
      pumpkin seeds
  8 sprigs fresh coriander, leaves only
  3 chiles serranos or any fresh, hot green chilies
  ½ small white onion
  1 tablespoon sweet butter
  ⅔ cup sour cream, preferably homemade (see page 235)

Put the uncleaned shrimps into a saucepan with the water, salt, and pepper and bring to a boil. Turn the flame down and simmer, turning the shrimps constantly so they cook evenly, for about 5 minutes, or until the shrimps are crisp-cooked (time will vary with size). Drain and reserve the liquid.

As soon as the shrimps are cool enough to handle, clean and devein. Return the shrimp debris to the pan, along with the reserved liquid, then cover and simmer for 10 minutes longer. Strain and again reserve the broth, discarding the shells.

In a heavy, ungreased frying pan, toast the seeds lightly, stirring them constantly, until they begin to swell up and start to pop about—do not let them brown.

Add the shrimp broth, coriander, chilies, onion, and last of all the toasted seeds to a blender jar and blend until smooth.

Melt the butter in the pan. Add the pumpkin seed sauce and sour cream (if homemade) and cook over a very low flame for about 10 minutes, stirring constantly and scraping the bottom of the pan. Stir the cooked shrimps into the sauce and heat through. (If commercial sour cream is being used, add it last or the sauce will become lumpy or have a curdled appearance.) You may need to dilute the sauce a little; if so add more broth or water.

6 to 8 servings

Relleno de Guavina Fish and Shrimp Sausage

(Don Victoriano, Tlacotalpan, Veracruz)

I don't know how it had escaped me during my many years of living in Mexico, but it wasn't until 1973 that friends told me about a very special restaurant, outstanding for its regional dishes. They are cooked with great care, my friends said, many using the sweet and delicate crayfish, crabs, and shrimps from the river that flows past the restaurant's door. Of course I had to go.

I had crossed the Papaloapan river, miles further down from my destination, in a boat that was small and crowded but that flaunted a little awning to protect us from the sun. I joined the other passengers waiting for the bus who, as they waited, ate tortillas crammed with *carnitas,* those small, delicious chunks of crisply cooked pork, or cracked the large white crab claws they had bought from the small food stands grouped around the ferry dock. The bus was standing by, empty, and it was beginning to seem that we would be there forever when suddenly, out of nowhere, the driver appeared at the wheel. There were two staccato hoots on the horn and we scrambled aboard, sensing the urgency of his message—and as the last ones clung to the hand rail and got a footing on the bottom step we went roaring off, in a cloud of dust.

On our left was the broad river, full to the brim, its muddy waters carrying logs, uprooted shrubs, and other debris swiftly down to the sea. The roadsides were alive with brilliant wild flowers; on the right, colorful birds skimmed over a narrow stream choked with pale mauve water hyacinth. And, on the marshes around the lagoons beyond, humped zebus grazed peacefully with their attendant herons standing watchfully by.

Half an hour later we were in Tlacotalpan, a small, compact town on the river bank. At first all you could see was a mass of low, tiled roofs weathered to a rich red-brown, accented by a white dome and spire, a few palm trees towering like sentinels above them all. As I stepped down from the bus, I found myself in a Mexico I didn't recognize. Many of the streets were unpaved. They were soft and grassy and so quiet, with flowering hibiscus and oleander bushes here and there. Many of the houses had recently been painted, in colors ranging from deep-hued pinks, greens, and blues to delicate pastels; their classical pillars and arches, picked out in white, gleamed in the midday sun. At every turn there seemed to be another little plaza—deserted, colorful, and almost unreal, as though one had stepped into a neglected set for an eighteenth-century movie. Along the river bank the fishermen's boats strained at their moorings in the swift current; the deserted docks nearby were a reminder of the days when the town was a flourishing port, and nineteenth-century ocean-going vessels brought in Spanish, Italian, and Portuguese passengers and cargo.

I established myself in the only hotel in town, and it was not long before I was deep in a conversation with the hotel owner about the local food. She was a mine of information, and very soon I began to realize that here was something very special indeed. For it was she who told me about Don Victoriano, who had taught the cooks in the famous little restaurant.

Without a moment's delay I set out to find his house—which I did, quite easily, for everyone knew him. In fact, he lived in two houses, adjoining and at right angles to each other, one painted a deep, violent red, the other a brilliant blue. I walked up to an open door and three people beckoned me in. I found them all seated in the locally made rocking chairs that seemed to be in every house, highly varnished, dark wooden frames with cane backs and seats, arms and headrests draped with spotlessly white antimacassars.

I was told to wait a moment, and very soon Don Victoriano came shuffling quickly into the room in his worn leather huaraches. He was of medium build, slim; his tightly curling black hair was receding and tinged with grey at the temples; his eyes were a lively blue-grey and his dark skin was mottled with pink. He was dressed like the fishermen of the town, in baggy blue pants and a white sweatshirt. He welcomed me in the open, friendly manner typical of the coast, as though I were an old friend and he had been expecting me.

No formal introduction seemed necessary. I loved good food; I loved to cook and wanted to learn about the regional specialties. "Come to lunch tomorrow at one o'clock. I am just cooking a *galápago en moste,* and by tomorrow it will be well seasoned and ready to eat."

The dish he had described, terrapin in a black sauce, sounded too good to miss, and the hollow, toneless church bell was just striking one o'clock when I returned the following day. Don Victoriano welcomed me by rushing out from the kitchen, noisily punctuating his greeting by sucking at the pineapple pulp that was lodged between his lower lip and teeth. We were very soon joined by an old lady and her companion, both carrying big black umbrellas against the afternoon sun.

Don Victoriano proudly ushered us into his new dining room, which was also the kitchen. The burners were set into a countertop that ran the width of the room and was completely tiled. The whole room, in fact, was covered with highly glazed blue and white tiles—floor, walls, buffet, stove, even the table.

The meal began. The fresh rolls that he himself had brought from the bakery only minutes before were carried into the room, along with a pile of carefully wrapped tortillas and a jug of iced, crushed papaya drink. The maid brought in large plates of shrimp soup—the small, sweet shrimps from the river, which reminded me of those I used to eat at home in England—then white rice and fried plantain. These were followed by the *pièce de résistance*, *galápago en moste quemado.*

The terrapin was delicious. Gelatinous and much more tender than sea turtle, it had been cooked in a thin, blackish sauce that had a musky flavor and was colored by the burnt, ground leaves of the *moste* bush that he had by his back door. "This dates from Zapotec times," said Don Victoriano.

I was beginning to feel very full—and then another steaming, fragrant dish was brought in. Don Victoriano apologized profusely for not serving something more elegant; apparently relatives had arrived unexpectedly, and because he had served them breakfast at ten-thirty that morning he couldn't get out to the market. He said the new dish was a duck in *lo que queda* sauce. I soon realized it was literally *lo que queda;* "that which was left over" had gone into the sauce, which resembled a light *pipián*, or pumpkin-seed sauce.

A huge mountain of sliced pineapple was now placed on the table, along with cookies made of unrefined sugar and grated fresh coconut, but the real dessert was on the buffet: enormous portions of a light egg custard thickened with finely ground almonds and topped with swirls of beaten egg white.

After the meal was over at last, I tried to concentrate on Don Victoriano's conversation and his never-ending string of recipes, while our lunch companions dozed, their heads bent over peacefully while their chairs rocked. He cooks and caters for hundreds—a baptism upriver, a wedding in the mountains, a breakfast for the President and his entourage. He never drinks or smokes, has never had a day's illness, and will soon be seventy-one.

"I want to give a large fiesta to celebrate that day and a good first year in my new house. I shall cook it all; come back then and cook with me and learn. The *galápagos* will be at their best and heavy with eggs, the wild ducks will be flying, and with any luck there will be fresh *tismiche* [newly hatched fish] from the river. We shall have to catch and skin the *galápago;* the best ones come from the river up near the mountains. Yes, come back then."

That December the house was due to be finished, so I wrote asking when the fiesta was to take place. I had a formally typed letter in reply, obviously composed and written by one of the town's official letter writers. It seemed the house was still not finished, and the inaugural fiesta postponed.

The following years were busy ones; I traveled but never to Tlacotalpan. Finally, three years later, I found myself once again on the road heading toward the little town to visit Don Victoriano. This time I was in a more predictable first-class bus, which roared along over the wide bridge that had now replaced the ferry.

When I got there, it didn't seem the same Tlacotalpan. Many streets were now paved and there was noise and activity, with young men screaming around on raucous motorcycles. I hurried along through the quieter back streets to Don Victoriano's. He no longer lived there. The man who had never had a day's illness in his life had died quite suddenly—and to this day nobody knows why.

This recipe of *relleno de guavina* is his. Nobody else I spoke to knows about it, and nobody remembers it.

You don't need an elegant and expensive fish for this recipe. Use whatever is the best buy—carp, sierra, or so forth.

You could use the sausage immediately, but the flavor will be greatly enhanced if you leave it to ripen in the refrigerator for 2 to 3 days. The broth could be frozen and used for poaching fish or as a base for a fish soup.

THE SAUSAGE

¾ to 1 pound fish, cut in ½-inch slices (about ½ pound boned), skin and bone removed and reserved
½ pound raw shrimp, cleaned and deveined, shells reserved
1 medium tomato (about 6 ounces), peeled and chopped
⅓ medium white onion, finely chopped
1 medium carrot, scraped and diced small
1½ tablespoons finely chopped fresh parsley
1 medium new potato, red bliss or other waxy potato, peeled and diced small
⅔ cup peas, preferably frozen
1 tablespoon lime juice
1 teaspoon salt, or to taste
6 tablespoons olive oil, approximately
4½ feet sausage casings (pork intestines, not plastic), approximately
1 chile jalapeño or any fresh, hot green chili, finely chopped
Freshly ground black pepper

THE BROTH

> *Reserved shells, skin, and bones from shrimps and fish*
> 2 *sprigs Italian parsley*
> 1 *stalk celery, roughly chopped*
> 2 *small carrots (about ¼ pound), scraped and sliced*
> 4 *cups water*
> 1 *small bay leaf (2 in Mexico)*
> ⅛ *teaspoon thyme*
> 1 *tablespoon lime or lemon juice*
> 6 *peppercorns*
> 2 *teaspoons salt, or to taste*

THE GARNISH

> ¼ *cup drained, chopped large capers*
> ¼ *cup pitted, chopped green olives*

Put the fish and shrimps into the freezer and leave for about 2 hours or until half frozen. While they are in the freezer, prepare the broth.

Put the debris from the fish and shrimps into a wide saucepan, together with the rest of the broth ingredients. Bring to a boil and simmer for about 1 hour. Strain the broth and return to the saucepan.

Put the fish and shrimps, a small quantity at a time to prevent the blades from clogging, into a blender jar or food processor and grind until fine. Mix the fish paste with the rest of the sausage ingredients, using only 2 tablespoons of the oil. Reserve the rest to fry the sausage after you have poached it. Fry one spoonful of the mixture now for taste, then adjust the seasoning if necessary and stuff into the casing, using any standard stuffing method; make two lengths about 1 inch thick, then prick all over with the sharp tines of a fork.

Reheat the broth, and when it starts to simmer add the sausages in flat coils. The broth should completely cover the sausages; if it does not, then add more hot water. Bring to a simmer and cook for about 15 to 20 minutes, then remove and drain. Let ripen in the refrigerator for a few days—this *will* improve the flavor—then proceed.

Cut the sausage into slices about ½ inch thick. Heat the remaining 4 tablespoons oil until it smokes, then lower the flame and fry the sausage slices until golden brown. Serve hot, sprinkled with the capers and olives.

6 servings

TAMIAHUA

Señora Santiago, the mother of a friend in Mexico City, had often talked to me about the small village on the Lagoon of Tamiahua, near Tampico, where she had lived for most of her married life and brought up her two children. She talked about her neighbors and friends and their peaceful, happy life: outings to the beach where they would catch and cook crabs and fish, boil potatoes to eat with them (an unusual local custom for Mexico), and make *enchiladas* of *pipián*, a sauce of pumpkin seeds. She told me about her daughter's *comadre*, or godmother, who was renowned for her *tamales* and shrimp balls; the women bakers of the village; and Leoncio Arteaga, who owned and ran a small restaurant, famed for its local food, called El Veracruzano. I began to dream, and, as so often happens, a few days later there I was, in Tampico.

The morning after my arrival I found myself speeding south down the narrow highway in a bus that, in the fashion that seems typical for long-distance Mexican buses, had no regard for any life in its path. I arrived breathless at my destination, Naranjos, or Orange Trees—such a pleasant name for what turned out to be a dismal village, sprawling and untidy and fearfully hot. Waiting for me across the street was one of those squat village buses, the glass long disappeared from the windows and springs sticking up from the tattered seats. The rack on top of the bus was already piled with baskets, cardboard boxes, and live poultry precariously tied on with string. It said "Tamiahua" boldly on the front of the bus—but one never knows in Mexico. In any case, I climbed up and paid my fifty cents to a poorly dressed but very serious young man all of nine years old. There were a few other passengers, and very soon we were off, bumping along a deeply rutted dirt road. We stopped occasionally to let somebody on or off—a young rancher who had left his horse tethered under a wayside shelter, a woman whose chickens were squawking on top—or to deliver one of the boxes to a waiting figure at the side of the road. To the right and left there were small ranches, which were marked out by smooth, red-barked fence posts that had taken root and were already sprouting on their way to becoming trees. The land had been cleared for cattle raising; charred, twisted trunks were all that remained of what had been tall, old trees, and they made a rather sinister landscape.

Trucks passing us in the opposite direction seemed to be warning our driver of something that lay ahead. Soon we would see for ourselves what it was all about. Although it was now mid-October and the rainy season was over, it had rained heavily the night before and the river was full. We forded it easily, but as we began to climb the opposite bank, the wheels began to spin and the engine choked into silence. The driver asked the men aboard to get down and push, which they did with vigor, but to no avail. They examined the engine, and everyone offered his piece of advice. The driver tried to start the engine again by running back into the river, precariously trying to avoid the deep-water side of the dividing concrete. It started with a rude jolt and we were off again—but once more the engine died as the wheels spun in the mud.

Time and time again we backed into the river—the only other woman passenger and myself exchanging fearful glances as the tries became more desperate, the men all the while insisting that we should not get down. An hour or more went by. We were joined by other drivers held up by our predicament. At least twenty voices were shouting advice now, and then twenty pairs of strong hands began pushing the bus from behind. The engine started up and the wheels bit into the earth. They held for one breathtaking moment, and then—amid resounding cheers and with mud churning up all around—we were finally off up the bank. About six miles further on we finally entered Tamiahua, two and a half hours after leaving Naranjos. My rosy vision of it soon faded amid the signs of bygone prosperity and respectability. I set off immediately in search of the *comadre,* and while there were no street signs, it was a small town, and everyone knew everyone else; by chance I came across a neighbor who lived next door to her. As we walked along talking, I found out that my companion was one of the bakers I had wanted to meet. She invited me to visit her house and see for myself.

As I went into the house I could see a huge shelter at the back whose roof adjoined the house itself, and under it was a huge, round brick oven about six feet across. The area was piled high with logs, and to one side a shelf of rough wooden planks held trays of rising dough and loaves of cooling bread. She broke a roll open for me to try—and I found I was disappointed. I suppose one expects something else from these "ideally primitive" conditions, but the bread was soft and doughy, as so much bread is along the Gulf Coast of Mexico.

I went next door and found the *comadre.* She was drawn and grey with prolonged illness, and, since it obviously fatigued her to talk, I left as soon as I could—but not before she had given me some guiding hints about the local food, its essential flavors, and how it should be cooked.

By this time it was late for lunch, so I found my way back to the *restaurante* El Veracruzano, which turned out to be a large, simple wooden shack set out over the water. Off to one side was the open kitchen, and behind that were long tables piled high with thousands of oysters, which were sheltered from the sun by a primitive roof of coconut palm. I sat down at a table and chose a fish soup, a spicy tomato broth thick with generous pieces of fish, crab, and shrimp from the lagoon (which, as I could see, was now a scene of frenzied activity as little boats sped from one side to the other, stopping as their occupants inspected the nets slung across the narrow waterway). Next came fish roe with green onions, chilies, and coriander, bound together by lots of beaten egg and fried into a large, flat cake, accompanied by the traditional *enchiladas de pipián*—made from the particularly large seeds of the pumpkins grown in the area—that are served with any fish dish in Tamiahua.

Finally Leoncio himself came to my table. He sat down and we talked for an hour or two about the local food, particularly the *tamales* of fish and shellfish that abound in the lagoon. Then with great pride he showed me his freezer, well stocked with fish; my heart sank at the thought of all that fresh seafood swimming right past his door.

It was now dark, and the restaurant was closing up for the night. I told myself I would try the oysters tomorrow, but I never did. After a miserable, fleabitten night I got up at five—and took the first bus out. Three of Leoncio's recipes follow: Saragalla de Pescado (page 104), Albóndigas de Camarones (page 106), and Pescado Enchilado (page 108). He would not divulge his recipe for *ostiones pimentados*, which was a closely guarded secret.

Saragalla de Pescado Shredded Fish Tamiahua

Sr. Leoncio Arteaga (restaurante El Veracruzano,
Tamiahua, Veracruz)

Jurel is the fish that was traditionally used for this particular dish, but in fact any firm-fleshed fish can be used; it is certainly ridiculous to buy expensive fish for it, although you can use crabmeat or chopped shrimps. I used shark, which was very good—it shredded well and is dry and not at all fatty. Monkfish on the East Coast and yellowtail or mahi-mahi (a type of tuna) on the West are other suggestions; as a matter of fact, any leftover fish would be fine.

The *saragalla* may be served hot or cold, along with freshly made tortillas, each person making his own tacos. Señor Arteaga says it should be served garnished with tomato and onion rings and strips of *chiles jalapeños en escabeche,* but I like it just as it is.

> 1 **small** chile ancho
> 12 *peppercorns*
> ¼ *teaspoon coriander seeds or* ⅛ *teaspoon cuminseed*
> ½-inch *piece cinnamon bark*
> ½ *teaspoon salt, or to taste*
> 2 *cloves garlic, peeled*
> ¼ *cup water*
> 3 *tablespoons peanut or safflower oil*
> 1 *medium tomato (about 6 ounces), peeled and chopped*
> ⅓ *medium white onion, roughly chopped*
> 2 *fresh* chiles serranos *or any fresh, hot green chili, finely chopped*
> 6 *green olives, pitted and finely chopped*
> 1 *teaspoon capers, roughly chopped*
> 1½ *tablespoons raisins*
> 2 *cups cooked and shredded fish (about 1 pound boned; see note above)*

Remove the seeds and veins from the *chile ancho,* cover with water, and simmer for 5 minutes. Soak for an additional 5 minutes, then drain and set aside. In a *molcajete* or mortar, grind together the peppercorns, coriander seeds, and cinnamon. Add the salt, garlic, *chile ancho,* and water and grind until smooth. (This is best done in the *molcajete* or mortar instead of a blender because there is not enough water for the blender to work efficiently, and the mixture must not be too watery.)

Heat the oil in a heavy saucepan and add the tomato, onion, *chiles serranos,* olives, capers, and raisins. Fry over a medium flame for about 5 minutes, stirring the mixture constantly. Add the spice mixture and cook, stirring from time to time, for about 5 minutes. Stir in the shredded fish and cook for 5 minutes longer.

Adjust the seasoning and serve either hot or cold, with freshly made tortillas (see page 246).

6 servings

Albóndigas de Camarones Shrimp Balls

Sr. Leoncio Arteaga (restaurante El Veracruzano,
Tamiahua, Veracruz)

THE SHRIMP BALLS

> 1½ pounds small shrimps, shelled, cleaned, and roughly
>   chopped
> ½ chile ancho
> ¼ teaspoon coriander seeds
> ¼ teaspoon peppercorns
> ½-inch piece cinnamon bark
> 1½ teaspoon salt, or to taste
> 1½ cloves garlic, peeled
> 3 tablespoons water
> 1 tablespoon peanut or safflower oil

THE TOMATO BROTH

> 3 tablespoons peanut or safflower oil
> 1½ pounds tomatoes, peeled and chopped
> ½ medium onion, finely chopped
> 3 cloves garlic, peeled and finely chopped
> 4 cups water
> 2 teaspoons salt, or to taste
> 5 peppercorns
> ⅛ teaspoon coriander seeds
> 1½ cups peeled, diced chayote (about ½ pound)
> 1 cup peeled, diced potatoes (about 6 ounces)
> 1 cup nopales, cooked (see page 147)

Put the shrimps into the freezer for about 2 hours, until they are slightly
frozen (this will make it easier to grind them in the blender or food processor).

Meanwhile, prepare the tomato broth. In a wide, heavy pan, heat the 3
tablespoons of oil and fry the tomatoes, onion, and garlic, stirring them from
time to time and scraping the bottom of the pan, until they are reduced to a
thick sauce. Add the 4 cups of water, salt, peppercorns, and coriander seeds

and bring to a boil. Add the *chayote* and cook for about 20 minutes, then add the potatoes and cook for 20 minutes longer. Add the *nopales* and just heat through. Adjust the seasoning.

Prepare the seasoning for the shrimp balls by first soaking the *chile ancho* in hot water for 15 minutes; then drain and put in a blender jar. Crush the coriander seeds, peppercorns, and cinnamon bark in a *molcajete* or mortar. Add the spices to the blender jar, along with the salt, garlic, and water, and blend to a paste. Heat the 1 tablespoon oil and fry the seasoning paste over a high flame for about 2 minutes. Set aside.

Blend the slightly frozen shrimps to a fairly smooth consistency. Add the fried seasoning and work it in well with your hands. Lightly grease your hands, then form the mixture into balls about 1½ inches in diameter—there should be 18 of them. Carefully place the shrimp balls into the simmering broth, then cover the pan and continue simmering for about 15 minutes, turning them once during the cooking time.

Serve three of the balls in each of six deep soup bowls, with plenty of the broth and vegetables.

6 servings

Pescado Enchilado Broiled Fish Seasoned with Chili Paste

Sr. Leoncio Arteaga (restaurante El Veracruzano,
Tamiahua, Veracruz)

One of Leoncio Arteaga's specialties is broiled *sargo*—a large local fish from the lagoon. On one occasion he had a four-pounder proudly displayed so you could see it immediately on entering the restaurant. A stake had been thrust up inside the fish, which had been liberally coated with a paste of *chile ancho* and broiled over a wood fire.

You can only do this dish successfully if the bars of your broiler are very thin, because, no matter how much you grease them, the chili paste tends to stick rather badly as it dries out over the fire.

I suggest that you use a red snapper or grouper for this recipe.

> *1 four-pound red snapper or grouper, gutted but*
> *head and tail left on*
> 4 chiles anchos, *cleaned of veins and seeds*
> 4 chiles piquin
> 3 cloves garlic, peeled
> 2 teaspoons salt, or to taste
> ⅓ to ½ cup wine vinegar
> 3 tablespoons peanut or sesame oil

Cover the *chiles anchos* with boiling water and leave them to soak until soft —about 15 minutes. Drain the chilies, then transfer to a blender jar. Add the *chiles piquin* (whole), garlic, salt, and vinegar and blend until smooth. (The mixture should be like a thick paste. If any more liquid is needed to release the blades of the blender, use some water, but as little as possible.)

Broil the fish briefly on both sides, unseasoned, and strip off the skin. Spread the outside of the fish with the chile paste, then baste with the oil and broil until cooked through.

Serve immediately, with hot, freshly made tortillas (see page 246).

6 servings

Light Meals,
Picnics, and Barbecues

We hear so much about the use of tortillas in Mexican food and the fact that their popularity has caught on north of the border—even if often in very strange ways. But what about the breads of Mexico, the *bolillos, teleras, semitas,* and *pambazos?* If they were better known, these crusty, salty yeast rolls, stuffed with all sorts of good and healthy things, might very well eclipse hot dogs and hamburgers—with their often synthetic fillings and soft, sweetish, bread, which I can only call "imitation"—and certainly give the hero sandwich, which they very much resemble, close competition.

Semitas

When next you go to Puebla, order *semitas*. They are round, salty rolls with a thick, dark crust—which means that they were baked in a wood-fired brick or adobe oven—and sprinkled with sesame seeds. Traditionally they are stuffed with potatoes, jellied calf's foot, and slices of avocado, all seasoned with fiery *chiles chipotles* and the fresh, pungent, round-leaved herb called *papaloquelite* (there is also a pointed-leaf variety). Alternatively, you can order them filled with mashed beans, avocado, cheese, and the same hot chilies, with a dash of good oil to boot.

Tortas

Tortas, which could be considered *the* well-stuffed sandwiches of central Mexico, are much easier to find. Flat, oval-shaped *teleras* are opened up and the inside crumb gouged out. The bottom half is filled with about 2 tablespoons of Frijoles Refritos (see page 37) and on top of that go as many strips as you like of canned *chiles serranos* or *jalapeños*, some sliced cold pork or shredded chicken—or whatever you have on hand—as well as sliced tomatoes, shredded lettuce, sour cream, plenty of avocado, and, of course, not forgetting a slice or two of good Chihuahua or Manchego cheese—or, failing these, mild Cheddar, jack, or Muenster. Admittedly I am biased, but this splendid, textured snack is far superior to any sandwich north of the border.

Molletes

A popular brunch dish known as *molletes* is made with the small, elongated, cushion-shaped rolls called *bolillos*. Since good *bolillos* are hard to come by, even in the Mexican bakeries in the southwestern United States, these could be made with sourdough rolls or four-inch lengths of good, crusty French bread.

> 6 bolillos, *hard rolls, or 4-inch lengths of French bread*
> 2 *cups Frijoles Refritos (see page 37)*
> ½ *pound Chihuahua cheese, mild Cheddar, or jack, grated*
> 2 *cups Salsa Mexicana Cruda (see page 158)*

Preheat the oven to 400 degrees. Butter a cookie sheet well; it should be large enough to accommodate the rolls when halved.

Cut the rolls in half. Scoop out and discard most of the doughy crumb inside and fill the hollows with fried beans. Sprinkle liberally with grated cheese and bake on the top shelf of the oven until the bread is nicely crisp around the outside and the cheese melted—about 10 minutes. Serve hot and pass the sauce separately.

6 servings

Guajolotes

Sra. María Luisa de Martínez (Mexico City)

Last, but by no means least, are the softer, round, bun-shaped rolls called *pambazos*. María Luisa de Martínez, who is constantly giving me new ideas and recipes, prepared *pambazos* for lunch one day after a strenuous morning swim in Cuautla. She made them into something she called *guajolotes* (lit., "turkeys"). They were very tasty, crunchy, and filling—but they do require a good digestive system.

(continued)

2 *canned* chiles chipotles adobados, *roughly chopped*
2 chiles anchos, *cleaned of stalks, seeds, and veins*
1 *teaspoon salt, or to taste*
¼ *small onion, roughly chopped*
1 *clove garlic, peeled and roughly chopped*
1¼ *cups cold water*
6 *large* pambazos *or hard rolls*
4 to 6 *tablespoons peanut or safflower oil, approximately*
4 chorizos, *sliced into 3½-inch lengths, then skinned and crumbled*
½ *pound potatoes, red bliss or other waxy variety, cooked and cut into ½-inch cubes*
4 *ounces Chihuahua cheese,* manchego, *mild Cheddar, or jack, grated*
2 *cups shredded lettuce*

Preheat the oven to 400 degrees. Place a baking sheet on the top shelf.

Toast the cleaned chilies lightly on a griddle or *comal.* Cover with boiling water and let soak until soft, then drain and transfer to a blender jar. Add the salt, onion, garlic, and cold water and blend until smooth. Pour into a shallow bowl and set aside.

Cut the rolls in half horizontally and remove and discard some of the crumb. Heat 2 tablespoons of the oil in a small frying pan. Dip one-half of a roll very quickly into the sauce—it should just have a light coating and not become too damp inside—and fry quickly on both sides, immediately afterward placing it on the hot baking sheet in the oven. Repeat the process until all the rolls are dipped and fried, adding a little oil at a time as necessary. (If you put too much oil in the pan at one time, the bread will absorb it and become very greasy.) Bake until the rolls become crisp—about 10 minutes.

Put the skinned, crumbled *chorizos* into a small frying pan. Cook over a gentle heat until the fat has rendered out and the meat is cooked, but take care not to keep frying until it is crisp and dried out. Drain off half of the fat and reserve for future use.

Add the cooked potato cubes and the blended chili mixture and fry for a few minutes longer, turning everything over constantly.

Fill the bottom halves of the rolls with some of the *chorizo*-potato mixture. Sprinkle them liberally with the grated cheese and top with a thick layer of shredded lettuce. Cover with the tops and serve immediately.

6 servings

Huevos Oaxaqueños Oaxaca Eggs

Sra. Domatila Santiago de Morales (Oaxaca)

I had been served *huevos en chilpachole* at La Flecha restaurant in Tlacotalpan, but checking up again on the recipe I couldn't find a Veracruzano who knew anything about them. Then, in Oaxaca, when I was cooking with Señora Domatila, she prepared them for a late breakfast. They were the same, with the addition of the *nopales* typical of that area and not of Veracruz.

It has always fascinated me to see just how recipes travel, and perhaps this one had gone by my most favorite route in all Mexico, across the Sierra Madre Oriental. It begins in the basin of the Papaloapan River and winds steeply and seemingly endlessly up through a dense and wonderfully lush rain forest that gives way at about nine thousand feet to silent pine forests, brilliant and fragrant in the crystal-clear air. As you look back toward the east you can see endless ranges of mountains and three snowy-capped volcanoes emerging through the light clouds that speck a brilliant blue sky.

> 2 small tomatoes (10 ounces), broiled (see page 262)
> 1 or 2 fresh chiles serranos *or any fresh, hot green chili,*
> *broiled (see page 261)*
> ¼ small onion, roughly chopped
> 1 clove garlic, peeled and roughly chopped
> ¼ teaspoon salt, or to taste
> 3 tablespoons peanut or safflower oil
> 3 large eggs
> ⅓ cup nopales *(optional), freshly cooked (see page 147)*
> *or canned in brine*
> ½ cup water
> 1 large sprig epazote

Blend the tomatoes with the chili, onion, garlic, and salt. Heat 1 tablespoon of the oil and fry the mixture for 5 minutes, stirring constantly.

Heat the remaining oil in a heavy pan. Beat the eggs briefly and cook very lightly in the oil, turning them constantly, until they are just set. Add the sauce and *nopales* to the eggs and continue cooking, stirring constantly for a few minutes. Add the water and *epazote* and cook for about 3 minutes more.

2 servings

Huevo a la Sorpresa Egg Surprise

Sra. Maura Rodríguez (Jalisco)

A student in a recent cooking class at Rancho Santa Fe brought along this recipe from her maid, who comes from Jalisco. Somewhere, sometime I had eaten this and forgotten just how delicious it is.

Make a tortilla so that it puffs up (see pages 246–49). Make a small slit in the puffed side to form a pocket, then crack open an egg and slide it into the pocket. Press the dough to seal in the egg and fry in hot oil until it is golden brown and crisp. Drain well and serve with Frijoles Refritos (see page 37).

Topped with some shredded lettuce, Salsa Mexicana Cruda (see page 158) or Salsa de Tomate Verde (see page 161), and slices of avocado, this makes a delicious light lunch dish.

1 serving

A PICNIC IN HIDALGO

Since the first day I was taken to María Elena Lara's restaurant, way up on Avenida Santa Lucía in one of the more remote sections of Mexico City, I had been impressed by the honest, well-cooked, hearty food, which had such great *sazon* (flavor). And since that day María Elena has generously shared her recipes and knowledge with me.

Early one September, María Elena's whole family was going on a picnic at their ranch in the state of Hidalgo, and they invited me to go along. María Elena said she would prepare the typical picnic meal of that region, *pollo en itacate* (lit., "chicken in a coarse string bag"; the word *itacate* has come to mean "provender"). This is prepared the day before, to improve the flavor, and then it is heated up in the fields over a wood fire the following day.

When I arrived to watch the preparations, it seemed that the kitchen was filled with baskets, all of them lined with white or red-and-white checked cloths. Ready to be packed were bottles of tequila and a dozen limes, *"Para abrir el apetito"* (to "open" the appetite), as María Elena explained, rather unnecessarily, *manchego* cheese to nibble on while sipping; red and green sweet *tunas* (prickly pears); hard-boiled eggs; and little pottery mugs—because someone was sure to bring fresh *pulque* from a neighboring ranch.

First María Elena simmered the chicken, a large fat one, with a whole head of garlic and salt, nothing else. While it was cooking she cut four fresh *jalapeño* peppers and four green onions, shredding the bottom of them in such a way that after a short time in iced water they opened like flowers. When the

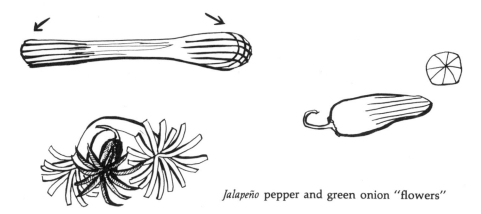

Jalapeño pepper and green onion "flowers"

chicken was tender, it was very lightly browned in hot lard. Then María Elena tucked a chili and onion into each of the four joints and tied the chicken up tightly in a large cloth while it was still hot.

With the chicken broth she made rice, frying it with the blended tomato, onion, and garlic as is customary, but adding some corn kernels. When it was cooked she scattered the top with sprigs of Italian parsley and decorated it with slices of hard-boiled eggs and whole, canned *chiles chipotles en vinagre*. The casserole was then covered tightly with yet another cloth, ready for the next morning.

María Elena then made red and green sauces, into which she dipped hot tortillas, folding them into neat packages (see the recipe for Tortillas Dobladas, page 117) with large napkins, after which she started to make fillings, four of them, for the *lolitos* (see the recipe on the following page), which are little stuffed cakes of tortilla dough. She seemed to go on endlessly mashing and frying chick-peas, dried fava beans, beans, and chilies; best of all was the sauce of *chile ancho* with lots of grated cheese. She beat tortilla dough with lard and salt and then, with wondrously dextrous hands, shaped a hundred little *lolitos* —diamonds, triangles, and ovals—each stuffed with one of the many different fillings. They puffed up invitingly on the *comal,* and a little cheese oozed out, sizzled, and quickly dried up with a tantalizing smell. It seemed too long to wait until tomorrow, so we sampled them one at a time.

Lolitos Savory Tortilla Cakes

Sra. María Elena Lara (restaurante Los Tres Migueles, Mexico City)

THE FILLING

> 2 *large* chiles anchos
> 1 *clove garlic, peeled*
> ½ to ¾ *cup water*
> ½ *teaspoon salt, or to taste*
> ½ *tablespoon peanut or safflower oil*
> 3 to 4 *ounces Chihuahua cheese or mild Cheddar, grated*

THE DOUGH

> 1 *teaspoon salt, or to taste*
> 2 *cups Quaker* masa harina *or ½ pound prepared* masa
> 3 *ounces (6 tablespoons) pork lard*
> 1½ *cups water (if using* masa harina*), approximately*

Prepare the filling first. Remove the stems from the chilies. Cut them open, remove the veins and seeds, and lightly toast on a hot griddle or *comal* (see page 259). Cover the chilies with hot water and let them soak for about 15 minutes, or until they are soft. Transfer to a blender jar. Add the garlic, water, and salt to the blender jar and blend until smooth.

Heat the oil in a small frying pan, add the chili puree, and cook over a fairly high heat, stirring constantly to prevent sticking, for 5 minutes, until it reduces and thickens. Stir in the grated cheese, adjust the seasoning, and set aside to cool off a little while you prepare the dough. Mix the salt and *masa harina* together. Chop the lard into the mixture and rub lightly between the fingers until it is well incorporated. Add the water and mix to a soft dough. Set aside for 5 minutes. (If you are using prepared dough, then work in the lard and salt thoroughly and omit the water.)

Roll the dough into balls about 1½ inches in diameter. Press each ball out, on the palm and lower fingers of your right (or left) hand, to a circular shape about 3 inches in diameter. If you have difficulty in handling the dough, grease your hands lightly and start again.

Put 1 good teaspoon of the filling into the center of the dough. Fold up the edges so they meet, then fold them over to seal and pinch them well together into a crescent-shaped turnover. Put the turnover on its side, flatten it until it is about ½ inch thick, and shape it into a square, rectangle, triangle, or circle, however the fancy takes you, taking care that the filling does not break out through the dough. Repeat with the remaining balls of dough.

Heat a *comal* or griddle, grease very lightly, and cook the *lolitos* over a slow flame until they are lightly browned and puffy and the dough is cooked well but not dried out—about 8 minutes on each side.

2 dozen lolitos

Tortillas Dobladas

Sra. María Elena Lara (restaurante Los Tres Migueles,
Mexico City)

This is how María Elena made the red sauce and prepared the *tortillas do-bladas* ("doubled over" tortillas, also called *paseadas*, or "passed through the sauce"). Some would have red sauce, some green (see the recipe for Salsa de Tomate Verde on page 161). A lot of pork lard went into the sauces, and for good reason—to make the tortillas soft and spongy when they were reheated at the picnic the following day.

She then spread out a large napkin, and in the center of it placed some plain tortillas, cut or broken up to form about an 8-inch square, the purpose of which was to protect the napkin from the rather messy *dobladas* stacked on top and to absorb some of the lard that would seep from them.

> 2 *large* chiles anchos, *cleaned of veins and seeds*
> 2 *cloves garlic, peeled and roughly chopped*
> ½ *teaspoon salt, or to taste*
> 1¼ *cups chicken broth or water, approximately*
> 3 *ounces (6 tablespoons) pork lard*
> 12 *freshly made tortillas (see page 246), still warm*

Open up the chilies and toast them lightly on either side on a hot griddle or *comal* (see page 259). Cover them with boiling water and leave them to soak

until soft—about 10 minutes, depending on how fresh or dry they are. Drain
and transfer to a blender jar. Add the garlic, salt, and 1 cup of the broth and
blend until smooth.

Heat the lard in a heavy pan, add the blended chilies, and cook over a fairly
high flame, stirring constantly, for about 4 minutes. Add ¼ cup more of the
broth and bring to the simmering point. Remove from the heat and set aside.

Put one of the tortillas, face down, into the sauce—which should be of a
medium consistency—and coat the tortilla well. Double the tortilla over with
the sauce inside and press the edges together, then dip the rounded edges into
the sauce so there is a border of sauce about ¼ inch wide. Place the *doblada*,
with the folded (unchilied) side parallel to the edge of the napkin, along one
side of the prepared square of tortillas already on the napkin. Repeat the
process with the second tortilla, placing it opposite the first one, with the
curved edges touching.

Make two more *dobladas* and place them on top of the first layer, with
curved edges touching, in such a way that the other sides of the square are
completed. Repeat until all the tortillas have been used up. Fold the edges of
the napkin over the top of the tortillas and store until the following day.

Reheat on a ungreased griddle or *comal*.

6 servings

BARBACOA

Meat cooked *en barbacoa* is Sunday food in Mexico, and varies tremendously
from region to region. The word *barbacoa* refers to pit barbecuing; meat
cooked on stakes over a wood fire is called *carne asada al pastor* ("roasted
meat shepherd style"). There are specialists who dedicate themselves to this
pit barbecuing, as it takes a great deal of preparation and long cooking. Perhaps the most popularly known *barbacoa* is that of central Mexico—the states
of Hidalgo, Tlaxcala, and Mexico—where the unseasoned meat, usually mutton, is cooked in a pit lined with *maguey* (century plant) leaves. The head of
the animal is included, as is the stomach—which is stuffed with the chopped
kidneys, liver, intestines, and so forth, and seasoned with salt and chilies. A
metal pan is placed under the meat to collect the juices, which are served
separately in small cups as *consomé de barbacoa;* thick, rich, and tasty, this is
almost the best part. Traditionally the very soft meat is eaten as tacos, wrapped

in soft, steaming tortillas and doused with a fiery sauce of *chiles pasillas* and *pulque* called *salsa borracha* ("drunken" sauce).

In Coahuila, in the north, the whole sheep, including the head—but not the stomach and innards—is wrapped in several layers of sacking and tied securely with cord, which is then wound into a strong handle for lowering the "bundle" into the hot pit. I am told—I have not been fortunate enough to try it yet— that the meat is particularly succulent.

I think that one of the most delicious ways of cooking in the ground is that done in the Yucatecan peninsula, in a *pib* (the Mayan word for "pit barbecue"). The young pig to be cooked is first seasoned with *achiote* ground with spices and diluted with Seville orange juice and finally wrapped in banana leaves, all of which gives the meat an exquisite flavor.

Another area where the *barbacoa* has always fascinated me is Oaxaca. And even there it varies within the state or region. I describe that of the northern part on pages 122–33, and here is the version from the area around the city of Oaxaca.

Barbacoa de Carnero Oaxaqueño Oaxaca Barbecued Mutton

Sra. Domatila Santiago de Morales (Oaxaca)

This is the "domestic" version of barbecued mutton from the central part of Oaxaca State. The chili seasoning, with its cinnamon and sesame seeds, has a wonderful flavor, and the fragrance that comes out of the oven—*masa*, chilies, and avocado leaves—is so tantalizing and satisfying in itself that you never want it to stop cooking.

If you can't prevail upon your friends in California or Florida to send you avocado leaves, then just leave them out. If you can't get a good *tamal* dough, or *tamal* flour, then use Quaker *masa harina*. Señora Domatila cooked her own parched corn with lime, left it to soak overnight, and sent it to the mill the following morning with specific instructions that it be very roughly ground so the broken pieces of the kernels would give the flour a lovely crunchy texture. When trying out the recipe in Mexico City, I couldn't find anyone nearby to do this for me, but I did find a wonderful, coarsely ground white hominy called *cacahuazintle,* which is traditionally used for *tamales* and made a delicious covering for the meat.

Obviously you don't need the more expensive cuts of lamb—mutton is preferable if you can get it. I have used lamb shanks and they were delicious. For this recipe you will want about 3 to 4 pounds of meat, depending, of course, on how much of it is bone.

THE MEAT

> *3 to 4 pounds mutton or lamb (see note above) or goat*
> *2 large sprays avocado leaves (optional)*
> *2 teaspoons salt*

THE BARBECUE SAUCE

> *3 chiles anchos*
> *8 chiles guajillos (chiles chilcostles in Oaxaca)*
> *2 tablespoons sesame seeds*
> *1¼-inch piece cinnamon bark*
> *2 tablespoons vinegar*
> *⅔ cup water, approximately*
> *3 large cloves garlic, toasted and peeled*
> *¼ teaspoon thyme*
> *1 teaspoon oregano*
> *1½ teaspoons salt, or to taste*

THE DOUGH

> *2 ounces (¼ cup) pork lard, softened*
> *2 teaspoons salt, or to taste*
> *2 pounds tamal dough or 4 cups Quaker masa harina*
> *plus 2½ cups water*

Slit the *chiles anchos* open and remove the seeds and veins; remove the stalks from the *guajillos,* but leave the seeds and veins. Toast the chilies well on a hot griddle or *comal* (see page 259), taking care that they do not burn (as the *guajillos* cool off, they should be crisp). Cover the chilies with water and bring them to a boil. Remove from the flame and let them soak for 5 minutes.

Meanwhile, put the sesame seeds into an ungreased frying pan over a low flame. Keep turning them over until they turn a rich golden color, then set them aside to cool. When they are cool, put them, together with the cinnamon, into a spice grinder and grind as fine as possible (this step may seem unnecessary, but if you put all the ingredients into the blender together the sesame seeds would remain whole for the most part).

Drain the chilies and put into a blender jar. Add the vinegar, water, garlic, herbs, salt, and ground sesame mixture and blend until almost smooth—the sauce should have a little texture, and it should be quite thick, rather like a paste. Add a little more water only if necessary to release the blades of the blender.

Salt the meat, then cover it liberally with the chili sauce, leaving about 2 tablespoons aside to add to the dough later. Set the meat aside to season.

Preheat the oven to 400 degrees. Have ready a roasting pan into which the meat and avocado leaves, if using, will just fit comfortably. Put a rack into the pan and add 1 cup of cold water. Pass both sprays of avocado leaves over the bare flame or a very hot electric burner—they should sizzle, crinkle, and send off a rich avocado smell. Place one of the sprays on the rack in the pan. Set the pan and the other avocado-leaf spray aside while you prepare the dough.

Work the lard, salt, and reserved chili sauce into the *tamal* dough. (If you are using *masa harina,* add these ingredients along with the water and mix to a soft dough.) Divide the dough into two equal parts. Pat each part out into a roughly circular shape about ¾ inch thick. Place the meat on one piece of dough and top with the second piece; press the edges of the dough together so that the meat is completely covered.

Place the dough-covered meat on the avocado leaves in the pan and cover with the second spray. Cover the pan with a well-fitting lid or foil tightly secured to the edges of the pan so that practically no steam will escape.

Place the pan on the middle rack of the oven and bake for 1 hour. Turn the oven down to 325 degrees and cook until the meat is tender—about 3 hours, depending on the quality and cut of the meat. During the cooking time make sure that there is still some liquid in the bottom of the pan—you may have to add ½ cup or so more of water to keep the dough moist (at the end of the cooking time the meat should be very soft; there should be some sauce around it and the dough should be spongy and moist).

Cut the meat and serve with plenty of the dough, along with freshly made tortillas (see page 246), some Frijoles Refritos (see page 37), and strips of *chiles jalapeños en escabeche.*

6 to 8 servings

A WEEKEND AND BARBECUE IN OAXACA

I could never resist an invitation to a barbecue and especially this one, which was to be held late in September to celebrate the ripening of the corn in a remote village in the state of Oaxaca. My mouth began to water at the very thought.

My hosts, Teofilo and his wife, Blanca, were the caretakers of the small but fairly elegant apartment house in Mexico City where I stayed with friends year after year. Teofilo was always neatly dressed, a stocky figure with a shock of greying black hair and large, owllike eyes behind thick horn-rimmed spectacles. He was for the most part monosyllabic but certainly pleasant, and whatever you said to him was always replied to with a smile. He also looked extremely well fed.

Doña Blanca, as the maids called his wife, had a great reputation as a cook. When I first heard this, I couldn't pass the opportunity up, and I hurried down to meet her formally. Doña Blanca is a monumental woman—*una mujer doble,* as the saying goes in Mexico—with heavy Indian features, soft, long wavy hair, and large, lustrous brown eyes, a constantly smiling woman with a soothingly soft voice.

From that first moment we were friends. I would proudly bring her some of the special breads I had personally baked in the nearby bakery, and she would send up to the kitchen door, much to the astonishment of my friends, a bowl of steaming stew or pungent *mole* from the family meal. We often cooked together, and we talked for hours about Teofilo's and her families and childhood in Tepzuitlán.

At first the invitations to visit their village had been tentative, but this summer the visit and barbecue were finally to take place—and I offered to pay for the goat.

It was a long drive, so we planned to be away for a three-day weekend. All Friday morning Teofilo had been packing things into the station wagon, a recycled job that, five years before, had literally been picked off the junk heap and that—unbent, reassembled, and with some minor additions—had been going strong ever since. It had been polished until it shone and was crammed full of linen and furniture for their new little house, still under construction in Tepzuitlán, and hideously colored plastic buckets and bowls for their rural relatives. The three of us sat in the front seat, while their adopted daughter, Francisca, who helped Doña Blanca with the housework and the cooking, sat huddled up in the back. And so we set off, punctually at midday, out through Mexico City and onto the Cuernavaca road. After about an hour we were halfway down the long descent into the valley of Morelos—a leisurely ride that gives one time to admire the breathtakingly beautiful panorama of fertile plains and distant mountains—at which point we turned off toward Cuautla. We drove past the dramatic overhanging rocks of Tepoztlán, past the tidy new resort developments of Cocoyoc and Oaxtepec, and for many miles through flat, fertile agricultural land, where vast tomato crops were being harvested and loaded into trucks at the side of the road.

Teofilo was always punctual about his meals, and at two-thirty it was time to stop, which we did at a pleasant, shady spot by a fast-flowing stream. Bordering the stream was a field of amaranth in flower. I had heard that the seed of the amaranth has been used since pre-Columbian times to make different types of confections, and what a sight those flowers were—a mass of velvety plumes in shades from gold to deep red, like the thick pile of some wildly colored carpet.

Teofilo unloaded a large basket covered with an immaculately laundered cloth. Everything inside it was wrapped with care in white napkins—*tortas* made from the flat, crusty yeast rolls called *teleras,* which had been cut open and stuffed to overflowing with well-fried beans, chilies, ham, cheese, lettuce, and tomato. These were followed by a sweet, juicy cantaloupe whose delicate flavor had been incredibly enhanced by the heat of the sun. It was such a simple lunch, but so good.

We were soon on the road again and passed near Matamoros in the state of Puebla, then through sugarcane fields, and very soon we began winding through rocky limestone hills that were sparsely dotted with mesquite, small palms, and towering organ cacti. There were no signs of life until the road approached a river, where we found clusters of primitive houses with palm-thatched roofs, surrounded by straggly plantings of corn and occasional brilliant patches of alfalfa. Here for the first time I saw the curious, small cone-shaped granaries with pointed thatched roofs I had only heard about; they were propped off the ground on stilts to protect the dried corn from predators.

We made a short stop in Huajuapan—a small town halfway between Mexico City and Oaxaca—and then turned off westward onto a dirt road. By now it was dark. The air was cool and fragrant after the noisy, smoggy city, and it was wonderfully quiet. The night was so clear I felt I could reach out and touch the stars, while all I could see around were the blurred outlines of rocky hills and brilliant patches of light from distant villages, which changed position constantly as the road twisted and turned. We drove on in complete silence.

It was late in the evening when we finally arrived at Tepzuitlán and the house of Blanca's sister, Petra. She and her husband, Pedro, a farmer, had nine children, and they were all there; two of the older sons who lived and studied in the city had made a special trip for the occasion with their wives. The family lived in a large, old rustic house set around a rectangular courtyard dotted with shrubs and flowers. The house was badly in need of repair, and the part of it that gave onto the main street and had once been the village store was now roofless and abandoned. There, set on a smoldering log fire, was a large pan containing parched corn kernels simmering in water, with a touch of lime to soften them, to be used for the *tamal* dough for tomorrow's barbecue. Nearby was another pan of corn, which had been put to soak until the following morning for a soup called *lligue.* And so my lesson began, and my many enthusiastic teachers were astonished that anyone from outside should take so much interest in the life and food that they took for granted.

We were called to supper, which was prepared and served, almost exactly as they might have done centuries before, by Petra, Francisca, and another young woman who had been adopted by the family at an early age. The "stove" was typical of those in Colonial *haciendas,* a broad, counterlike construction of adobe brick whose cementlike finish was the color of terra cotta. Set into the counter, in a row, were small clay wells to hold the smoldering charcoal, and off to each side were counters on other levels, one just the right height for grinding on the *metate,* the rectangular grinding stone of volcanic rock; another for the *cazuelas* and *ollas,* the glazed earthenware cooking dishes and pots; and others for storing baskets of fruit and vegetables. There was a large pot of black beans simmering away next to a pan of milk with its thick, yellow crust of cream, and another earthenware pot contained coffee boiling with cinnamon and brown sugar.

Petra was at the *metate,* mashing and rolling curds of cheese that had been clabbered that morning. When she was satisfied that the curds were smooth enough, she packed them firmly into a wooden ring about six inches in diameter and one inch deep; then, picking up the ring with both hands, she began pressing the cheese between her palms, first on one side and then the other, as though she was making a tortilla. When it was ready, she gently tapped the ring all around on the table and the cheese was loosened, a compact, creamy *queso fresco* (that fresh cheese sometimes called *queso de metate*), ready to be eaten for supper.

Most of the visitors chose to eat *cecina* (beef jerky), which had been salted and dried only two days before by the butcher, who lived a few doors away. It was simply flung onto the glowing charcoal and allowed to sizzle for about a minute on each side. There was a powerful but fragrant sauce of fresh chilies in the *molcajete* to complement the meat. Of course there were tortillas, and sweet yeast rolls fresh that evening from the bakery, and hot chocolate.

Petra had made the chocolate herself of toasted cacao beans, unskinned almonds, cinnamon, and sugar, crushing and grinding them on the *metate,* which had some hot charcoal beneath it to give the chocolate just the right consistency. Once ground, it was pressed into small round molds and left out in the sun to dry. The chocolate, now stored in a huge glass candy jar, was ready to be boiled with water and beaten with a hand-carved wooden beater, the four loose rings of which, carved from the same block of wood, would give the chocolate an appetizing, frothy top.

Teofilo and Blanca had not been home for some months, so there was a lot of gossip to catch up on, and we were not allowed to go on our way until quite late. But there was one more stop, this time at Teofilo's sisters' house, where we were to leave the car. Jealous that we had had our supper elsewhere, they insisted that we at least have a nightcap before we turned in, and as exhausted as I was, with a throbbing headache besides, I found it to be a surprisingly good homemade brandy, an infusion of Jamaica sorrel *(Hibiscus sabdariffa)* in alcohol.

At last we were able to be on our way, to unpack the car and haul the things up the street, a steep incline of massive rocks, that led to Teofilo's and Blanca's house. It seemed that the whole village was asleep, and only the incessant barking of dogs broke the silence. We had to shout for some time before we could rouse the old lady looking after the house, but she finally came to unlock the gate and let us in.

Teofilo and Blanca proudly showed me their home, still unfinished, of concrete with an asbestos-tiled roof. It was immaculately clean. It seemed an age before the things we had brought had been stowed away, the gas cylinder connected, and the water turned on. Fresh linen was found and beds made, and then, in my room, Blanca discreetly set a chamber pot on a small wooden stool and placed a carefully folded clean white mat in front of it so my feet wouldn't get cold on the cement floor.

It was a very short night. At five o'clock I was awakened with a start as *las mañanitas,* a special birthday song, boomed into my ears. Outside soft footsteps and low voices sounded as devout villagers climbed up the hill to the chapel, not more than two hundred yards away, while four loudspeakers set up on the church tower blared forth sentimental songs and Strauss waltzes. This was just one day in the month-long celebration in honor of the Virgin of the Rosary.

By now sleep had gone; there was obviously nothing else to do but get up. By the time we had dressed and walked down to Petra's house, foaming buckets of milk were being carried in. Some of it was put aside for breakfast, while the rest was immediately clabbered for cheese (this is not done with rennet tablets, but with a natural coagulant—an infusion made with a piece of dried cow's stomach). Almost immediately I was hustled off to the *molino,* the mill where the corn is ground for tortillas and *tamales,* with the two batches of corn for the barbecue. Meticulous instructions were given to the young man who was operating the grinder. The corn that had been cooked the night before was to be ground, but not too fine, for the *tamal* dough, while the soaked corn had merely to be broken up for the *lligue.* The young man kept stopping the machine and handing us a little piece of the dough so we could feel it and tell him when just the right point had been reached.

Then to breakfast. Petra offered us more of the same food we'd had the night before, along with some eggs that had been gathered that morning and *bolillos,* the crusty oval rolls. But time was getting on, and there was still a lot to be done.

A lot of rattling and shouting in the street announced the arrival of the truck that was to transport us, along with the food, to the fields where the barbecue was to take place. The loading began: a large sackful of fresh ears of corn, huge earthenware *ollas,* cases of beer and soft drinks, great branches of wood for the fire, chilies, salt, spices, and handfuls of fresh herbs—it seemed endless. At last all was packed in and we drove off through the streets, slowing down every few yards to greet yet another relative. Everybody stared at me curiously but was too polite to ask who I was and why I was there.

About fifteen minutes' drive from the village, the dirt road stopped abruptly at an unfinished bridge over a narrow, fast-flowing river. There we began to unload, and in relays we carried everything through a field where the corn towered above our heads until we came to a clearing further up the river. There, very near a huge, shady tree, a pit had been dug, about about a yard square and a yard deep. Teofilo, Pedro, and I were left there by the others, who went home to finish the rest of the day's chores, but we were shortly joined by three other people, two men who helped the family work their land and Señorita—as everyone called her.

Señorita was a woman in her fifties. Her grey hair, tightly plaited, hung down from under her wide-brimmed, man's straw hat. Her face was lined and weatherbeaten, her bright blue eyes sparkled, and she was lithe and muscular. She was the village specialist in preparing goats for barbecue.

Very few words were spoken between us; none were needed, for everybody knew what to do and I just tagged along and helped them collect small rocks from the river bed to cover the bottom of the barbecue pit. We gathered kindling and cut up the wood we had brought along and threw it all into the pit until it was piled high up over the edges. Someone found some matches and we lit the fire.

Pedro told me that the man who was selling us the goat had gone to fetch it. I somehow expected him to return with large hunks of meat ready to be cooked, but no—I soon saw him returning through the haze of smoke carrying a long, thin machete in one hand and leading a pretty little cinnamon and white goat by the other. It let out some ladylike bleats when it saw us, and when it caught a whiff of the smoke it rolled its eyes nervously. "Now you can learn how to kill a goat," said Petra's husband with a chuckle as the man sharpened his machete on a stone.

I berated them all for not choosing an ugly, cross-eyed animal, and then, covering my ears tightly, I turned my back and walked away along the river bank, trying hard to concentrate on a large black butterfly with superb red markings that was hovering around a clump of purple cosmos. When I finally turned around and came back, they began laughing at me and telling me that I had missed an important part of my lesson.

By this time Señorita was supporting the goat's head, now quite limp, with one hand, while in the other she held a bucket under its pulsating neck as the brilliant, paint-red blood gushed out. When she was satisfied that she had got enough, she quickly beat some rough crystals of salt into it, to prevent it from clotting.

In minutes the men had skinned the animal and were deftly removing the organs. With accurate aim they threw the intestines and stomach onto a rock in the river, a few steps from where Señorita was standing, knee deep in the water, her long skirts tucked up into her waistband. I shall always remember her standing there, skillfully turning yards and yards of the intestines inside out as they floated downstream, all the time being pounded and washed by the swift current against the stones. She then picked up the stomach, tossed out the undigested fodder and began to scrub it, rubbing it all over with cut limes to remove the strong odor. Very soon everything was washed, scraped, and cut, and the meat and entrails neatly hung along a bare branch in the shadiest part of the tree.

By this time the wood had burned down to ash, and more was piled on. With the renewed blaze, Teofilo decided that we had earned our first snack. He threw some of the ears of corn, still completely covered with their sheath of green leaves, onto the fire. Within minutes he was fishing them out again with a forked stick, and as soon as he could handle them he unfurled the leaves at the tip and blew hard into the husk. "It helps the final cooking of the corn," he explained. It was crisp and sweet, far more delicious than the overstewed corn we were offered later that afternoon.

Up until this point everything seemed surprisingly well organized, but then came the unforeseen delays so typical of life in Mexico. Someone had forgotten the lard, the avocado branches had not been cut from the neighbor's tree, and the *molcajete* was missing. Two of the men were sent off to get them, while we gossiped and watched Señorita prepare the filling for the stomach. The blood was thoroughly beaten once again, with more salt and water to smooth out the lumps. The small intestines of the goat were cut into short lengths; fresh mint and marjoram were chopped and cuminseed was ground with garlic and onion. All these were stirred into the blood, and as I held the stomach open Señorita poured the mixture into it. She then gathered the uneven edges of the stomach together tightly and tied them with a strip of fiber torn from an agave leaf, securing it firmly around a specially cut peg of wood about four inches long.

Teofilo's sisters had now arrived and were lending a hand. One of them beat the *tamal* dough with lard and salt until it was light and puffy. She then spread it "two fingers deep" onto a shallow baking pan that had been lined in overlapping layers with the heart-shaped leaves called *hoja santa* (*Piper sanctum,* whose fragrant, aniselike flavor is touched with something else beyond description). The leaves extended well up over the sides of the pan, and were folded back over the edges of the dough. Another layer of leaves covered the top of the dough and it was ready.

One of the guests had contributed chickens, another rabbits, and again there was a slight delay while the seasoning was made for them—fiery dried chilies ground with vinegar and herbs. This was thickly smeared over the little bodies, and they were set aside until the fire was hot enough.

By now Señorita had started the *lligue.* The roughly broken corn had been soaking in water brought up from the river, and she began to rub it hard between her palms, so that the tough, transparent outer skins of the kernels were loosened and floated up to the surface. These were carefully skimmed off and saved to be fed to the cattle. There were three more washings and much discussion before the corn was pronounced ready for the pot. By now the two large earthenware pots had been filled about two-thirds of the way up with water. Most of the water in which the corn had been soaking was saved to feed to the pigs that evening, but some of it went into the *lligue.*

(Almost 8 pounds of corn were used to feed forty-five guests with some left over for the family.)

Blanca's mother now joined the helpers. She rinsed some dried chilies, *guajillos* and *costeños* (a thin, orange-red chili grown in the coastal area, as the name implies, and much esteemed by the Oaxaqueños) and ground them for a few minutes in the *molcajete* before straining the fiery sauce that resulted into each of the two pots. Someone else picked up some small sprays of avocado leaves and held them for a moment over the hot ashes so that the leaves sizzled and crinkled, letting off a burst of wonderful anise-avocado scent before they were plunged into the soup. Finally some rough salt, a little of the goat fat, a vigorous stirring, and that was it.

The wood had once again burned down to ashes, and the stones were now hot enough to begin the cooking. Two of the strongest men lifted the pots and, staggering a little under the weight, almost ran toward the pit, where they gently lowered their burden onto the hot stones below. Some of the men cut branches from the *cazahuate* trees across the river—a wood traditionally used since it chars but does not burn—which they trimmed into thin stakes; these they laid in crisscross fashion over the top of the pots to form grids. The thick, pointed leaves of the mescal agave were laid on top of the grids, and on these were placed the haunches, shoulders, and the doubled-over sides of the goat, along with the filled stomach and its whole liver. Then the chickens and rabbits went on, and lastly the two flat pans of *tamal*. Someone had forgotten the goat's head, and on it went as well. It had been trimmed of its horns, skinned, and scrubbed, and a small peg—the end of a corn cob—had been stuck, rather picturesquely, in the top of the skull to prevent the brains from falling out. Another large avocado branch had been placed over the top of the meat, and then two of the men dragged a couple of smoke-blackened *petates*, or locally woven straw mats, that had been soaking in the river over the top of it all. Several of the younger men set to enthusiastically and shoveled on the loose earth that had been excavated from the pit, covering the *petates* completely. A wisp of smoke was seen to escape, but this was quickly smothered with a final shovelful.

By now the party was growing. A big cattle truck had just driven up to the bridge, and we could hear the distant laughter of a group of young people just arriving, together with innumerable aunts, in-laws, and godparents; even Grandmother, who never stirred from her room in the family house, came, carried across the cornfield by two of the strongest young men.

Now the agonizing wait for food began in earnest. We had been up since five, it was now past one, and we had had no more than the corn and a tangerine to snack on since that early breakfast. Still with a throbbing headache, I decided to nap, but when I curled up under a tree the flies attracted by the killing, as well as some local bloodthirsty insects whose name I can't spell or pronounce, attacked me mercilessly. I gave up.

It was a brilliant day, but the water was too cold for me to even wade in, let alone bathe like the rest of the women. After brief greetings and introductions, I watched them troop upstream to find their favorite bathing place in the deeper pools. A hum of their chatter, and occasional shrieks as they dived into the icy water, reached us, punctuating the quiet conversation of the men, who were drinking Mexican brandy, neat and steadily, in the hot sunlight.

By the time the women had dressed themselves and wandered back in small groups to keep vigil over the barbecue, an hour or so had passed. It was now the mens' turn for bathing. Sluggishly they walked off, some decidedly under the weather by now. The bracing water took its toll, and after a time we saw Teofilo, supported by the arms of his companions, stumbling along until he finally collapsed on the river bank a hundred yards or so from us—and he didn't stir again until we were ready to leave.

By now it was about four-thirty. We were all ravenous, and the children were complaining loudly that they couldn't wait any longer to eat. After some argument it was decided to open up the pit, and as the loose earth was pushed aside and the *petates* drawn off, an incredibly fragrant smell emerged, the herbs, meat, chilies, and avocado leaves all contributing their share. A few of the older children snatched morsels as the meat was taken out, but most of them sat patiently around a huge rectangular cloth that had been spread out on the ground.

Two other fires had been set. On one a pot of corn was boiling (to its ultimate death), and on the other a *comal*, a huge, thin disk of unglazed clay, had been heating, ready for the tortillas.

Petra by this time was hurriedly making a sauce of charred chilies and tomatoes. Blanca's mother was stirring up the *lligue*, which had gained even more from the meat drippings, and began to serve powerful bowls of the broth with some of the tender, broken white corn from the bottom of the pot. I cut the *tamales* into squares, while Señorita sliced the stuffed stomach with her sharp knife and Blanca presided over the meat. There was no lack of enthusiastic help, and for a while a contented silence fell over the group.

The meat was succulent and wonderfully flavored, with a smoky avocado flavor. The broth, I must confess, was a little too pungent for my taste, but the *tamal*—rich and spongy and marvelously fragrant with *hoja santa*—was, to me, along with the stomach and its rich, savory stuffing, the height of gastronomic excellence. I helped myself time and time again, just a little bit more each time to make sure I wasn't imagining anything.

"The barbecue could have done with another hour at least," said Petra's husband, who was a brooding, sober pessimist. "And what's more, Señorita didn't beat the blood enough. It's lumpy"—this said as he ate sparingly, considering every mouthful. But he was alone with his comments. Everyone else came back for second and third helpings, until they could hold no more.

Some of the tastiest pieces of the meat were tucked away for Blanca to take back to the city. I suddenly remembered the head. Where was it? That was the part I really wanted to try, remembering as I did the delicate little heads that I had eaten in Monterrey, where *cabrito al pastor* (kid roasted over wood) is prepared par excellence, and as nowhere else in the Republic. But the head, too, had been discreetly tucked away, for, since the picnic was being held on her land, Blanca's mother had laid claim to it.

When we were stuffed and could hold no more, we sat around joking and singing, gossiping, and belching, until the shadows lengthened and the fires died down to grey ash. Just before the sun disappeared behind the mountains, we began to stow things away into huge baskets, which were hoisted up into the truck until there was hardly one inch of standing room left. Off went the truck, rocking precariously home along the dusty, uneven track, while the few of us who had decided to walk enjoyed the cool evening air and the extravagant blue brilliance of the evening sky.

By the time we had reached the house I wanted only to sleep, but no sooner had I laid my head on the pillow than the wretched loudspeakers blared forth their evening greetings to the Virgin of the Rosary. I felt desperate—but then, since I was the guest of honor for the weekend, Blanca's young nieces were sent hurrying up to the church with an unprecedented request, that the volume of the music be lowered. And to our surprise it was.

The weekend was far from finished, and to enjoy it to the full, Blanca had decided that we would have to join in the spirit of things: get up with the *mañanitas* in the morning and go up to the *peñas,* the rocks, to bathe.

It was barely light when we set off the following morning, carrying towels, shampoo, soap, and containers for water. Blanca had mentioned this trip several times, but I wasn't quite sure what she meant. As we walked up the hill past the church we could hear the congregation praying. The streets were deserted, and only the huge zebu cows tethered in a neighbor's yard turned to look at us curiously. Most of the houses we passed were constructed in the same rustic style and of the same materials—adobe brick with roofs of large, curved terra-cotta tiles that overhung to form broad eaves, and these supported by strong timbers to form galleries around the houses. There was a scent of burning in the air from fires started early to cook the first tortillas of the day.

We were now on the outskirts of the village. Climbing up between tall, overhanging rocks for a few hundred yards, we suddenly found ourselves in a landscape of huge, smooth boulders that sloped down for perhaps half a mile to flat grassland beyond. A few people had been there before us and were driving their donkeys, laden on both sides with tin cans filled to the brim with fresh water. Ahead of us were two small boys, who were balancing buckets of water suspended from the homemade yokes of rough timber across their shoulders.

We went first to the main spring of water, which seemed to be hardly more than a trickle as it came out of the crevice between two huge boulders but that soon gathered in a small catch basin below, to form a small but very clear pool. We bent down to drink from a hollowed gourd and found the water icy cold and delicious. Little wonder people came from miles around to collect it daily, and would drink nothing else.

Blanca and I left our water containers with Teofilo while the two of us climbed further up to find a pool in which to bathe. Satisfied with the place, Blanca unself-consciously stripped off all her clothing and sat in the pool like some life-sized Zuñiga sculpture, throwing cold water over herself with abandon and washing her long black hair. At that hour it seemed to me as cold as any English bathroom (which I have abhorred since childhood), but as the sun rose higher I, too, found myself a deep, clear pool. The shock of the bracing water made me shiver, but it was wonderfully refreshing, and it did leave my skin and hair soft and satiny. As we strolled back to relieve Teofilo of his watch, Blanca casually told me that she had kept a sharp eye open while I was bathing, for, as she said, water snakes hide in the pools, and when disturbed they hurl themselves out of the water and, with a lightning movement, wrap themselves around the intruder.

When we returned to the house, Francisca had a substantial breakfast waiting for us, and after that began a day so packed with activities that it would put any well-organized group tour to shame. First we went to the marketplace, where the Indians from distant villages high up in the Sierras, dressed in shabby but colorfully embroidered native garb, were selling their meager produce of corn, squash, chilies, or herbs. They collected their money in, or sold tortillas from, tall, narrow, round baskets called *tenates.* More often than not they would carry several of these, one set inside the other, the outer, largest one having a strong leather thong stitched to it to hang over the shoulder. Sitting around gossiping, or tending their animals in the fields, their hands would be in constant motion as they wove these baskets and broad-brimmed hats, holding under their armpits a roll of fiber made from stripping and drying the small local palm that grows prolifically in semiarid areas of Oaxaca. These Indians greet each other by touching, not shaking, hands and, always smiling, chat incessantly to each other in their soft Indian tongue.

After our trip to market there was mass to attend, a visit to the father's grave, lunch with Teofilo's sisters, who had prepared a special Oaxacan stew called *amarillo*—chicken or pork with many vegetables prepared in a thin sauce flavored and colored with a dried orange-yellow chili. They had prepared *tamales* steamed in corn husks, and to finish the meal a delicious, grainy-textured paste of local guavas.

As soon as the meal was over and we could excuse ourselves, Teofilo, Francisca, and I went in search of provisions to take back to Mexico City while Blanca went to console her mother because we had not stayed there for lunch. First to the butcher's. At the back of his store we entered a small room completely screened against flies and hung densely with drying, thinly cut beef, *cecina*. The smell was overpoweringly strong, and I was glad when they had finally chosen several pounds of meat and folded it neatly into a basket as though it were the finest laundry. From there we went to the *barrio*, as everyone called it, about half a mile from the village. This was a small area of rich, black soil at the foot of a rocky escarpment. The smallholders there had planted it thickly with orchards, vegetable plots bordered with bushy rows of coriander, and flowers. We bought bushels of guavas, a hundred sweet limes to make *agua fresca* (literally "fresh water," but in this case limeade, Blanca's and Teofilo's favorite mealtime refreshment), pumpkins, onions, and roses.

From there we went across the village to the tomato fields on the other side, where hampers of sweet, fresh tomatoes—plum-shaped ones for sauces and green ones for ripening later—were given to Teofilo and Blanca, who had now joined us. Petra had added homemade cheeses, protectively wrapped in fig leaves, and some cakes of her famous drinking chocolate. Hundreds of tortillas completed the store of good country food to last them through the next few months, when they would return to stock up again. Surrounded by heady aromas, we drove slowly back to Mexico City the following morning, Teofilo still feeling the effect of his unaccustomed drinking bout.

Vegetables

I remember so well an old man sitting on a sack of chilies in Mercado Juarez in Mexico City. As I admired and exclaimed over the variety and beauty of the chilies, herbs, and edible flowers that his wife was selling, he said, *"Sí, señora, aquí comemos a pie de la vaca* (Yes, *señora,* here we eat at the foot of the cow)!"

Coliflor en Aguacate Cauliflower in Avocado Sauce

This recipe comes from *Recetas de Cocina,* a 1911 Mexican cookbook I have discussed elsewhere. The idea of cooking cauliflower with aniseed was rather intriguing; it does give an interesting flavor. This could be served as a vegetable dish or salad, but since it doesn't look too attractive by itself I prefer to serve it in the form of a dip—crisp-cooked cauliflower with *guacamole*—or masked with *guacamole* as a salad or side dish.

This should all be prepared at the last moment. If not, the *guacamole* will lose its color and become rather watery and the cauliflower will become somewhat bitter and the subtle anise flavor will be lost.

THE CAULIFLOWER

    1 *pound cauliflower, trimmed of the outer leaves*
      A large pinch of aniseed, tied in a small piece of
        cheesecloth
    1 *teaspoon salt*

THE GUACAMOLE

    2 *fresh* chiles serranos *or any hot, fresh green chilies*
    3 *sprigs coriander, leaves only*
    2 *tablespoons finely chopped onion*
    ½ *teaspoon salt or to taste*
    1 *large tomato (about ½ pound), broiled and skinned (see*
      page 262)
    2 *avocados*

THE GARNISH

    2 *ounces* queso fresco *or farmer cheese*

Rinse the cauliflower well and divide it into florets. Bring a large pan of water to a rolling boil. Add the cauliflower, aniseed, and salt and cook until just tender—about 10 minutes. Drain and let cool.

While the cauliflower is cooling, make the *guacamole*. Crush the chilies, coriander, onion, and salt to a paste. Add the tomato and blend a second or so longer. Skin and mash the avocados until smooth. Add the blended ingredients and mix together well.

To serve as a vegetable dip, place the *guacamole* in a small bowl and garnish with the crumbled cheese. Put the bowl onto a large platter, on which you have arranged the cauliflower. To serve as a vegetable dish or salad, place the cauliflower in one layer on a shallow serving dish. Mask with the *guacamole* and garnish with the crumbled cheese.

6 servings

Chiles Rellenos de Elote con Crema Chilies Stuffed with Corn and Cream

Of all the combinations of chilies, corn, and cream, this is by far the most luscious. It makes a wonderfully rich and exotic first course. Use frozen corn if you cannot get very fresh, tender corn. *Crème fraîche* or homemade sour cream (see page 235) should be used, as the commercial sour cream curdles when cooked.

You can make the corn stuffing ahead and refrigerate it. If you do, just heat it through a little before filling the chilies. Cover the dish with foil and put in a 350-degree oven for 20 to 30 minutes.

> *4 tablespoons sweet butter*
> *1 medium white onion, finely chopped*
> *2 cloves garlic, peeled and finely chopped*
> *4 cups corn kernels (if frozen, measure before defrosting)*
> *1½ teaspoons salt, or to taste*
> *⅓ cup water, if necessary*
> *3 tablespoons finely chopped* epazote *(optional)*
> *12 small* chiles poblanos, *charred, peeled, and cleaned (see page 260)*
> *½ pound* queso fresco *or farmer cheese, cut into thick slices*
> *2 cups homemade sour cream (see page 235) or* crème fraîche
> *3 ounces Chihuahua cheese or mild Cheddar, grated*

Melt the butter and fry the onion and garlic gently, without browning, until soft. Add the corn kernels and salt, then cover the pan and cook over a gentle heat until the kernels are tender (if the corn is very dry, then add about ⅓ cup water)—15 to 20 minutes, depending on whether fresh or frozen corn is used. Add the *epazote* and adjust the seasoning. Set aside to cool a little.

Preheat the oven to 350 degrees.

Clean the chilies carefully, leaving the top and stalk intact. Stuff the chilies well with the corn mixture. Put a slice of the cheese in the center of the filling (the *chilies* should be fat but must close where they were slit open).

Place the chilies in one layer in a shallow ovenproof dish into which they will just fit comfortably. Pour over the sour cream and bake until well heated through, then sprinkle with the grated cheese and continue to bake until the cheese is melted.

6 servings

Rajas de Chile Estilo Oaxaqueño Chili Strips Oaxaca

Sra. Domatila Santiago de Morales (Oaxaca)

In all my years in Mexico, I had never come across this recipe until I was cooking with my friend Señora Domatila in Oaxaca last August. The chili strips are traditionally eaten over white rice, which makes for a most unusual combination of flavors and textures. Like all rice dishes in Mexico, this rice is eaten as a "dry soup" or pasta course.

The long, light-green *chiles de agua* are used in Oaxaca, but you can substitute fresh *chiles poblanos* or *Anaheim*, or canned, peeled green chilies.

> 3 tablespoons peanut or safflower oil
> ½ cup whole epazote *leaves*
> 9 chiles poblanos *or* Anaheim, *charred, peeled, cleaned (see page 260), and cut into strips, or canned, peeled, green chilies*
> 1 teaspoon salt, *or to taste (depending on the cheese)*
> 1½ cups milk
> 12 ounces queso fresco *or domestic block Muenster cheese, teleme, or jack, cut into thick slices*

In a heavy, shallow pan about 10 inches in diameter, heat the oil until it smokes. Add the unchopped *epazote* leaves and fry until they wilt, stirring all the time—about 2 minutes. Add the chili strips and salt and fry for about 3 minutes, stirring all the time. Over a low flame, gradually stir in the milk, then add the pieces of cheese and cook until they melt. Serve hot, over Arroz Blanco (see page 32).

6 servings

Chiles Rellenos con Calabacitas Chilies Stuffed with Zucchini

This recipe caught my eye when I was leafing through a little book called *Recetas de Cocina*, published in Mexico City in 1911. Like many cookbooks of its time, it was a compilation of recipes contributed by groups of women for some charitable cause. This one was for raising funds to build a temple to the Archangel San Rafael. I have included several of the most interesting recipes, such as Coliflor en Aguacate (see page 134). They are always vague; the one for this dish directs the cook as follows: "Having roasted and cleaned [chilies], fill with cooked zucchini squash, onion, oregano, etc." Here the recipe is, a little more clearly and concisely:

> 2½ *tablespoons peanut or safflower oil*
> 1½ *pounds zucchini, trimmed and diced small*
> ½ *medium white onion, finely chopped*
> 2 *cloves garlic, peeled and finely chopped*
> 1 *teaspoon salt, or to taste*
> ¼ *teaspoon oregano*
> 2 *tablespoons wine vinegar*
>   *A good squeeze of lime or lemon juice*
> 2 *tablespoons fruity olive oil*
> 6 *ounces* queso fresco *or farmer cheese, crumbled*
> 6 *medium* chiles poblanos, *peeled and cleaned (see page 260)*
> 2 *tablespoons sweet butter*

THE GARNISH

> *Romaine lettuce leaves*
> 6 *radish flowers*

Put 1½ tablespoons of the peanut oil, zucchini, all but 2 tablespoons of the onion, half the garlic, and the salt into a heavy pan, then cover and cook over a medium flame for about 8 minutes, turning them from time to time so they do not stick. (The squash should steam in its own juices, but if it seems very dry, add a *little* water. Remember too that squash vary in moisture content, so if there appears to be too much water exuding from them, remove the lid, turn up the flame and reduce the liquid.)

While the mixture is still warm, add the remaining 2 tablespoons chopped onion, the remaining garlic, the oregano, vinegar, lime juice, olive oil, and cheese. Adjust the seasoning. Stuff the chiles until they are full but will still meet at the opening. (There should be about ⅓ to ½ cup of the stuffing left over, depending, of course, on the size of the chilies.) Fasten each opening with a toothpick. Melt the butter and remaining 1 tablespoon peanut oil together. Add the stuffed chilies and fry them over a medium flame, turning them over gently so the stuffing does not fall out, until lightly browned.

Arrange the chilies on a serving dish and garnish with lettuce leaves and the radish flowers. Sprinkle with the remaining stuffing. They can be served either hot or cold as a first course.

6 servings

Esquites Corn Cooked with Epazote

The name *esquites* comes from the Nahuatl word *izquitl,* meaning "toasted corn." It probably referred to the corn that popped open when toasted, but is now used very loosely to describe corn that is prepared very simply and sold from street vendors.

Indeed, you can eat *esquites* on any street corner in Mexico. Sometimes the kernels are shaved off the cob and sometimes the whole ear is cut into thick rounds. But it is that *epazote* again. . . .

The corn itself should be very fresh and tender.

> *6 small ears of corn*
> *2 tablespoons sweet butter*
> *3 tablespoons pork lard or peanut or safflower oil*
> *1½ teaspoons salt*
>   *1* chile serrano *or any fresh, hot green chili, finely*
>   *chopped*
>   *3 heaped tablespoons chopped* epazote *leaves*

Cut through each ear of corn at the stalk end and remove all the leaves and tassle. Cut the ears into slices about 1½ inches thick.

Heat a heavy pan into which the corn will just fit in one layer. Melt the butter and lard together, then add the corn, salt, chili, and *epazote.* Cover the pan and cook the corn over a medium flame, shaking the pan from time to time and turning the corn over once, until it is tender and slightly browned —about 15 minutes.

6 servings

Huitlacoche con Calabacitas Estilo Querétaro Corn Fungus with Zucchini

Obdulia and AnaMaría Vega (Querétaro)

Huitlacoche, the delicious, exotic-looking greyish fungus that grows on corn, has become a luxury to many people. The price has almost trebled in recent years, but AnaMaría and Obdulia Vega tell me that it was one of the cheapest meals at the small ranch in Querétaro where they were born and raised. Cooked in this way, it makes a wonderful filling for tacos; it can also be served as a vegetable.

> ¼ *cup peanut or safflower oil*
> 2 *large green onions or* ¼ *medium white onion, finely chopped*
> 1 *clove garlic, peeled and chopped*
> 1 *pound zucchini, trimmed and diced small*
> 1 *cup corn kernels*
> 1 *pound* huitlacoche, *shaved from the corn cob and roughly chopped (about 3 cups)*
> 2 chiles jalapeños, chiles serranos, *or any fresh, hot green chilies, cut into thin strips*
> ½ *teaspoon salt, or to taste*
> 1 *heaped tablespoon roughly chopped* epazote *leaves*

Heat the oil and fry the onion and garlic gently, without browning, until soft. Add one-quarter of the diced squash and cook for a few seconds over a fairly high flame, turning constantly, then add another quarter, and so on. When all the squash is in the pan, fry for a few minutes more.

Add the corn kernels by degrees, the same way you did the squash. Add the *huitlacoche* in the same manner. Add the chili strips and salt, then cover the pan and cook over a low flame, stirring from time to time, until the vegetables are tender—about 15 minutes. (The vegetables should remain moist and cook in their own juices, but if they do get rather dry, sprinkle liberally with water.)

When almost cooked, add the *epazote* leaves and simmer a few seconds longer.

6 servings

Lentejas Guisadas Stewed Lentils

Lentils cooked in this way may be served as a soup or as an accompaniment to the main dish, served in a separate bowl. If you are serving it as a soup, you may have to dilute it with water. It can then be served with fried croutons or, better still, crisp-fried tortilla pieces (see page 251).

I cooked this in Mexico City, in an earthenware bean pot, and found I used 10 to 14 cups of water for the same amount of lentils (see page 25).

> ½ pound (1 cup) dried lentils
> 8 cups cold water
> 2 teaspoons salt, or to taste
> 3 tablespoons peanut or safflower oil
> 2 cloves garlic, peeled
> 1 medium white onion, finely chopped
> 1 large tomato, peeled and chopped
> 2 chiles güeros, largos, or jalapeños, or any fresh, hot green chilies
> 2 tablespoons chopped coriander leaves

Rinse the lentils in cold water, then drain and put into a large saucepan with the water. Bring to a boil, lower the flame, and simmer until soft. Season.

Heat the oil and lightly brown the garlic. Discard the garlic, then, in the same oil, fry the onion gently, without browning, until soft. Add the chopped tomato and cook over a fast flame, stirring constantly and scraping the bottom of the pan, until the mixture has reduced to a sauce.

Add the tomato sauce to the lentils and cook over a medium flame for 15 minutes longer. Cut a cross in the bottom of the chilies and add them to the lentils. Cook for another 15 minutes, then add the coriander leaves and cook for 5 minutes longer.

6 servings

Lentejas con Piña y Plátano Lentils with Pineapple and Plantain

Sra. Godileva Castro (Mexico City)

When I rented a house for part of the summer in Mexico City, it was a great joy to know that Godileva, my old maid (whom I wrote about in *The Cuisines of Mexico),* was living just three blocks away. She often popped in to help me and give her opinion on the recipes I was test-cooking. She came up with this recipe, which is unusual and delicious served as a vegetable with broiled or roasted meats.

> ¼ *pound (½ cup) dried lentils (see page 25)*
> 6 *cups cold water*
> 1 *large tomato (about ½ pound), peeled and chopped*
> 1 *clove garlic, peeled and roughly chopped*
> ⅓ *medium white onion, roughly chopped*
> 1½ *tablespoons peanut or safflower oil*
> 1 *thick slice pineapple, peeled, cored, and cut into small cubes*
> ½ *medium-sized, very ripe plantain (about ½ pound), peeled and cut into thin rounds*
> 2 *teaspoons salt, or to taste*

Rinse the lentils well in cold water and drain. Cover with the 6 cups of water and bring to a boil, then lower the flame and simmer until soft—2½ to 3 hours, depending on how dry they are. Drain and reserve the broth (there should be about 1½ cups; add water if necessary to make up to this amount).

Blend the tomato together with the garlic and onion until smooth. Heat the oil and fry the tomato puree over a high flame for about 3 minutes, stirring constantly and scraping the bottom of the pan. Lower the flame, add the pineapple and plantain, and continue cooking for 5 minutes more.

Add the lentils and 1½ cups of the reserved broth to the pan, then add the salt and cook until the fruit is tender—about 20 minutes (the lentil mixture should neither be too thick nor too runny).

6 servings

Hongos Guisados con Chile Estilo Querétaro Mushrooms in Chili Sauce, Querétaro

Obdulia and AnaMaría Vega (Querétaro)

It was mushroom time when AnaMaría and Obdulia Vega from Querétaro were looking after me. The mushrooms started to come in in July, first the small, succulent little brown *clavitos,* from which we made soup and filling for tacos; then the *huitlacoche* (corn fungus; see page 240); the delicate, orange-yellow *yemas,* reddish *enchilados,* and earth-colored *tecamaniles;* and the fibrous mass of little stalks called *pata de pájaro* (lit. "bird's foot") or *escobilla* —named for the little bunches of dried roots used for scrubbing dishes or vegetables. And as the rainy season progressed, there were more and more, black, blue, and white, the clumsy-looking cèpes and finally the morels. (The mushrooms of Mexico are a study in themselves, and I hope to go into them in detail in a future book on Mexican vegetables and herbs.)

We actually prepared this recipe with *pata de pájaro,* which we had to boil in salted water for about 20 minutes until it was tender. However, there is no reason why you can't do it with cultivated mushrooms. It would make a very good filling for tacos or an accompaniment for plainly cooked meats.

To be more authentic, do use the pork lard for frying the sauce.

> 1 tablespoon peanut or safflower oil
> ½ pound mushrooms (see note above), well washed and
>   thickly sliced
> 1 teaspoon salt, or to taste
> 3 chiles guajillos
> 3 chiles pasillas
> 1 whole clove
> 3 peppercorns
> ⅛ teaspoon cuminseed
> 1 small clove garlic, peeled
> 1½ tablespoons pork lard or peanut or safflower oil
> 1 large sprig epazote

Heat the oil in a saucepan and add the mushrooms and salt. Cover the pan and cook over a medium flame until the mushrooms are just tender—about 10 minutes. Drain the mushrooms, reserving the juices, and set aside.

On a hot griddle or *comal,* toast the chilies well (see page 259), taking care they do not burn. Remove the stalks, slit the chilies open, and remove the seeds and veins. Cover with hot water and soak for 15 minutes, or until soft. With a slotted spoon, transfer the chilies to a blender jar. Crush the spices, then add, along with the garlic, to the blender and blend until smooth, adding a little water only if necessary to release the blades.

Heat the lard until smoking, then add the sauce and fry over a fairly high flame, scraping the bottom of the pan so it doesn't stick, until reduced and seasoned, about 5 minutes.

Add sufficient water to the reserved juice from the mushrooms to make ¾ cup. Add this, the *epazote,* and mushrooms to the chili sauce, then adjust the seasoning, and cook over a medium flame for about 10 minutes (the sauce should be of a medium consistency, not too watery, nor too thick).

Serve immediately.

6 servings

Hongos en Salsa Verde Estilo Querétaro Mushrooms in Green Sauce, Querétaro

Obdulia and AnaMaría Vega (Querétaro)

The Vega sisters and I cooked a large, smooth, orange-hooded mushroom called *tecomate* in this green sauce (in Querétaro it is known by the delightful-sounding name of *caximoses*). You, however, will find it to be an attractively different way of cooking the ordinary, commercially grown mushroom.

To be more authentic, do use the pork lard for the frying.

1½ *tablespoons pork lard or peanut or safflower oil*
¼ *medium white onion, thinly sliced*
½ *pound mushrooms, well washed and thickly sliced*
2 chiles serranos *or any hot, fresh green chilies, cut into thin strips*
⅛ *teaspoon cuminseed*
8 *small* tomates verdes, *freshly cooked (see page 245) or canned, drained*
1 *clove garlic, peeled and roughly chopped*
½ *teaspoon salt, or to taste*

Heat the lard or oil and fry the onion, without browning, until soft. Add the mushrooms and chilies and fry for a few seconds more, stirring all the time.

Crush the cuminseed, then blend, along with the *tomates verdes* and the garlic, until smooth; add, with the salt, to the pan. Fry for a few seconds longer. Cover the pan and cook over low heat until the mushrooms are tender—about 20 minutes (they should not be too dry).

6 servings

Nopales al Vapor Estilo Otumba Steamed Cactus
Paddles Otumba

The longer I live in Mexico, the more varied my recipe sources become. This one was given to me by a bus driver from the village of Otumba (near the pyramids of Teotihuacán) who loves to cook. His brother-in-law, also a bus driver, was driving the bus that was to take a group of us to the Merced market to buy our varied and exotic provisions for the week's cooking class I was holding. Curiosity got the better of the cook and he wanted to meet me, so he came with us for part of the journey. He told me that he had set up his "kitchen"—a small charcoal stove, two *cazuelas,* and a *comal*—in the bus garage, and with these he turns out, when time permits, a full midday meal for his fellow drivers. Judging by their stomachs, it must be good—and also judging by this recipe, which is, to my mind, the tastiest way of preparing *nopales.*

> 2 tablespoons peanut or safflower oil
> 2 cloves garlic, peeled and finely chopped
> 1 pound prepared nopales, *cut into small cubes*
> ¼ large white onion (1 large cebolla de rabo *in Mexico*),
>   finely chopped
> 2 chiles jalapeños *or any hot, fresh green chilies, seeds and*
>   veins left in, thinly sliced
> 2 large sprigs epazote, roughly chopped
> 1 teaspoon salt, or to taste

Heat the oil in a heavy pan until it smokes, then lower the flame and sauté the garlic, without browning, for a few seconds. Add the rest of the ingredients, cover the pan, and cook over a low flame, stirring the mixture from time to time, until the *nopales* are almost tender; they should be very juicy at this stage.

Remove the lid from the pan and continue cooking over a slightly higher flame until all the sticky liquid from the *nopales* has dried up—about 20 minutes, depending on how tender the *nopales* are.

To serve, fill a freshly made hot tortilla (see page 246) with some of the *nopales* and add a little crumbled *queso fresco* or farmer cheese, if desired.

2½ cups, enough to fill 12 tacos

Legumbres en Pipián Oaxaqueño Vegetables in Oaxacan Pumpkin-Seed Sauce

Sra. Domatila Santiago de Morales (Oaxaca)

While we were cooking in Oaxaca last summer, my friend Señora Domatila suggested that a vegetable *pipián*—of *nopales* and peas—would be an unusual choice for my new book. It does make an excellent vegetarian main course, deliciously satisfying in color, texture, and flavor.

I call Domatila *la regañadora*, "the scolder," because she is forever complaining and chiding as she cooks. As she was toasting the seeds for this dish, I asked her to what point they should be browned. *"Ni muy, muy, ni tan, tan* (neither too much nor too little)," she said with a click of her tongue, which indicated that I should know better than to ask. And later, as she was grinding the seeds on the *metate*—enough to make anyone complain, as I know from experience—she said that the preparation of Mexican food was *"dura pero segura* (hard but sure)." (The ground seeds, by the way, were strained through a small decorated gourd with small holes perforated in the bottom.)

Of course, this *pipián* can be made with poached chicken, stewed pork, or rabbit, and during the Lenten period with dried shrimps. I made it with cubed

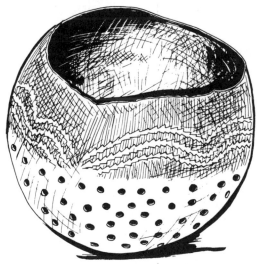

Gourd strainer

zucchini and quartered mushrooms precooked for a few minutes and it was very good.

You can make the sauce ahead, since it both refrigerates and freezes well. After you defrost it, put it back into the blender and blend for a few seconds before reheating.

> ½ *pound raw, unhulled pumpkin seeds (see page 242)*
> 1 **chile ancho**
> *1 to 2* **chiles chilcostles** *or* **chiles guajillos**
> 1 *clove garlic, peeled*
> 4 *cups cold water, approximately*
> ¼ *teaspoon cuminseed*
> 3 *tablespoons peanut or safflower oil*
> 2 *teaspoons salt, or to taste*
> 1 *pound* **nopales**, *crisp-cooked (see page 147), and diced*
> ½ *pound shelled, crisp-cooked peas*
> 2 *large sprigs* **epazote** *or 1 avocado leaf*

Put the seeds into a heavy frying pan over a medium flame. Turn them constantly until they are evenly browned, keeping a lid handy, as they are apt to pop about fiercely. Set them aside to cool.

Remove the seeds and veins from the *chile ancho;* leave the *guajillos* or *chilcostles* whole. Cover all the chilies with water and simmer them for 5 minutes, then leave them to soak for 5 minutes longer. Drain and transfer to a blender jar. Add the garlic and 1 cup of water to the chilies and blend until smooth.

When the toasted seeds are cool, grind them, along with the cuminseed— preferably in a coffee/spice grinder—until they are rather fine but still have some texture. Transfer to a bowl and stir in 2½ to 3 cups of water until smooth. Pass through the medium disk of a food mill and set aside.

Heat the oil in a heavy pan. When it is hot, but just before it begins to smoke, lower the flame and fry the chili sauce, scraping the bottom of the pan constantly, until it has reduced and seasoned—about 4 minutes. (You will know the sauce is done when the oil floats to the surface.)

Gradually stir in the pumpkin-seed sauce and cook over a low flame for about 15 minutes, stirring and scraping the bottom of the pan from time to time. Add the salt and vegetables and heat them through for 15 minutes longer, adding the *epazote* or avocado leaf just before the end of the cooking time.

Serve hot, with freshly made tortillas (see page 246).

6 servings

Calabacitas Rancheras "Farmhouse" Zucchini

A very simple way of cooking zucchini, and delicious—especially for those who love the taste of *epazote* as much as I do.

1½ pounds small zucchini, trimmed and thinly sliced
1 medium white onion, finely chopped
2 cloves garlic, peeled and finely chopped
3 tablespoons roughly chopped epazote *leaves*
4 chiles poblanos *or* chiles Anaheim, *charred, peeled, and cut into strips (see page 258), or canned, peeled green chilies*
2 teaspoons salt, or to taste

Put all the ingredients into a heavy pan and cook over a low flame, stirring and turning from time to time so the mixture won't stick. The squash should be tender in about 15 minutes. (It should cook in its own steam, but if it appears to be very dry, then add just a little water.)

6 servings

Sauces, Relishes, and Salads

Anyone would get the impression from reading the recipe for *salsa de muchos chiles* on page 152 and my suggestions for substitutions in the recipes throughout this book that all chilies go together. But they don't. A friend of mine from Yucatán, who shall be nameless, told me of an incident concerning *chiles peleados,* or "chilies that fight." His mother had not been enthusiastic about some droppers-in and didn't want them to stay. She did, however, offer them some refreshment, a snack that included a special sauce of *chiles verdes* and *chiles habaneros.* Very soon the visitors were excusing themselves to go home, looking decidedly unwell. I also heard, and this was further north, of a woman who saw her husband returning to the house with some companions who were drunk and quarrelsome. She hurriedly made a sauce of *chiles peleados*—and before long they were on their way.

I have asked many cooks about this in central Mexico, and while (so far, at least) they say they have never heard of it, there must be a variation of *chiles peleados* in that region, because the combination of *chiles serranos* and *chiles pasillas,* which are used more generally in central Mexico, have that reputation.

Salsa de Muchos Chiles Sauce of Many Chilies

Sra. María Elena Lara (restaurante Los Tres Migueles,
Mexico City)

This is another of those *picante*, uncooked table sauces that are used as a condiment, as opposed to a cooked sauce, which becomes an integral part of a dish. There are so many excitingly different chili flavors here that, along with my *chile cascabel* sauce in *The Cuisines of Mexico* (see page 303), it has become a firmly established favorite in my kitchen.

María Elena Lara, of whom I have written elsewhere, always serves this sauce (which she calls simply *salsa*) at her restaurant, Los Tres Migueles, in Mexico City, with wonderfully rich *gorditas* that she stuffs with crumbled *chicharrón*. A wonderful start, with a shot of tequila, to one of those wickedly enticing and fattening Sunday *comidas*.

If you don't have all the chilies called for in the recipe, then substitute from your stockpile, remembering always, of course, that *chiles anchos* and *mulatos* are rarely, if ever, used for this type of sauce.

>   *2 chiles cascabel*
>   *2 chiles moritas*
>   *2 chiles de árbol*
>   *1 chile chipotle*
>   *1 chile guajillo*
>   *1 large tomato (8 to 10 ounces), broiled (see page 262)*
>   *¼ teaspoon salt, or to taste*
>   *½ cup cold water*
>   *1 large clove garlic, peeled*
>   *2 heaped teaspoons chopped coriander leaves*

Heat an ungreased frying pan or *comal* and toast the chilies (see page 259), turning them constantly so they do not burn. Let them cool, then crumble (which they should do easily), seeds and veins and all.

Put the broiled tomato, salt, and water into the bottom of a blender jar, then add the garlic and the crumbled chilies and blend until you have a rough sauce (pieces of the chili skins should be visible).

Stir in the coriander and serve the sauce with broiled meats or snacks, or use for *sopes* (see *The Cuisines of Mexico*, pages 115–16).

About 1½ cups

Salsa de Chile de Arbol I Chile de Arbol Sauce I

Sra. Clara Zabalza de García (Guadalajara)

This is probably the best way of using the very fierce *chile de árbol* in a sauce
—and even then you may wish to reduce the number of *chilies* to the proportion of tomatoes.

> 5 chiles de árbol
> 1 tablespoon peanut or safflower oil
> 2 medium tomatoes (about 10 ounces), broiled (see page 262)
> 5 medium tomates verdes (about ½ cup), freshly cooked (see
>   page 245) or canned, drained
> 1 teaspoon salt, or to taste

Slit the chilies open and remove the seeds and veins. Reserve the seeds and
discard the veins. Heat the oil and fry the chilies and seeds until they are well
browned, but do not let them burn or the sauce will have a bitter taste.

   Put the tomatoes, *tomates verdes,* and salt into a blender jar. Add the fried
chilies and seeds and blend briefly. (Do not overblend; the sauce should have
some texture.) Eat with discretion as a condiment for tacos or as a seasoning
for plainly cooked Mexican foods.

About 1¼ cups

Salsa de Chile de Arbol II Chile Arbol Sauce II

This is the type of uncooked table sauce that is used as a condiment with broiled meats and eggs, in soups, or as a topping for *antojitos*. It could also be diluted with water and fried with shredded meat to make a taco filling. It is fearsomely hot, so reduce the number of chilies to suit your own taste.

If *chiles de árbol* are not available, use any small, dried hot chilies, like the *serranos secos* or *japonés*, that are more commonly found. Use the same number.

> **9** chiles de árbol
> *1½ cups* tomates verdes, *freshly cooked (see page 245) or canned, drained*
> *½ cup water*
> *¼ teaspoon salt, or to taste*
> *1 clove garlic, peeled*

Toast the chilies well on a hot griddle or *comal*, turning them constantly so they do not burn (see page 259).

Put the *tomates verdes* into a blender jar with the water, salt, and garlic. Remove the stems from the chilies and crumble them, with seeds and veins, into the blender jar. Blend the mixture until almost smooth. (Do not overblend; the sauce should have some texture and there should be some evidence of the chili skins.)

Serve as suggested above.

About 1½ cups

Salsa de Chile Guajillo Chile Guajillo Sauce

This sauce, from central Mexico, makes a wonderful accompaniment to plainly broiled meats and any tacos.

> 6 chiles guajillos
> 1 cup water, approximately
> 1 medium tomato (about 6 ounces), broiled (see page 262)
> 1 slice white onion, roughly chopped
> 1 clove garlic, peeled and roughly chopped
> ½ teaspoon salt

Slit the chilies open and remove the seeds and veins. Heat a griddle or *comal* and toast the chilies well on both sides (see page 259)—when they cool off they should be almost crisp—but be careful not to burn them, or the sauce will have a bitter taste.

Put the water into your blender jar first. Add the rest of the ingredients and blend until almost smooth (small pieces of chili skin should be evident in the sauce).

About 1½ cups

Salsa Arriera "Mule Drivers'" Sauce

The very simplest of tacos, reputedly eaten by mule drivers, consists of a hot tortilla, some rather strong white cheese *(añejo)*, and a *small* amount of mouth-searing sauce.

> **20** **chiles serranos**
> **¼** *small white onion, finely chopped*
> **1** *clove garlic, peeled and roughly chopped*
> **3 to 4** *tablespoons cold water*
> **½** *teaspoon salt, or to taste*

Remove the stalks from the chilies. Toast the chilies on a hot griddle or *comal* (see page 258), turning them from time to time until they are blistered and charred. While they are still hot, grind them with the rest of the ingredients to a rough paste, preferably in a *molcajete* or mortar.

Serve as suggested above.

About ½ cup

Salsa de Chile Serrano Rojo Red Chile Serrano Sauce

Sr. José Meza (restaurante El Pastor, Monterrey)

When I was in Monterrey at the end of October, the markets were filled with shining piles of ripe *chiles serranos,* their preferred condition for sauces in this part of Mexico. (Further south, on the other hand, the most popular sauces are made of *serranos* when they are green and have a sharp, pungent flavor.) One could almost call this particular sauce a violent one, as many are in the north, but it seemed to go very well with the *cabrito al pastor* (goat) I ate while I was there. That *cabrito,* by the way—cooked over a wood fire, the specialty of Monterrey and that part of Mexico—was just as good as I had remembered it. I ordered a steamed head, too, just to prove that my memory wasn't exaggerating how delicious it was, and then some *machitos* (the small intestines wound into a skein and broiled over the fire). Everything went so well with a *taro,* or mug, of draught beer and then a bowl of *frijoles rancheros* to finish up with (the best *frijoles rancheros,* incidentally, I have ever eaten).

> *2 ounces ripe* chiles serranos *(about 18)*
> *1 medium tomato (about 6 ounces)*
> *¼ cup water*
> *½ teaspoon salt, or to taste*

Remove the stalks from the chilies and put the chilies into a small saucepan, together with the tomato. Cover with water, bring to the simmering point, and cook for about 15 to 20 minutes, or until soft.

Drain the chilies and tomatoes and transfer to a blender jar. Add the water and salt to taste and blend briefly. (Do not overblend; the sauce should have some texture.)

Serve with broiled or roasted meats.

1¼ cups

Salsa Mexicana Cruda Fresh Mexican Sauce

This sauce can be made up ahead of time, but it tends to lose its crispness and fresh flavor if left to stand more than about 3 hours. It goes with just about everything.

> 1 *medium tomato (about 6 ounces), unpeeled, finely chopped*
> ½ *medium white onion, finely chopped*
> 6 *sprigs coriander, leaves only, finely chopped*
> 3 chiles serranos *or any fresh, hot green chilies, finely chopped*
> ½ *teaspoon salt, or to taste*
> ⅓ to ½ *cup fresh tomato juice or cold water*

Mix all the ingredients together well and serve.

About 1½ cups

Salsa de Jitomate Yucateca Yucatecan Tomato Sauce

This is a simple sauce that is used in many Yucatecan recipes. Here it is used with Pan de Cazón (see page 93) and Frijol con Puerco (see page 51).

The same old argument goes on about the best way to cook it. It seems that traditionally, after cooking the tomatoes over hot charcoal or wood, they were just mashed and never fried—but times have changed and the consistency of the sauce is better this way. Despite the fact that the *chile habanero* has the reputation of being one of the hottest of chilies—if one really can compare at this stage—it has a delightful flavor, and this is supposed to be imparted to the sauce, not its heat. But, then again, some cooks blend a little piece of the chili with the tomato.

The sauce keeps well for a few days and will freeze, although it does tend to separate a little.

> *1½ pounds tomatoes, broiled or boiled (see page 262)*
> *3 tablespoons peanut or safflower oil*
> *⅓ medium white onion, roughly sliced*
> *1 whole* chile habanero *or any fresh, hot green chili*
> *½ teaspoon salt, or to taste*

If the tomatoes are broiled, then remove any very blackened pieces of the skin and leave the rest on; if they are boiled, then remove the skins, as boiled skins tend to be tougher. Mash or blend the tomatoes briefly—there should be some texture to the sauce.

Heat the oil and fry the onion over a low flame, without browning, until it is translucent. Add the tomatoes, whole chili, and salt and cook the sauce over a medium flame, stirring from time to time until it has reduced and thickened.

Serve as described above.

About 2 cups

Salsa Ranchera Country-Style Sauce

This is the sauce traditionally used on *huevos rancheros,* which are eggs that are fried and then served on tortillas. It can be as *picante* as you like. There will always be arguments among cooks as to whether broiled or boiled fresh tomatoes should be used. I prefer the flavor of the sauce when they are broiled, although it is a little more trouble to make. This sauce can be made ahead, of course. It freezes quite well but does tend to separate.

Salsa ranchera is used for Queso Flameado (see page 10) and Molletes (see page 111).

> *1 pound tomatoes, broiled or boiled (see page 262)*
> *3 chiles serranos or any fresh, hot green chilies, broiled (see page 261) or boiled*
> *1 clove garlic, peeled and roughly chopped*
> *2 tablespoons peanut or safflower oil*
> *¼ small white onion, finely chopped*
> *½ teaspoon salt, or to taste*

Blend the tomatoes, chilies, and garlic together until fairly smooth.

Heat the oil, and fry the onion gently, without browning, until it is translucent. Add the blended ingredients and the salt and cook over a fairly brisk flame for about 5 minutes, stirring and scraping the bottom of the pan until the sauce has reduced a little and is well seasoned.

Serve as described above.

About 1 cup

Salsa de Tomate Verde Mexican Green Tomato Sauce

This is the raw version of a sauce that is so popular in central Mexico. It is undoubtedly superior when made in a *molcajete,* the Mexican volcanic-rock mortar. So often when it is made in the blender it becomes watery and separates.

If you are using fresh *tomates verdes*, the water in which they were cooked can be used for the sauce. If you are using the canned ones, then they should be drained and fresh water added, since the canning liquid tends to be acidy and salty.

This sauce can be made ahead—about 3 hours maximum—but tends to lose the fresh flavor of the coriander if left for too long. It will thicken up as it stands and may be diluted with more water before serving.

If you are using a blender, take care not to overblend (there should be some texture, and pieces of skin evident in the sauce).

> 2 chiles serranos *or any fresh, hot green chilies, finely chopped*
> ¼ *small white onion, finely chopped*
> 1 *small clove garlic, peeled and chopped*
> ¼ *teaspoon salt, or to taste*
> 2 *large sprigs coriander, leaves only*
> 1 *cup* tomates verdes, *freshly cooked (see page 245) or canned, drained*
> ⅓ *cup water or cooking liquid (see note above), approximately*

THE GARNISH

> 1 *teaspoon finely chopped coriander (optional)*

Preferably in a *molcajete* (see note above), grind together the chilies, onion, garlic, salt, and coriander to a paste. Add the *tomates verdes* and water or cooking liquid and grind briefly. Adjust the seasoning, sprinkle with the remaining coriander, if desired, and serve as a seasoning for tacos, eggs, rice, sausages . . . It's a universal sauce in the best sense of the word.

About 1¼ cups

Chiles de la Sierra "Mountain" Chilies

This very simple way of preparing *chiles anchos* to serve with roast or broiled meats, or as a relish with cold cuts, comes from the Sierra de Puebla. The chilies can be eaten the day they are made or, perhaps better still, when they have been left for a day or two to season at the bottom of the refrigerator.

> 6 *medium* chilies anchos
> 3 *tablespoons peanut or safflower oil*
> 1 *small white onion, thinly sliced*
> ½ *cup vinegar*
> ½ *teaspoon salt, or to taste*
> ½ *cup water*
> 2 *ounces* queso añejo, *Romano, or Sardo cheese, finely*
>   *grated*
> ¼ *teaspoon oregano*

THE GARNISH

> 1 *small white onion, thinly sliced*
> 6 *romaine lettuce leaves*
> 1 *medium tomato, sliced*

Heat an ungreased frying pan or *comal* over a medium flame and let the chilies heat through, turning them over from time to time, until they have softened and become flexible. Flatten each chili out as much as possible, then make a slit down one side and halfway around the top, to which the stalk is attached. Flatten out as much as possible and remove the seeds and veins.

Heat the oil until it smokes. Lower the flame, and pressing the inside of one chili at a time into the oil, let it fry for a minute or so—its color will turn to an opaque tobacco brown. (Take care that the flame is not too high or the chili will readily burn.) When all the chilies have been fried, drain off the excess oil.

Add the sliced onion to the pan and cook gently until it is translucent; do not let it brown. Add the vinegar, salt, water, and chilies and simmer for about 10 minutes, or until the chilies are completely soft. Remove the chilies from the pan and set them aside to cool.

Sprinkle the inside of each chili with a little of the cheese. Re-form them by folding the edges back in place, then set them in one layer in a serving dish and pour the liquid from the pan over them. Sprinkle them with oregano and top with onion rings, both cooked and raw. Just before serving, garnish the sides of the dish with the lettuce and tomato.

6 servings

Chiles Serranos en Escabeche Pickled Serrano Peppers

Important note: Partially cooked chilies grow a lot of bacteria, so it is important to make sure that the chilies have been cooked through thoroughly if they are to be kept for any length of time.

> *1½ pounds* **chiles serranos** *or* **chiles jalapeños**
> *¾ cup olive oil*
> *2 medium white onions, thickly sliced*
> *3 medium carrots, scraped and thickly sliced*
> *1 head garlic, cloves separated but not peeled*
> *3 cups mild vinegar*
> *2 tablespoons salt*
> *1 bay leaf (2 to 3 in Mexico)*
> *½ teaspoon oregano*
> *3 sprigs fresh marjoram or ¼ teaspoon dried*
> *3 sprigs fresh thyme or ¼ teaspoon dried*

Wash the chilies, leaving the stems intact. Cut a cross in the tip end of each chili so the vinegar can penetrate.

Heat the olive oil until it smokes, then lower the flame, add the onions, chilies, carrots, and garlic, and fry over a medium flame for about 10 minutes, turning them over from time to time. Add the vinegar, salt, and, herbs, and bring to a boil. Lower the flame and simmer for 5 minutes longer. Pack 6 sterilized pint jars with the chilies, vegetables, and herbs, top with the vinegar, and seal.

6 pints

Rajas de Chiles Jalapeños Frescos Fresh Chile Jalapeño Relish

Sra. Arcelia Vázquez de Valles (Durango)

This fresh and *picante* relish always appears on the table of homes and restaurants in Durango. It is eaten with broiled meats, on top of rice, or with beans. The *rajas* can be used after about 2 hours but are better the next day. They will keep well up to about a week in the refrigerator.

> ½ *pound* chiles jalapeños *(about 13)*
> 1 *medium white onion, thinly sliced*
> 4 *cloves garlic, peeled and left whole*
> 1½ *teaspoons salt, or to taste*
> ½ *teaspoon oregano*
> ¾ *cup mild vinegar*
> ¼ *cup salad oil*

Wash and dry the chilies well. Cut off the stalk and slice in half. Remove as many of the veins and seeds as possible and slice thin. Mix with the rest of the ingredients and set aside to marinate for at least 2 hours (see note above).

About 2 cups

Original Ensalada Alex–Cesar Cardini The Original Alex–Caesar Cardini Salad

Alex Cardini, Sr. (Mexico City)

Three years ago one of the best-loved restaurateurs in Mexico, Alex Cardini, Sr., died. He had started in the restaurant business in Italy at the age of ten and by his late teens had worked in some of the most distinguished restaurants in Europe. As an ace pilot in the Italian air force, he was decorated for his courage and daring during World War I.

In 1926 Alex, Sr., joined his brother Caesar in Tijuana, where Caesar had a thriving restaurant business and where he had invented a famous salad dressing. Using this dressing and a unique combination of other ingredients, Alex invented his salad in honor of the pilots of Rockwell Field Air Base in San Diego. First known as Aviator's Salad, it then became popularly known and copied as Caesar, but I shall call it as it should be called: Alex–Caesar Cardini Salad.

A few months before he died, I had one of those long and wonderful lunches with the Cardini sons and their friends. We talked for hours about the rare and fascinating things in Mexican food, and Alex, Sr., prepared his salad for us.

10 romaine lettuce leaves, approximately
6 half-inch slices French bread
¼ cup olive oil
3 cloves garlic, peeled
6 anchovy fillets
1 egg, in shell
1 tablespoon fresh lime juice
1 teaspoon Worcestershire sauce
¼ cup freshly grated Parmesan cheese
Salt and freshly ground pepper to taste

Wash the lettuce, spin dry, wrap in a dry towel, and set aside in the refrigerator to crisp up.

Preheat the oven to 400 degrees. Put the bread slices onto a ungreased baking sheet and bake until crisp—45 minutes to 1 hour. Brush with 1½ tablespoons of the oil and return to the oven to brown—about 15 minutes.

Crush together the garlic and the anchovies and gradually add 1 tablespoon of the oil. Spread this mixture onto the bread slices and set aside.

Cover the egg with boiling water and cook for 1 minute; the white should be opaque and just setting.

Put the lettuce leaves into the salad bowl, add the remaining ingredients, and toss until all the ingredients are well incorporated.

2 servings

Chiles en Escabeche Colimenses Pickled Chilies Stuffed with Beans

This is a deliciously different version of stuffed chilies given to me by a distinguished cook from Colima. You should start three days ahead for best results. One chili per serving should be plenty, as it is a very filling salad or first course.

THE CHILIES

     6 medium-sized chiles poblanos
     3 tablespoons peanut or safflower oil

THE PICKLING MIXTURE

     5 cloves garlic, peeled and halved
     1 medium purple onion, thinly sliced
     1 medium carrot, scraped and thinly sliced
     ½ cup wine vinegar
     2 tablespoons water
     1 teaspoon salt, or to taste

THE FILLING

     *½ pound pinto or California pink beans (*canarios *or* flor de mayo *in Mexico), cooked (see page 36), with their broth*
     3 small chorizos *(3 to 4 ounces each)*
     2 tablespoons pork lard or bacon fat
     1 small white onion, finely chopped
     1 medium tomato (about 6 ounces), peeled and chopped

> **3 tablespoons grated** queso ranchero seco, añejo, *Sardo, or*
>   **Romano cheese**

THE GARNISH

> **6 slices** queso panela *or feta cheese*
> **12 romaine lettuce leaves**

Heat the oil until it smokes, then lower the flame and fry the chilies over a medium flame, turning them from time to time, until they are blistered and well browned. This should take about 10 minutes. Remove the pan from the flame, cover, and let the chilies "sweat" for about 5 minutes. Remove the chilies from the pan, drain, and set them aside to cool while you prepare the pickling mixture.

Sauté the garlic gently in the same oil until the cloves are lightly browned. Add the other ingredients and bring to a boil. Reduce the heat and let the mixture simmer, stirring from time to time, for about 2 minutes. Transfer the contents of the pan to a glass or china bowl.

Remove the skins from the chilies (if you have fried them sufficiently, they should slip off easily). Carefully slit the chilies open and remove the seeds and veins, taking care to keep the top and stalk intact. Add the chilies to the ingredients in the bowl and store at the bottom of the refrigerator for 2 or 3 days, turning them over at intervals so they become evenly impregnated with the seasoning.

On the day you plan to serve the chilies, prepare the filling. Blend the beans and their broth together (do not overblend, as they must have some texture). Set aside.

Skin and crumble the *chorizo,* then heat the fat and cook the *chorizo* pieces gently—they will burn easily—until the fat has rendered out—about 5 minutes. Remove the *chorizo* pieces and set aside.

In the same fat, fry the onion gently, without browning, until translucent. Add the tomato and fry for 3 minutes longer. Add the blended beans and *chorizo* and fry the mixture, stirring and scraping the bottom of the pan, until it is reduced to a thick paste. Remove from the flame and set aside to cool, then stir in the grated cheese.

Stuff the *chilies* with the bean mixture and arrange them on a round platter lined with romaine lettuce leaves. Cover each chili with a strip of the cheese and the onion and carrot pieces from the pickling mixture.

6 servings

Desserts and Sweet Snacks

Flan de Naranja Orange Flan

Sra. María Luisa Camarena de Rodríguez (Tehuacán, Puebla)

Sra. María Luisa Camarena de Rodríguez invited me to stay with the family in Tehuacán for a few days at the end of October to try the local specialty, *mole de cadera,* which is prepared each year at the time of the mass killing of goats. (I was fascinated by it—a strong, soupy stew made from the spine and hip bones of the goats and seasoned with chilies and avocado leaves—but I confess that I couldn't eat anything after the first mouthful.) However, during the few days I was there, Señora Rodríguez took me to meet the well-known cooks of the town and lent me the family cookbook, to choose and copy any recipes that I liked. Many were almost completely Spanish in origin, and this one, for an orange flan, particularly caught my eye.

I think it's quite sensational. However, if the oranges are very sweet you will need to add a little more lemon or lime juice. I have also made it with a proportion of tangerine juice, and this was delicious. I have reduced the sugar to ¼ cup (aside from the sugar for the caramel), and added the grated rind, which I think improves the flavor. Don't be surprised at how much the mixture reduces during the cooking time. And if you do not let the froth from the beaten eggs subside sufficiently before you put it into the oven, it will puff up and stick to the lid of the flan mold (see page 254).

> ¾ *cup granulated sugar*
> *Finely grated rind of 2 oranges and ½ lemon*
> *1 cup orange juice plus juice of ½ lemon*
> *6 eggs, separated*

First make the caramel. Melt ½ cup of the sugar in a heavy pan over low heat. When it has completely melted, turn the flame up and stir the syrup with a wooden spoon until it darkens (the color will depend on how dark you like your caramel). Pour the caramel into the flan mold if you are using it, or a 1-quart charlotte mold, and turn it around quickly, tipping the mold from side to side until there is an even coating of caramel over the bottom and halfway up the sides. Set aside.

Preheat the oven to 350 degrees. If you are not using the flan mold as illustrated, set a water bath on the lowest shelf of the oven (improvising with a roasting pan into which the mold will fit and putting in hot water to a depth of 1½ inches, or so that it will come almost halfway up the side of the mold *after* it has been filled with the flan mixture).

Add the grated rind to the juice and stir the remaining ¼ cup sugar in gradually so that it dissolves.

Beat the egg yolks until they are thick, then, in a separate bowl, beat the whites until stiff. Gradually add the yolks to the whites, beating all the time. When they are thoroughly incorporated, gradually beat in the orange juice. Let the froth subside before pouring the mixture into the prepared mold. Grease the lid of the mold, cover, and set in the water bath. Bake until the flan is set—about 2 hours. (Test by inserting the blade of a knife into the center of the custard, taking care not to pierce the bottom of the flan. If the blade comes out clean, then it is cooked.) Set aside to cool, *not* in the refrigerator, before attempting to unmold.

6 servings

Crema de Piñon o Nuez Encarcelada Pine Nut or Pecan Cream

This is clearly one of those desserts of Spanish origin that were often changed, embellished, or adapted to local ingredients by the nuns in Mexico during the Colonial period. Although I personally find them too cloying, I have included this one example to appease my Mexican friends who have accused me of leaving out some of their favorite desserts.

I have changed the recipe slightly. Because I have reduced the amount of sugar, which helps thicken the mixture, I have included two egg yolks—which is not atypical—and I have suggested rum or brandy rather than the innocuous white wine, and pecans as a possible substitute for the pine nuts. Pine nuts in Mexico have reached a prohibitive price; still, unlike those generally available in the United States, they do give a delicately lovely flavor and pale pink color to the dish, since the papery pink skin is always left on them.

> *3 cups milk*
> *4-inch piece cinnamon bark, roughly broken up*
> *¾ cup granulated sugar*
> *2 tablespoons rice flour or cornstarch*
> *½ pound pine nuts or pecans (2¼ cups, approximately), roughly chopped, plus a few whole nuts for decoration*
> *2 egg yolks, well beaten*
> *⅓ cup brandy or rum or ⅔ cup white wine, or to taste*
> *10 ladyfingers, roughly broken up*

Well butter a shallow dish, ideally about 9 inches in diameter and 1½ inches deep.

Bring the milk to a boil, then add the cinnamon and stir in most of the sugar, reserving a little to grind with the nuts. Lower the flame and stir until the sugar is melted. Stir ¼ cup of the warmed milk into the rice flour and work to a smooth paste. Stir this into the milk/sugar mixture and continue cooking, stirring all the time, until it thickens slightly.

Grind the nuts with the reserved sugar until very fine and stir into the boiling milk mixture. Cook until the mixture has reduced and thickened—about 20 to 30 minutes. Add about 1 cup of the hot mixture to the egg yolks and beat together well. Return to the pan and continue to cook, stirring and scraping the bottom of the pan constantly, until the mixture thickens to the extent that you can see the bottom of the pan as you stir. (It should coat the back of a wooden spoon thickly.) Stir in about two-thirds of the brandy or wine.

Pour half of the mixture into the prepared dish. Cover with the ladyfingers, sprinkle with the rest of the brandy or wine, and cover with the remaining cream. Decorate the top with the whole nuts and set aside to cool off to room temperature—do not refrigerate—before serving.

6 servings

Capirotada I Bread Pudding I

One of the favorite Lenten desserts of Mexico is *capirotada,* using slices of the small yeast rolls called *bolillos* (slices of French bread would do equally well). It is preferable to slice the bread and leave it overnight on a wire tray to dry out, or you can dry it out in a slow oven.

In all the Mexican recipes for this, you are told to fry the bread. This means that an enormous amount of fat is absorbed, so I have changed the cooking method here.

Don't look askance at the fig leaf listed below; it gives a distinctive and delicious flavor to the pudding. (The fig is a very decorative tree and grows quite far north; I even know of one growing on New York's Upper West Side.) And if you are using *piloncillo,* the raw sugar of Mexico, I suggest that you leave it to soak in the water several hours ahead of time, as it tends to be rather hard.

Traditionally, *capirotada* is eaten as a dessert or with a glass of milk at supper.

(continued)

*4 bolillos, sliced, or 16 half-inch slices French bread,
    dried out (see note above)*
¼ cup melted pork lard
¼ cup peanut or safflower oil
½ pound piloncillo *(see note above) or dark brown
    sugar*
1 cup water
4-inch piece cinnamon bark or 1 large fig leaf
4 ounces queso añejo *or farmer cheese*
¼ cup raisins
¼ cup slivered almonds or pine nuts
3 tablespoons butter, softened and cut into small pieces

Preheat the oven to 350 degrees and place the oven rack on the middle level. Well butter a shallow dish just large enough to accommodate half of the bread slices in one layer (a Pyrex dish 8½ × 8½ inches should be perfect).

Choose a cookie sheet onto which all the bread slices will just fit comfortably. Mix the melted lard and oil together and coat the cookie sheet well. Arrange the pieces of bread on the cookie sheet and paint the top of them liberally with the rest of the oil/lard mixture. Bake for about 10 minutes, then turn the pieces over and bake for 10 minutes more, or until the bread is crisp and a deep golden color.

Over a low flame, melt the *piloncillo* or sugar in the water, along with the cinnamon or fig leaf (if using the *piloncillo*, see the note above). Bring the resulting syrup to a boil and cook for 8 minutes *only* (the syrup should have some body but not be too thick).

Put one-half of the bread slices into the prepared dish and very slowly pour about one-third of the syrup onto the bread (*not* the dish), then sprinkle with one-half of the cheese, raisins, and nuts. Dot with half the butter. Cover with the remaining bread slices and syrup and sprinkle on the rest of the cheese, raisins, and nuts, and dot with the remaining butter. (Note: it is particularly important to pour the syrup little by little onto the bread, waiting for each batch to be absorbed before adding more. If you don't do this, the syrup will run to the bottom of the dish and the top layer will remain dry.) Cover the dish with foil and bake for about 20 minutes, by which time the bread should be soft but not mushy and the top slightly browned.

Serve hot or cold.

6 servings

Capirotada II Bread Pudding II

Sra. María Elena Lara (restaurante Los Tres Migueles,
Mexico City)

This is a more elegant version of the preceding recipe for *capirotada*. While that one calls for stale *bolillos* or French bread, this version calls for the slightly sweet yeast bread called *pechuga* (a suitable substitute for which would be any semisweet yeast bread made with eggs, such as challah). This bread, too, is sliced and left to dry out overnight—or is dried out in a slow oven.

Señora Lara uses chopped *acitron* (candied *biznaga* cactus) between the layers, but I find this too sweet—a problem I have with most Mexican desserts—and prefer using about ⅓ cup extra white raisins and currants as a substitute, harking back, I am sure, to my youth in England and the bread-and-butter pudding that was an inevitable favorite at home.

An ideal dish for this recipe would be a round Pyrex dish about 8½ inches in diameter and 2½ to 3 inches deep.

> *2½ cups milk*
> *⅓ cup granulated sugar*
> *2-inch piece cinnamon bark*
> *⅓ cup mixed white raisins and currants*
> *⅓ cup blanched, sliced almonds or pine nuts*
> *5½ tablespoons safflower or peanut oil*
> *3 six-inch tortillas, preferable dried out*
> *4 tablespoons sweet butter*
> *15 slices sweet yeast bread (see note above), each*
>   *approximately 6 inches long, 2 inches high, and ½*
>   *inch thick*
> *½ cup cubed* acitron *(see note above)*

THE TOPPING

> *4 large eggs*
> *Pinch of salt*
> *2 tablespoons granulated sugar, approximately*

Put the milk, sugar, cinnamon bark, raisins, and almonds into a saucepan and bring to a simmer. Continue simmering until the sugar has melted, then set aside to cool.

Heat 1½ tablespoons of the oil and fry the tortillas on both sides; they should be leathery. Drain on paper toweling, then cut them into pieces so that they completely cover the bottom of a round Pyrex dish.

Melt 2 tablespoons of the butter in 2 more tablespoons of the oil. Quickly dip both sides of the bread slices into the mixture so they are lightly covered but do not absorb too much. Add the rest of the oil and butter and repeat the process for the remaining slices. Put the pieces back into the frying pan, a few at a time, and fry over a low flame until golden on both sides. (The original recipe used up a great deal more fat because the slices were just fried. This is a more laborious method but uses less fat.)

Put one-third of the fried bread into the prepared pan in one layer, completely covering the bottom. Pour over about one-quarter of the sweetened milk, raisins, and almond mixture, then sprinkle on one-third of the *acitron*. Cover with another layer of the bread. Pour about one third of the remaining milk and fruit evenly onto the bread, then sprinkle on another third of the *acitron*. Repeat the layers with the remaining ingredients and set aside for the bread to absorb the milk—about 15 minutes.

Place an oven rack on the lowest shelf of the oven; preheat the oven to 350 degrees.

Beat the egg whites together until fluffy. Add the salt and beat until stiff (you should be able to turn the bowl upside down without the eggs sliding out). Add the yolks, one by one, beating well after each one is added until they are well incorporated.

Spread the top of the pudding evenly with the beaten eggs, then sprinkle with the sugar and set in the oven to bake for about 30 minutes. When cooked, all the liquid should be absorbed and the top lightly browned.

Serve either hot or cold.

6 servings

Buñuelos del Norte Buñuelos from the North of Mexico

Alma Kauffman (Chihuahua)

Somewhere, every day in Mexico, churches celebrate the day of their patron saint. Small stands appear out of nowhere overnight, and by morning have set themselves up in business on the sidewalk outside the church, ready to feed the early worshippers. They may be gaily hung with elaborately decorated fiesta breads of all sizes, they may be cooking up the usual *enchiladas* and tacos —but no matter what, there will always be a *buñuelo* stand.

In the villages of Michoacán the *buñuelo* seems to have become daily food. As evening falls, there is a hum of activity under the arches of the central plazas as everyone gathers to gossip over a bowl of *pozole* (pork and corn soup) or eat *buñuelos.* It is the tradition there to break them up into a hot syrup flavored with cinnamon bark, and you are even given a choice of having them *acaramelizados* (still crisp), or *garritos* (cooked in the syrup until soft). And no Christmas Eve supper in Mexico is complete without hot chocolate and *buñuelos.* This is the time of year when the family recipes are brought out and everyone helps to stretch out the paper-thin rounds of dough, which are then fried crisp and sprinkled with sugar and cinnamon or perhaps a vanilla-flavored syrup. Naturally, every recipe varies slightly, and families vie with each other, proclaiming theirs to be superior *and* authentic. Alma Kauffman, who was born in Chihuahua, showed me how to make the *buñuelos* traditional to her family.

As she sat, cross-legged, pulling out each piece of dough to a paper-thin circle with rapidly moving fingers, she reminisced about her childhood. Every Christmas she went to visit her grandmother in the Sierra de Chihuahua, and would watch her sitting in the sun, stretching out the dough either over her knee or over an inverted pottery jug. She believes that there is something very special about the air and sun at that time of year that contributes toward making the festive *buñuelos* superior to those made during the rest of the year. Her grandmother always made hundreds of them for family and friends, but they were kept under lock and key from the children, whose appetites knew no limits, and for the few days before Christmas frantic efforts were made to try and discover where the key had been hidden.

Señora Kauffman mentioned that her grandmother's original recipe used an infusion of the papery husks of *tomates verdes* to both mix the dough and provide the acid raising agent now supplied by baking powder. And because the family prefers to eat their *buñuelos* just as they are, instead of sprinkling them with sugar and cinnamon or a cinnamon-flavored syrup, the dough has a larger proportion of sugar than most recipes call for. (They can also be made with butter, or pork lard, or a mixture of shortenings, according to one's taste.)

The furniture in the room was piled with pale golden disks, and Señora Kauffman's son was just finishing off the last batch from twelve pounds of flour. He was punching and pulling it until it reached its *punto*. To test this, he formed the dough into a thick circle and put it over his clenched fist. The dough rolled softly over his hand, covering it like a closely fitting cap. Another way he tested the dough was to form it into a thick roll and slash it to a depth of about 1½ inches with a sharp knife. If the dough sprang back immediately like elastic, it was ready.

THE BUÑUELOS

> *1 cup cold water, approximately*
> *5 heaped soupspoons granulated sugar (if not using the syrup; only 1 heaped soupspoon sugar if using the syrup)*
> *½ teaspoon salt*
> *1 pound unbleached all-purpose flour*
> *½ heaped soupspoon baking powder*
> *4 tablespoons pork lard or butter, cut into small pieces*
> *1 large egg, lightly beaten*
> *Vegetable oil for frying*

THE SUGAR SYRUP (optional)

> *1 cup light brown sugar*
> *½ cup cold water*
> *2½-inch piece cinnamon bark, broken in half*

Put the water into a small saucepan. Add the sugar and salt and warm through over a low flame until the sugar has melted. Let the mixture cool off to lukewarm while you start the dough.

Sift the flour and baking powder together, then rub with the fat through your fingertips until the mixture resembles fine crumbs. Add the beaten egg, then, gradually, the sugared water. Work the dough very hard, kneading, pulling, and throwing it down onto the table until it is smooth and elastic. (Test by making a cushion of the dough and slashing it with a knife to a depth of about 1 inch; the dough should spring back immediately.) This will take about 10 to 15 minutes, depending, of course, on how much strength you put into it.

Press the dough out to a thick oval, then roll up into an elongated sausage shape. Tuck both ends in to form a "cushion" and place inside a polyethylene bag. Set the dough aside, in a warm place, for a minimum of 3 hours.

After the dough has rested, divide up and roll into balls approximately 1 inch in diameter. Place the balls on a tray, cover first with polyethylene wrap and then with a damp towel, and set aside in a warm place for at least 30 minutes.

Cover your table with a cloth. Sitting in a comfortable chair, cross your legs and put a dry, clean kitchen towel over your knee. Press one of the balls of dough firmly between your palms until you have a circle about 2½ inches in diameter. Take the dough between the thumbs and forefingers of both hands and gently stretch it out into a larger circle about 4 inches in diameter; do this in such a way that the center will be almost transparent while the edges are still thick.

Place the center of the dough on your knee and, using the thumbs and forefingers of both hands, gently ease out, rather than pull, and at the same time stretch, the thick edge in quick little movements, working clockwise, until you have a circle about 10 inches in diameter. Place the *buñuelo* carefully onto the tablecloth to dry (you can hang them around the edge of the table, too) while you proceed with the remaining balls of dough.

It will take about 45 minutes for the *buñuelos* to dry out on one side; they will then feel dry and papery to the touch. Turn them over and let them dry out completely on the second side. The drying process should take about 1 hour 15 minutes, depending, of course, on how humid the air is, and so forth.

Pour oil to a depth of ½ inch into a large, heavy frying pan and heat until it is hot but not smoking. Spread a large tray with a double layer of paper toweling.

Put one of the *buñuelos* carefully into the hot oil—it will most probably balloon up—and holding a sharp-tined fork in each hand, prick the dough in various places and lift up the edge at one side to let the air out. In perhaps 2 seconds light golden spots will appear through the dough, or at the edge— the sign that the *buñuelo* should be turned over and cooked for a few seconds more on the other side. The *buñuelo* should be pale gold in color, with some creamy-colored patches. If it is too dark in color (commercially made ones usually are), lower the flame and let the oil cool off a little before cooking the next one.

(continued)

As each *buñuelo* is cooked, drain well of any excess fat by holding it over the pan and then lay on the paper toweling to drain further. Serve immediately or keep hot if you are going to dribble them with syrup first.

If you are using the sugar syrup, put the ingredients for the syrup into a small saucepan. Set over a slow flame and stir, until the sugar has melted. Raise the flame and cook fast until the syrup reduces and forms a soft thread—120 degrees on a candy thermometer. Dribble the syrup over the hot *buñuelos* and serve.

About 22 ten-inch buñuelos

Buñuelos Chihuahuenses Buñuelos from Chihuahua

Sra. Rosa Margarita J. de Mejía (Chihuahua)

These *buñuelos* are from Chihuahua, as are Señora Kauffman's in the preceding recipe, but how different the two are! These are sprinkled with granulated sugar and cinnamon while they are still hot and can be eaten hot or cold. At Christmas time in Chihuahua they are served with *café con leche,* as chocolate is rarely drunk in the north.

The leavening agent, as in many parts of Mexico, is *tequesquite* (a natural salt used as a raising agent), for which I have substituted cream of tartar.

> ¾ *pound unbleached all-purpose flour*
> 2 *teaspoons baking powder*
> ¼ *teaspoon cream of tartar*
> ¼ *teaspoon salt*
> 3 *tablespoons grated Chihuahua cheese or mild Cheddar*
> 1½ *tablespoons solid vegetable shortening, cut into small pieces*
> 2 *small eggs, lightly beaten*
> ⅓ *cup warm water, approximately*
> *Vegetable oil for frying*

THE TOPPING

> *½ cup granulated sugar, approximately, mixed with 2*
> *tablespoons ground cinnamon*

Sift the flour, baking powder, cream of tartar, and salt together. Stir in the cheese. Add the shortening and rub in lightly with the tips of the fingers until it is well incorporated.

Gradually stir in the eggs and water, then knead the dough lightly until it is soft and pliable—about 2 minutes. Cover the dough with waxed paper and set aside for about 2 hours. Do not refrigerate—unless, of course, the weather is very hot and sticky.

Divide the dough into 12 equal balls about 1½ inches in diameter. Lightly sprinkle a pastry board or cloth with flour, and using a thin rolling pin (see page 184), roll four of the balls of dough out very thin; they should each make a circle about 8 inches in diameter.

Pour oil into a heavy 10-inch frying pan to a depth of 1 inch and heat until smoking. Carefully place a thin round of dough in the hot fat and fry until it is a deep golden color on the underside (you may need to use two spatulas toward the end of the frying period to keep the *buñuelo* down in the fat); this should take about 2 minutes. Turn it over carefully and fry the second side. (The whole process should take from 3½ to 4 minutes.) Remove and drain on paper toweling. While still hot, sprinkle with the sugar and cinnamon.

Repeat with the remaining 3 circles, then roll out 4 more balls of dough and continue until the remainder of the *buñuelos* have been fried.

Serve the *buñuelos* immediately or let cool and store in an airtight container.

12 eight-inch buñuclos

Sopaipillas

For years I have been denying to aficionados of the *sopaipillas* of New Mexico that they have a Mexican counterpart. I have now discovered that they *can* be found, though rarely, in the state of Chihuahua. Made of the same dough as wheat-flour tortillas, they are rolled out thin, cut into small pieces, and fried puffy and crisp. They are then sprinkled with powdered sugar or cinnamon and eaten, cold, in the early evening with coffee. I have yet to see them on any restaurant menus in the north.

Don't be discouraged if all the *sopaipillas* don't puff up like little cushions, especially when making them for the first time. The thickness of the dough and the heat of the oil will determine whether they puff up or not. The dough should be very thin but not transparent; each 1¼ inch ball of dough should be rolled out to a circle between 5 and 5½ inches in diameter. The oil must not be too hot or the outside of the dough will harden and brown too quickly and therefore not puff up. You will need to adjust the heat constantly, lowering it as each piece of the dough is put in and letting it return to full heat as each batch of cooked *sopaipillas* is removed.

Do one at a time to begin with so you can press down with the back of a fork and make them puff up properly. After about 2 seconds—if the oil is the correct heat—the dough will start to bubble and puff up. If you see that it's bubbling but not puffing up, then turn the *sopaipilla* over and keep pressing with the fork.

When finished, the *sopaipillas* should be crisp but palest gold in color.

When rolling out the dough, try not to pick up too much extra flour. It will sink to the bottom of the frying pan and burn, and eventually you will have to strain the oil and start again—which is a nuisance, and very messy besides.

> ½ *teaspoon salt*
> 1 *cup warm water*
> 2 *ounces (¼ cup) pork lard, cut into small pieces*
> 1 *pound unbleached all-purpose flour*
> *Peanut or safflower oil for frying*
> *Confectioners' sugar and ground cinnamon for dusting*

Dissolve the salt in the water and set aside to cool to lukewarm. Rub the fat into the flour with your fingertips until it resembles very fine breadcrumbs.

Add the salted water to the flour and mix the dough with your hands until it comes cleanly away from the sides of the bowl. Turn the dough out onto a lightly floured surface and knead and pull it out for about 5 minutes. Knead the dough into a round cushion shape, put into a polyethylene bag, and set aside for a *minimum* of 2 hours, but preferably overnight. Do *not* refrigerate.

Cover a tray with a smooth, clean cloth. Remove the dough from the bag and knead for a minute or so on a lightly floured surface, then divide into small balls approximately 1¼ inches in diameter; there should be about 30 of them. Set them onto the tray and cover with a slightly damp cloth or polyethylene wrap so the outside of the balls does not dry out and form a crust.

Have ready a small frying pan containing peanut or safflower oil to the depth of ½ inch. Have ready another tray, covered with two layers of paper toweling. You will then need an ordinary kitchen fork, a metal spatula, and a thin rolling pin (see page 184).

Dust your working surface *very lightly* with flour (see note above). Roll out one of the balls until it is about 5 to 5½ inches in diameter (don't worry if it is an uneven circle, as *sopaipillas* can be cut into any shape). Cut the dough into 4 or even 6 small triangles and set them aside until you have repeated the process with 3 more balls and are ready to begin frying the first batch.

Heat the oil. Just before it begins to smoke, lower the flame as you put *one* piece of the dough into it. Keep pressing the dough down lightly with the back of the fork—it should then start to bubble and puff up. Turn the *sopaipilla* over and cook on the second side. The whole process should only take a few seconds, and the *sopaipilla* should be barely golden in color. Drain on paper toweling.

Quickly fry the remainder of the batch, sprinkle with confectioners' sugar and cinnamon while still hot, then let them cool off.

Repeat the whole process with the remainder of the dough, working in batches.

About 120 sopaipillas

Mexican Baking

GENERAL NOTES

Apart from liking to eat Mexican pastries, I found that I was fascinated by the very different techniques of making them, techniques I had never seen elsewhere. I know they sound terribly complicated. Try them once and the instructions will become clearer; after several tries you will become quite expert. I hope these recipes won't be ignored by all but the real *aficionados* and homesick Mexicans.

You really have to be in the mood, with an undisturbed weekend ahead, to embark on a new type of baking such as this for the first time. (Once in the mood I myself find it hard to break out of. I like my own bread and cakes, I like dough rising around the kitchen and a yeasty smell permeating the house. I even happen to like the crusty coating of flour on every handle and knob in the kitchen!) You will find that once you get in the habit you can arrange your baking time to stretch over work, play, or shopping periods; you will become critical of the oversweet, overrefined baked goods of this type generally

182

around and your palate will begin to demand the real thing.

As you can see by reading through the recipes, you need a bit of patience, but they all incorporate rather different and, I think, quite fascinating techniques; they are certainly not boring. Here are some general tips that should help simplify the various processes for you.

1. While I have no time for dough hooks in regular bread making, I do recommend a heavy-duty mixer with a dough-hook attachment for all these yeast recipes (with the exception perhaps of the *biscuits de queso* on page 200). They require long, hard beating, which I certainly wouldn't do by hand.

2. You will need a warm, draft-proof area to prove the doughs, ideally at a temperature of 80 degrees, so I suggest you keep a room thermometer handy.

3. You may wonder why I make a starter and then only use half of it in a recipe. First of all, the half quantity is hard to mix and beat in the standard bowl the heavy mixers provide, and besides, it will encourage you to try the recipe a second time.

4. Why aren't they rich in butter? In Mexico *pan dulce* are bought and eaten in great quantities daily. They would be too rich, too heavy, and too expensive eaten on such a scale with morning and evening *café con leche* or chocolate.

5. All breads baked with a high proportion of yeast such as these tend to dry out quickly. Eat as many of them as you can freshly baked and then follow the ways I have suggested of freezing, reheating, or toasting wherever feasible.

6. Weather affects this sort of baking. A damp, heavy, warm day will not produce the same nice, light dough as a clear, dry day, so be warned.

7. To make the nice, lumpy sugar used in decorating some of the *pan dulce*, spread a good, thick layer of granulated sugar on a large baking sheet. Dampen it thoroughly with water and let it dry out completely before crumbling it roughly, ready to use.

8. Never use your fingers when working and kneading dough, only the flat of your hands and the heels of your palms. When the dough is strong, use your whole forearm to break it down.

SPECIAL EQUIPMENT FOR MEXICAN BAKING

A kitchen scale indicating both pounds and kilos if possible—to start the changeover to the metric system in your mind and daily baking.

A postal or diet scale for weighing small quantities, if your ordinary scale does not measure these accurately.

In addition to a normal-sized wooden rolling pin, a skinny wooden rolling pin, 12 to 15 inches long and just under 1 inch in diameter. You probably won't find this anywhere, so do what the Mexican bakeries do: buy a broom handle or dowel cut to the appropriate length and have the ends smoothed off.

A plastic dough scraper. Nothing else can really take its place.

A cutter for decorating Conchas (see page 202 and illustration below), not essential but nice.

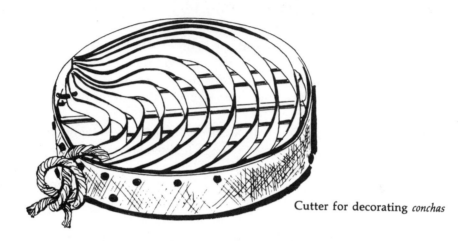

Cutter for decorating *conchas*

A room thermometer to enable you to judge and adjust temperatures when your dough is rising.

2 large rubber spatulas with *wooden* handles.

2 thick pieces of old toweling and some large polyethylene bags for raising the doughs.

A heavy-duty electric mixer with dough-hook attachment. (I don't think it would be honest of me not to give the result of my experience in so many kitchens with so many different pieces of equipment, in England, the United States, Mexico, and France. I much prefer the KitchenAid. So many mixers are designed for design's sake—and this is particularly true of English and German machines. A particular feature to watch is the design of the mixing bowls. Those with bulbous bottoms—although the beater may be designed for them—very rarely beat as thoroughly and as quickly as the more tapered mixing bowl that the KitchenAid offers. And, when the bowls are well designed, you do not need two of different sizes.)

INGREDIENTS FOR MEXICAN BAKING

FLOUR

Except where otherwise specified, use unbleached all-purpose flour. Always have some finely ground white corn meal or presifted flour on hand for dusting baking sheets to prevent the dough sticking. In this section, amounts of flour are specified in terms of weight, for accuracy's sake.

FAT

In Mexican bakeries they use vegetable shortening and margarine. If you want to improve the flavor, then use butter for one-quarter of the specified amount of fat. No more, or your pastries will become too rich and heavy.

Note also that the amounts of fat are specified in terms of weight, in ounces rather than tablespoons or cups.

YEAST

I personally choose to use cake yeast; it takes less time to develop a good flavor in the rising stage, and apart from that I find the dried stuff rather unaesthetic. If you cannot find the 2-ounce packages it generally comes in, then buy a whole 1-pound block. Cut it into 1-ounce pieces and freeze it until ready to use. You will not have to let it defrost before using; simply mash it with a wooden spoon until it breaks up and starts to liquefy.

EGGS

For any recipe here I have allowed for 2-ounce eggs. Get used to weighing your eggs, especially for the baking of delicate sponges, *génoise,* and so forth. The names given to eggs in the United States are totally misleading. You will notice there are almost never any small ones. The smallest generally available, resembling pullets' eggs, are called medium, then come large, extra-large, and jumbo!

LA PANADERIA (The Bakery)

Let me say at the outset that I love all manner of baked goods, from heavy British fruitcakes to cream puffs, so little wonder that I can always remember from my childhood in England the fascination of bakeries. That wonderfully yeasty smell would waft out of the bakehouse door as trays of freshly baked teacakes, scones, and currant buns were brought out, all ready to be rushed home, toasted on a brass toasting fork over glowing coals and slathered with butter to make teatime such a consoling affair. Depending on where you were, there would be pikelets, crumpets, lardy and eccles cakes, or coiled Chelsea buns generously filled with currants.

It is no wonder, then, that when I first came to Mexico in 1957 I found it very difficult to walk past a bakery. I almost automatically stopped, entered, took up my metal tray and pair of tongs, and began the round, mentally savoring all the different types of sweet breads and finally emerging with tray piled high—far too many, but I had to try them all, just once more.

In Mexico you eat freshly made breads every day. From early morning to late afternoon constant streams of sweet rolls, shiny pastries, crusty, white rolls, croissants, and cupcakes are loaded onto the already full trays in the windows and around the walls of the bakery. All shapes and sizes, intricately worked doughs with sugar toppings or sprinklings of sesame seeds and candied peel, they bear the entrancing names of *besos* ("kisses"), *novias* ("brides"), *monjas* ("nuns"), *tortugas* ("turtles"), *bigotes* ("mustaches"), *yoyos, suspiros* ("sighs"), and so on without end, as far as I can discover.

For years I favored a bakery in Mexico City, very near where, year after year, I stayed with friends, and one day it occurred to me to go in and ask to be shown how to make the pastries. Like many other bakeries in Mexico City, this one was owned and operated by a Spanish family. They provided the premises, sales staff, supervisor, and bakehouse equipment and contracted with a master baker *(el maestro)* and his team to make bread on a piecework basis. My bakery had a particularly formidable supervisor, who always snapped and never smiled. However, heartened by a wave of publicity on television and in the papers about my work, I approached him. He said he would have to ask the *maestro* and led me through a door at the side of the shop into the huge bakehouse.

The bakehouse, as big as a warehouse, was stacked to the ceiling with large sacks of flour. There were two huge, diesel-fired ovens, worktables, large mixers, and various machines to cut and roll the dough, as well as movable racks containing trays full of rising or freshly baked breads. One group of about eight men were working around a rectangular table making hundreds of the elongated Mexican yeast rolls called *bolillos,* while at the back of the room, at workbenches set at right angles to one another, were my future teachers and friends. They were all dressed in aprons and caps in different shades of white. Maestro Miguel was a quiet-spoken man, and I could hardly hear him above the roar of the ovens. But he agreed to let me come in and learn, and thus began an apprenticeship I shall never forget.

The *maestro* and his son Jorge started every morning at three o'clock to prepare some of the more complicated doughs ahead of time, readying them for the arrival of the rest of the team at six. The first sweet rolls had to be baked by the time the store opened at seven, or sometimes even earlier. A lot of the slow-rising doughs had been prepared the day before and had to be taken out of the cooler rooms in which they were stored (the temperature in the main room was well over 80 degrees). So, when I arrived that first morning at eight, everything was in full swing. An old sack was torn up for my apron and a bit of old cloth to cover my hair. I was told to measure out the ingredients for the starter for *conchas,* those round, spongy, sugar-topped buns. And so my apprenticeship began in earnest.

I soon settled into the daily routine, and I rapidly came to admire my hard-working colleagues. The team, with no more than a quiet word to each other, went about their work each morning with a dedication and coordination that many a department in government would be wise to emulate. The *maestro* whispered a few instructions and answered an occasional question, but that was all; during the months I worked there I never heard a quarrel or cross word. As the morning wore on, the workers began to gossip and tease each other, with an occasional guffaw or a piercing whistle of approval when one of the shop girls came in. Occasionally the radio would be turned on, and those making the *bolillos* would fall into a hypnotic rhythm of pounding, kneading, and rolling the dough without stopping to catch a breath for hours on end. I came to be fascinated by the terminology I heard as these busy mornings flew by so rapidly. I found it curious how the terms for mixing dough were related to heat and cold. When a dough was mixed to the right point and had to be worked into shape immediately, someone said, "Don't let it get cold *(no se deje enfriar)."* To beat the dough to its correct consistency, it was "Let it get warm *(se calienta la masa)."* And the admonition "Don't let it burn *(no se queme)"* meant that the dough should not be allowed to go past its correct point in beating.

The mornings were so busy that I was always relieved to see ten o'clock drawing near, for it was then that Ruben, the special pastry cook, who was in charge of the food for the *almuerzo,* started his preparations. It fascinated me to see what he would do next with only a baking tray to cook on. Often he would cut tortillas into strips and fry them lightly in the doughnut fryer (to do which, of course, he always asked permission). He would broil tomatoes and chilies under the jets of the oven and pound them into a sauce in an ingeniously improvised *molcajete* (after putting the broiled ingredients into an empty tin can, he would place a plastic bag over the top so it dipped down inside, covering the contents, and then he would pound them with an empty Coke bottle!). The sauce went over the fried tortillas, was topped with lots of crumbled cheese, and then back it all went into the oven once more. There were always fresh *teleras*—flat, crisp rolls—which were torn open and stuffed with the *chilaquiles* Ruben had made. I was always expected to help myself first, and they would wait to see my expression. How they laughed when I found my *torta* too *picante* for me.

I never failed to look with awe on Miguel's incredible expertise. There were two huge drawers under the worktable for flour. I could never get right which drawer I was to use or what the difference was in the flours, but the *maestro* just had to run his fingers through the flour once to tell whether the amounts of salt, yeast, or water should be increased or diminished for that particular lot. He would inspect each new shipment of flour to judge the quality of the grain and milling and would occasionally make up one batch of dough with it, to test it. I often saw him with Jorge, breaking open the new-baked bread and discussing at some length just what adjustments were necessary for that shipment.

I soon found that the baking processes were not without their impediments. Something was missing on the scales, for which we always had to compensate when we weighed something. I sometimes forgot, but just as I was about to make a mistake a quick hand would come out of nowhere and make the adjustment for me. There was a large hole in the bottom of the mixer, so I was warned to put flour and sugar in first and then the eggs and liquids. There were no bowls or spoons; we used hands and table—and I found it disconcerting at first to roll out dough in the deep, curved well that was the working surface of our table deformed by constant use.

Nothing was thrown away in the bakehouse, either. I was taught how to fold and cut brown paper bags to make icing decorating bags that were simple, strong, and efficient. Every little chili can was kept from the *almuerzo,* too. They were just the right height to use as supports for stacking trays of rising dough when there was not enough room in the special racks. New uses were found for other old containers as well. Hundreds of eggs were cracked, ready for the day's work, into a recycled lard drum. They were measured out for the rich doughs with an old tin can—seventeen eggs to the can—about three-eighths of a liter, I believe it was. And I shall never get over our *biscuits de queso.* In that bakery they were cut out with hollowed tin cans, and the characteristic little circle in the top stamped with an empty, upended Coke bottle!

As far as ingredients went, I learned never to waste one teaspoon of flour or sugar. On completing a batch of dough I was handed a small dustpan and brush to sweep the surface clean; the gathered crumbs went into a special bin, to be used again. And once, when I held up impossibly greasy hands with a helpless look on my face, a large lump of soft dough landed in front of me, thrown by someone from the other table who had seen my plight. Most efficient and ecological, too—no greasy towels to wash up, and that surplus grease went to enrich some other dough that would be used later in the day.

The days sped on, and it seemed to me that my apprenticeship came to an end almost before it had begun. My hands, though, were proof of the work I had put them through. The strenuous kneading and pulling and stretching of dough in which they had engaged themselves had softened them, had emblazoned them with the badge of the baker (had Jorge not told me you could always tell a baker by his hands?), a badge I bore proudly in the less hectic—in fact I would almost say boring—days that followed.

Campechanas Sugar-Glazed Flaky Pastries

Next time you go into a bakery in Mexico, look for those shiny-topped, oval pastries that break into a thousand flaky pieces as you bite into them. Those are *campechanas*. I had always wanted to make them, and it was such a proud day for me when trays full of my very own *campechanas* were drawn out of the bakery oven. Everyone in the place craned their necks, curious to see how they had come out, and congratulated me as the pastries were whisked away into the front shop, actually to be sold.

Once you get the knack of rolling and stretching the dough, they are not difficult to make. I always think of this as an exercise in dexterity. If you look at it like that, perhaps it won't be so frustrating the first two or three times you make them! The baking procedure, however, has to be just right or you will end up with whitish layers of uncooked dough in the middle; or the sugar on top will not melt and caramelize as it should. The commercial *campechanas* are always made with a mixture of vegetable fat and margarine—in Mexico I have never tasted them made with butter—but I have used a bit of butter here to improve the flavor.

You really have to use an electric mixer; 15 minutes beating by machine is at least half an hour by hand. . . .

THE BASIC DOUGH

> *1 pound unbleached all-purpose or strudel flour*
> *¼ heaped teaspoon salt*
> *1 ounce granulated sugar*
> *1⅓ cups cold water*
> *1 ounce vegetable shortening (U.S. only)*

FAT FOR HANDS AND WORKING SURFACE

> *8 ounces solid vegetable shortening, approximately, for heavy greasing of hands and working surface*

THE FAT/FLOUR MIXTURE

> *5 ounces unbleached all-purpose or strudel flour*

4 ounces sweet butter, at room temperature
4 ounces salt-free margarine, at room temperature
2 ounces solid vegetable shortening, at room temperature

THE TOPPING

1 cup granulated sugar, approximately

Put all the ingredients for the basic dough into the mixing bowl of a heavy-duty mixer and beat with the dough hook until you have a stiffish, very smooth, very elastic dough that cleans itself in thick skeins from the side of the bowl. (Test by stretching a piece of the dough. If it breaks easily, then it needs some more beating.) It will take 15 minutes or even a little more.

Grease your working surface well with some of the extra fat. Turn the dough out onto it. Grease your hands well and divide the dough into two equal parts. Roll each part into a large ball. Grease your hands again and press each ball out to a flat, even circle about 8 inches in diameter and ¾ inch thick. Smear the dough liberally with fat and set it aside to rest for about 10 minutes. Meanwhile, prepare the fat/flour mixture.

Work the flour and softened fat together with your fingertips until the mixture is completely smooth. Divide into two equal portions. The mixture should be soft enough to spread easily, but on no account let it become oily. Refrigerate briefly, if necessary. Set aside.

Smear your hands and the working surface with plenty of the extra fat. Pick up one of the disks of dough and turn it upside down (that is the rough side; you can see the joins of the dough that resulted from rolling it into a ball). Flatten the dough out as evenly as possible to a rectangular shape about ¾ inch thick, with the width toward you and the length extending away from you. Well grease a thin rolling pin, ideally 15 inches in length (see note page 184), and roll the dough out thinner, still keeping the rectangular shape, until it is about ⅛ inch thick.

Take one portion of the fat/flour mixture and smear it, with your hands, as evenly as possible over the top of the extended dough. Smear the rolling pin again with more fat, and carefully pulling out the near end of the dough, press it onto the rolling pin. Give a turn to the rolling pin, covering it with a thin layer of the dough and leaving about 3 inches of the pin uncovered at each end so you can grasp it firmly.

Taking the rolling pin in one hand, smooth the dough out evenly over the pin with the other. Then, very carefully, start the rolling and stretching movement, lifting the dough up quite high off the counter as it stretches out. Your hands will quite naturally be working like pedals as you roll the dough, working them backward and forward. Stretch the paper-thin dough out as much as you can without tearing it. (Note, however, that even the most expert bakers do have tears in their dough at times, so if it does happen, don't despair. It will also happen if the dough has not been beaten enough in the first place.) The last few inches of the dough must be rolled and stretched very carefully, since they will form the outer layer of the *campechanas*.

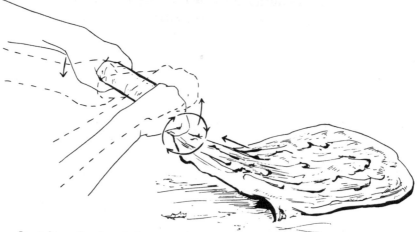

Stretching the dough for *campechanas*

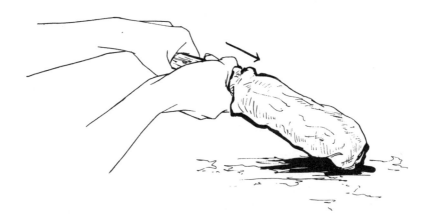

Removing the dough from the rolling pin

Grease your hands with more fat, and smear it liberally over the outside of the rolled dough. Grasping the end of the rolling pin with one hand, with the other push the roll off the pin—it will be in the form of a sausage about 3 inches in diameter. Grease your hands once more and gradually stretch the roll, easing it at different parts until it is extended to form a longer, thinner roll about 28 inches long and 1½ inches in diameter. Set the roll onto a well-greased surface while you repeat the procedure for the second roll. Leave the dough to rest for about 20 minutes.

To form the *campechanas,* grasp the roll, between your left thumb and forefinger, about 2½ inches from the end. Flatten that small section of dough with your other hand until it is about ½ inch thick. Then—squeezing the dough hard between your thumb and forefinger—give a quick twist, severing it from the rest of the roll. (Maestro Miguel would not hear of using a knife or other convenient cutter. He says it spoils the form of the *campechanas* and they would have ragged edges.)

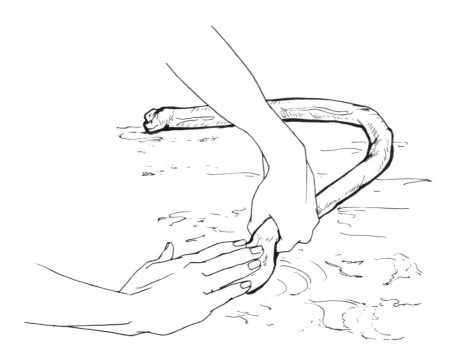

Pinching off the dough

(continued)

Have ready some ungreased baking sheets. Place the piece of broken-off dough on one of them. Greasing your hands very well, flatten the dough out into a thin oval shape about 5½ × 2½ inches. Smear another good layer of fat over the flattened surface. Repeat the procedure until all the dough has been used up—each roll should yield about 16 pastries. (Mathematically it doesn't look correct, but the dough stretches out even more as you work with it.)

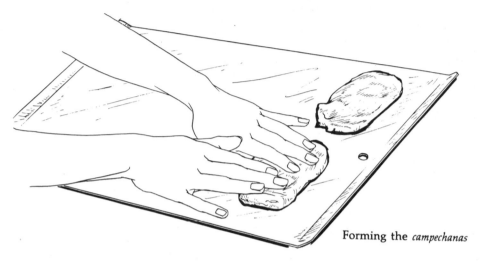

Forming the *campechanas*

Preheat the oven to 375 degrees, setting the oven racks in the top half of the oven. Sprinkle the sugar for the topping liberally over the finished trays of flattened dough. Turn the trays upside down and give them several sharp taps in different places so that the excess sugar falls off. (Note: If you have not greased the top of the dough sufficiently, the sugar will not adhere properly and make a nicely glazed topping.)

Unless you have a very big oven, bake one tray at a time, on the second shelf of the oven, until the pastry has puffed up and browned lightly—about 15 to 20 minutes. Turn the oven up to 450 degrees, move the tray to the top shelf, and bake for another 5 minutes, by which time the sugar should have melted and caramelized. (Be careful—the baking is tricky, and as every oven is different you will have to experiment a bit with the first tray for the desired result. Far too many gas ovens I have known and worked with run out of control at 450 degrees and the sugar burns.)

About 32 pastries

Cuernos Croissants

The large, fat, well-browned croissants made in Mexico are one of the most popular *pan dulce*. Eaten with *café con leche* or chocolate at breakfast or suppertime, when they are always brought fresh and hot from the bakery, they are made of a rich brioche dough and given plenty of slow rising time to develop flavor and character. They need a lot of beating, so I do advise you to use a heavy-duty mixer with dough-hook attachment.

In Mexico, for economy's sake they are made with margarine and vegetable shortening. I have compromised and put in some butter to improve the flavor.

Start at least twelve hours ahead.

THE STARTER

> *1 pound unbleached all-purpose flour, plus extra for*
> >   *dusting*
> *1 ounce cake yeast*
> *2 tablespoons lukewarm water, approximately*
> *3 large eggs, lightly beaten*

THE FAT MIXTURE

> *7 ounces sweet butter, at room temperature*
> *4 ounces salt-free margarine, at room temperature*
> *2 ounces solid vegetable shortening, at room temperature*

THE FINAL DOUGH MIXTURE

> *1 pound unbleached all-purpose flour, plus extra*
> *1 cup eggs (about 5 large ones)*
> *3½ ounces granulated sugar*
> *½ teaspoon salt*
> *2 ounces salt-free margarine, at room temperature*
> *¼ cup lukewarm water*

THE GLAZE

> *2 large eggs, well beaten*

Sift the flour into the mixing bowl of a heavy-duty mixer. Crumble the cake yeast into a small bowl, add the warm water, and press out the lumps with the back of a wooden spoon until it has the consistency of a thin, smooth cream. Add the eggs and yeast cream to the flour and beat with a dough hook at high speed until the dough forms a cohesive mass and starts to come away cleanly from the side of the bowl. The dough should then be soft, sticky, smooth, and shiny. This should take about 5 minutes.

Throw a little more flour around the edge of the bowl and beat for 2 seconds longer. Flour your working surface well and scrape the dough out onto it. Flour your hands and quickly work the dough into an oval-shaped "cushion." Butter a small baking sheet and sprinkle it with flour. Place the dough on it and make three deep diagonal slashes across the top. Cover with a piece of buttered paper and then with a length of toweling and set it aside in a warm, draft-free place to rise until it has more than doubled in size—1 hour at 80 degrees.

During this time, prepare the fat mixture. Mix the fats together with your fingertips until they are well incorporated and smooth. Refrigerate briefly; when it is ready to use, the fat mixture should be soft and pliable, neither hard nor soft and oily.

Divide the risen starter into two equal portions. Store one half in the refrigerator for the next batch of *cuernos* (it will last 3 days refrigerated and about a month frozen). The other half should be broken up roughly and put into a mixing bowl. Add the rest of the ingredients (but *not*, of course, the mixed fats) and beat at high speed with the dough hook until the dough forms a cohesive mass and starts to come away from the sides of the mixing bowl—about 10 minutes.

Stop the mixer occasionally during this time and scrape off the dough that collects at the top of the hook. The dough should now be soft, sticky, smooth, and shiny. Throw a little more flour around the edge of the bowl and beat for 2 seconds more.

Flour your working surface well and scrape the dough out onto it. Flour your hands and quickly form the dough into an oval-shaped "cushion." Let it rest for 1 minute.

Flour your hands again and flatten the dough out into a rough rectangular shape with the long side toward you. Then, with a thick rolling pin, roll the dough out to a rectangle about 19 × 10 inches and ¼ inch thick, lifting the dough constantly as you roll it out to make sure that it is not sticking. Throw more flour underneath when necessary.

Starting from the right side, smear the mixed fats, as evenly as possible, over two-thirds of the dough (there will be quite a thick layer of fat), leaving a

1-inch border free of fat around the edge of the dough. Sprinkle the fat liberally with flour. Starting from the left-hand side, fold the ungreased third of the dough over onto the greased middle third. Then fold the right-hand third over on top of them both to form a neat rectangular "package." Make sure that all the edges meet as evenly as possible, as if you were ironing a cloth. Press the edges together firmly with the rolling pin so that the fat will not be able to ooze out. Give the dough one turn to the right *clockwise,* so that the long side will again be toward you.

Again, flour your working surface well. Roll the dough out a second time into a rectangular shape. Sprinkle flour over the surface of the dough, fold as before, and give one turn clockwise. Flour your working surface again and once more roll out the dough—although this time the rectangle will be a bit smaller, about 17 × 8 inches or thereabouts. By this time the yeast will be in action and the dough becoming thicker and more resilient. Sprinkle with flour and fold for the third time.

Set the dough aside to rest for about 10 minutes. Do not refrigerate unless the day is very hot and sticky. (For this type of baking, the ideal temperature in the working area of the kitchen is 75 to 80 degrees; this will not be too hot for working and resting the dough.)

Flour the surface again and roll the dough out twice more, folding and turning it in the same way. Cover the folded dough with a buttered piece of waxed paper and a thick piece of toweling and store in the bottom of the refrigerator, to allow the dough to rise very slowly, for at least 6 hours (a maximum of 12).

At the end of the rising time, remove the dough from the refrigerator. Flour your working surface well and turn the dough onto it. If the dough is very cold and stiff and hard to roll, then let it sit at room temperature for about 15 minutes. Roll the dough out until it is about ¼ inch thick. Using a plastic pastry scraper or knife, cut the dough into strips 5½ inches wide. Then cut each strip into triangles with a 3-inch base (see the illustration on page 198).

Pick up one of the triangular pieces of dough and stretch the wide base gently outward to form elongated "ears." Gently pull the pointed end to stretch the dough a little. Place the triangle of dough down on the surface, with the point toward you, and then, using your palms, quickly and lightly roll it up, from the "ears" down toward the tip, making an even, compact roll. Curve the ends around to complete the crescent shape; make sure that the pointed tip is visible on top of the *cuerno.* (See the illustrations on pages 198 and 199 for all these steps).

(continued)

Place the *cuernos* about 2 inches apart on lightly greased baking sheets and set aside in a warm place, free from drafts but uncovered, until they have doubled in size—about 3 hours in a temperature of 80 degrees.

Just before the end of the rising period, place the oven racks in the top half of the oven. Preheat the oven to 425 degrees.

Brush the *cuernos* liberally with the beaten egg and bake until they are a deep brown (*not* golden brown)—about 12 minutes. Halfway through the baking time, reverse the position of the trays so the *cuernos* will bake and brown evenly, top and bottom.

20 to 24 croissants, about 4½ inches across when baked

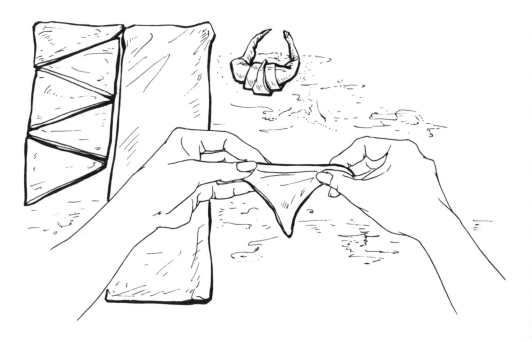

Forming a *cuerno*

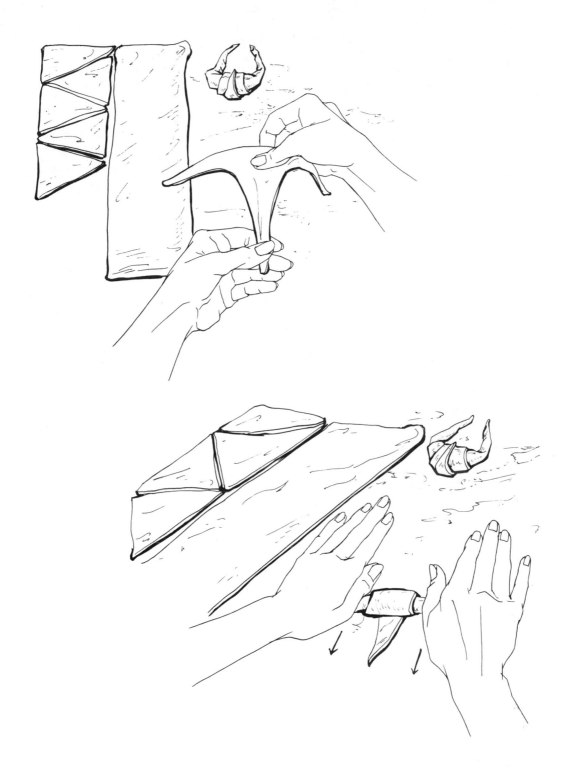

Biscuits de Queso Cream Cheese Biscuits

These rich, yeasty biscuits, or scones, are a favorite *pan dulce* in Mexico. Of course they are better eaten the day they are made, and preferably straight from the oven, but they freeze perfectly well and can be reheated or cut in half and toasted. Those that are not frozen and have become a little dry should be quickly dipped into milk and reheated in a 400-degree oven for about 15 minutes, or, without being dipped into milk, cut horizontally into thick slices and toasted. They are very good either by themselves or with preserves for breakfast or tea.

For reasons of economy, *biscuits de queso* are made in the Mexican bakeries with all margarine. For reasons of flavor, as they are really rich enough with the cream cheese and large number of eggs, I substitute a small amount of butter for part of the margarine. Ordinary packaged cream cheese could be used, but I prefer, if possible, to buy the best but most reasonable loose cream cheese available in the delicatessen section of specialty shops or supermarkets. To buy the best French cream cheese for this sort of recipe seems to me to be needlessly extravagant and unnecessary.

Start at least five hours ahead.

THE STARTER

> 6 *ounces unbleached all-purpose flour, plus extra for*
> *dusting*
> 2 *ounces granulated sugar*
> ¼ *teaspoon salt*
> 1 *ounce cake yeast*
> 1 *tablespoon lukewarm water*
> 2 *large eggs, lightly beaten*
> 2 *ounces salt-free margarine, softened*

THE FINAL DOUGH MIXTURE

> 8 *ounces granulated sugar*
> 8 *ounces cream cheese (see note above)*
> 2 *teaspoons salt*
> 9 *large eggs*
> 1 *cup milk*

> 2½ *pounds unbleached all-purpose flour*
> ¼ *cup baking powder*
> 8 *ounces salt-free margarine, at room temperature*
> 5 *ounces sweet butter, at room temperature*

THE GLAZE

> 2 *large eggs, well beaten*

Put the flour, sugar, and salt together into a mixing bowl; mix well. Crumble the cake yeast into a small bowl, add the warm water and smooth out the lumps with the back of a wooden spoon until it is the consistency of a thin cream. Add the yeast cream, eggs, and softened margarine to the flour and mix just until the eggs are well incorporated and you have a soft, sticky dough—about 3 minutes.

Scrape the dough out onto a floured surface. Let it rest for 1 minute, then, with well-floured hands, shape it into an elongated cushion shape. Grease and lightly flour a small baking sheet and place the "cushion" of dough on it. Make 3 deep, diagonal slashes across the top of the dough, then cover with a piece of buttered waxed paper and a thick towel and set in a warm place—80 degrees is ideal—to rise and almost double in volume. This will take about 2 hours.

Tear the starter up roughly and put into a mixing bowl. Add the sugar, cream cheese, salt, and eggs and mix until all are well combined, which should take about 3 minutes. Add the milk and mix for 1 minute longer, then set aside.

Sift the flour and baking powder together. Cut the fat into the flour, and when it is in small pieces rub lightly with your fingertips until the mixture resembles fine breadcrumbs. Gradually add the flour mixture to the rest of the ingredients, mixing only until just combined. The result should be a soft, sticky dough.

Throw a good dusting of flour—no dainty little sprinkle from a perforated metal can—over your working surface. Scrape the dough out onto this and let it rest for 1 minute, then flour your hands well and quickly work the dough into a round cushion shape. Leave for 1 minute more. Flour your hands again and press the dough out to a thick rectangular shape. Then, with a thick rolling pin, flatten the dough to a rectangular shape—long side toward you—about 21 × 13 inches and about ½ inch thick.

Dust the surface of the dough lightly with flour. Starting from the left-hand side, fold one third of the dough over onto the middle third, making sure that the edges meet neatly, then fold the right-hand third over on top to form a neat "package." Lift the "package" up and dust the working surface well with flour. Give the dough one turn to the right, clockwise. Roll out again, roughly to the same size. Dust the surface of the dough with a little more flour, fold as before, and again give a turn to the right. Repeat this process once more, to give three turns in all. Leave the dough to rest for 1 minute.

Dust the surface of your counter again liberally with flour and roll the dough out until it is about ¾ inch thick. Using a plain, round cookie cutter about 2½ inches in diameter, cut the dough out into rounds and place about 1½ inches apart on greased baking sheets. Gather up the remaining dough, press together well, and roll out again until it is ¾ inch thick; cut into biscuits. When all the biscuits are cut out, flatten them slightly with the palm of your hand and then stamp each one in the center with a circular cutter about ½ inch in diameter. Set the biscuits aside to rise, uncovered, until they almost double in size—about 2 hours in a temperature of 80 degrees, free from drafts.

Arrange two oven racks in the top half of the oven. Preheat oven to 375 degrees.

Brush the surface of the biscuits liberally with the beaten egg and bake, two trays at a time, for about 10 minutes. Reverse the position of the trays—the one on top to the second shelf, and so forth—and bake for another 5 to 10 minutes, or until they are spongy, cooked throughout, and golden brown on top.

Remove the trays from the oven and let the biscuits cool off away from drafts and cold air.

About 40 biscuits, 3½ inches across when baked

Conchas Sugar-Topped Sweet Buns

Conchas (lit., "shells") are probably the most generally known and popular of the sweet Mexican yeast rolls. They are round, spongy buns with a thin, sugar topping etched with a curved, shell-like design, from which their name is derived. Others are topped with a crisscross design and should strictly speaking be called *chicharrones* (the same name, interestingly enough, that is given to the fried pork skins), although they are usually all lumped together and called *conchas*. They are delicious when fresh and well made and the dough has been given the long, slow rising that develops the flavor. Like all bread with a higher percentage of yeast, they dry out very quickly, and instead of reheating them I prefer to cut them into thickish horizontal slices and toast them. They are also very good sliced thick, put onto well-buttered cookie sheets, and toasted crisp like Swedish rusks—to be eaten with tea or coffee or even with ice cream.

You really do need to use a mixer with a dough-hook attachment for this type of dough, which requires such a lot of beating, unless, of course, you have a very strong arm and are a glutton for punishment!

Start one day ahead.

THE STARTER

     ½ *pound unbleached all-purpose flour, plus extra*
     ¾ *ounce cake yeast*
     3 *tablespoons lukewarm water, approximately*
     2 *large eggs, lightly beaten*

THE FINAL DOUGH MIXTURE

     1 *pound unbleached, all-purpose flour, plus extra*
     6 *ounces granulated sugar*
     ½ *teaspoon salt*
     1 *ounce sweet butter, softened*
     1 *cup eggs (about 5 large ones), lightly beaten*
     ¼ *cup lukewarm water, approximately*

THE SUGAR TOPPING

     4 *ounces unbleached all-purpose flour*
     4 *ounces confectioners' sugar*
     2 *ounces salt-free margarine, at room temperature*
     2 *ounces solid vegetable shortening, at room temperature*
     1 *ounce unsweetened cocoa powder*
     1 *ounce ground cinnamon*

Sift the flour into a mixing bowl. Crumble the yeast roughly into a small bowl. Add the warm water and press out the lumps with the back of a wooden spoon until it has the consistency of a thin, smooth cream. Add the eggs and yeast cream to the flour and beat with the dough hook for about 2 minutes—the dough should be fairly stiff and sticky. Throw a little extra flour around the bowl and beat for 2 seconds longer so the dough comes away cleanly from the side of the bowl.

Flour the working surface well. Scrape the dough onto the surface and let it rest for 1 minute, then flour your hands well and quickly shape the dough into an oval "cushion." Place on a well-greased and floured baking sheet and make 3 deep diagonal slashes across the top. Cover with a piece of buttered waxed paper and a thick towel and set to rise in a warm place—it should double its size in 1½ hours at a temperature of 80 degrees, which is ideal.

At the end of the rising period, cut the dough into two equal parts; weigh to make sure they are equal. Put part into the refrigerator for a later batch of *conchas* (it will last about 3 days refrigerated or 2 months frozen). Tear the other half of the starter into rough pieces and put the pieces into a large mixing bowl.

Add the ingredients for the final dough, except for 2 ounces of the sugar, to the starter in the bowl, and beat with a dough hook at high speed for 5 minutes. Add the rest of the sugar and beat for 5 minutes longer, or until the dough is soft, sticky, and shiny and forms a cohesive mass. Throw a little more flour around the edge of the bowl and beat for 2 seconds more so that the dough cleans itself away from the side of the bowl.

Flour your working surface and hands well. Scrape the dough out onto the surface and quickly form it into a round, even cushion shape. Let it rest for 1 minute while you butter and flour another large mixing bowl, leaving your mixer bowl free for other purposes.

Put the dough into the bowl, cover with a piece of buttered waxed paper and a thick cloth or towel, and set aside in a warm, draft-free place—about 80 degrees—for 2 hours. At the end of the rising period, place the covered bowl with the dough into the bottom of the refrigerator and leave it to rise more slowly for 16 hours.

Just before the end of the long rising period, prepare the sugar topping for the buns. Sift the flour and confectioners' sugar together. Cut the fat into the flour mixture and work it in with your fingertips until thoroughly and evenly incorporated and you have a soft, pliable mixture. Divide the mixture into two equal parts. Add the cocoa to one part and cinnamon to the other and mix each one until the flavoring is evenly distributed. Set aside.

After the dough has completed its long rising period, turn it out onto a well-floured surface and let it rest for 1 minute. Flour your hands and quickly work the dough into a round cushion shape. With a plastic dough scraper or a sharp knife, cut the dough into 4 equal portions. Divide each portion again into four, making 16 portions. (I like to make sure that each portion is equal, so I weigh each one and cut off any dough over 2 ounces; this way I usually end up with 18 pieces.)

Butter some cookie sheets well.

Dust your hands very lightly with flour, and taking a ball of the dough in each hand, cup your palms and fingers around each of them and press them down firmly onto your working surface. Move your hands in a circular motion to form, very quickly, completely even, round balls of dough. (This is a baker's trick, and it takes a little practice before you can do it perfectly. If the counter-top has too much flour you can't get any traction; if it is too sticky, then the dough will stick and have an uneven surface.)

Place the balls of dough onto the prepared sheets about 3 inches apart. When they are all set out, grease your hands well and press each ball down firmly to flatten them slightly. Then take a small piece of the sugar topping and roll it into a ball about 1 inch in diameter. Dust your hands with flour and with the fingers of your left hand—or right, whichever the case may be—press the ball of topping out onto the palm of your other hand until you have a flattened disk about 3 inches in diameter. Press this disk very firmly onto one of the balls of dough so that it adheres well. Repeat until all the balls of dough have a sugar topping, some of cinnamon, some of chocolate. Cut a crisscross or curved pattern in the sugar toppings with a knife, or use an authentic cutter (as illustrated on page 184).

Set the *conchas* aside to rise, uncovered, in a warm, draft-free place until they are almost double in size—about 3½ hours in a temperature of 80 to 85 degrees.

Set two oven racks in the top half of the oven. Preheat the oven to 375 degrees.

Bake the *conchas* until the dough is light and springy and a golden color appears around the sugar topping—about 12 minutes. If possible, serve immediately.

16 to 18 buns, about 5 inches across when baked

Empanadas de San Cristóbal de las Casas Savory Pastries Filled with Chicken

Señora Rode (San Cristóbal de las Casas)

In *The Cuisines of Mexico* I wrote about the delicious, flaky *empanadas* filled with chicken and sprinkled with sugar that I had eaten on a previous visit to San Cristóbal. On a very recent visit there I was introduced, by a gourmand taxi driver called El Tigre, to Señora Rode, one of the few women remaining who make these *empanadas* commercially, preserving the same quality and tradition for which her aunt was renowned for many years before her.

There was no mistaking her house; walking along the street there was a sudden welcoming, savory smell of baking on the cool evening mountain air. Señora Rode, still quite young, plump, with rosy cheeks, was patiently finishing off a last batch of five hundred *empanadas* for a wedding the next day.

She had been working in her kitchen since five o'clock that morning. The kitchen was warm and the dough very soft, yet she still managed with wonderful dexterity to turn the edges of the dough around the *empanada* into neat, even little pleats. For local tastes she was filling some with potato, others with tuna, a solid custard, or just a sprinkling of grated, dry cheese. But the really luxurious ones were filled with chicken, and this is the recipe she gave me for them.

Following the recipe just as Señora Rode gave it to me I got a very tough pastry, so I have had to adjust the recipe for ingredients in this country. It makes a very short crust, which is most delicate to handle.

THE DOUGH

15 ounces unbleached all-purpose flour
1 ounce cornstarch
¾ teaspoon salt
6 ounces pork lard, at room temperature
2 ounces solid vegetable shortening
1 ounce sweet butter
1 to 2 tablespoons water
3 whole eggs plus 3 egg yolks
3 tablespoons or more melted lard for brushing

THE FILLING

> 1 tablespoon peanut or safflower oil
> ¼ small white onion, chopped
> 2 chiles serranos *or any fresh, hot green chilies, finely chopped*
> 1 large tomato (about ½ pound), peeled and chopped
> ½ cup cooked, cubed zucchini
> ½ cup cooked, cubed carrots
> 2½ cups finely chopped, poached chicken (¾ pound skinned and boned)
> ½ teaspoon salt, or to taste
>   Freshly ground black pepper

THE TOPPING

> *2 ounces granulated sugar*

Sift the flour, cornstarch, and salt together, then put on a clean, smooth working surface and make a well in the center. Put the soft lard, shortening, and butter, together with the water, eggs, and egg yolks, into the well and work them together with your fingers until you have a smooth emulsion. Gradually work in the flour and knead the dough well until it is soft and smooth.

Divide the dough into three equal balls about 10 ounces each. Brush them liberally with melted lard, cover with a towel, and set them aside (not in the refrigerator) for at least 2 to 3 hours.

One by one, flatten each of the balls and roll them into 9 × 9 inch squares about ¼ inch thick. Brush the surfaces liberally with melted lard, sprinkle with flour, and put one on top of the other. Roll them out to make one slightly bigger square, about 11 × 11 inches. (Señora Rode rolls out one ball, brushes it with lard and flour, and then rolls the second one out on top of the first and the third on top of that. The way I suggest is much easier.)

Carefully roll the three layers together, not too tightly but not too loosely, into a sausage shape about 1½ inches in diameter. Brush the roll with plenty of the melted lard and set aside for another 2 hours.

Meanwhile, prepare the filling. Heat the oil and fry the onion, chilies and tomato together until they are well cooked and have a saucelike texture. Stir in the vegetables and chicken, season, and let the mixture cool off thoroughly before filling the *empanadas*.

Preheat the oven to 425 degrees.

Cut the roll into rounds about ½ inch thick and roll each one out into a circle about 4 inches across. Put about a heaped tablespoon of the filling onto one side of the dough, then fold the other side over to cover the filling. Pinch the semicircular edges together firmly, twisting with your fingers to form little scallops around the edge. Place the *empanadas* well apart on an ungreased baking sheet and bake for about 25 minutes, until well browned.

Sprinkle with the sugar and serve immediately, as a light supper dish or hors d'oeuvre.

2 dozen pastries

Polvorones Mexican Shortbread Cookies

Sra. María Luisa de Martínez (Mexico City)

Polvorones are small, round cookies, so short that they crumble to the touch. Traditionally they are made with all lard, but that is dying out—I myself find the flavor too strong and the texture too greasy—and solid vegetable shortening and butter seem to be a better combination. Owing to the great difference in the vegetable shortening in the United States and Mexico, and some difference in the flour, I have provided slightly different quantities and instructions for each country.

Polvorones may be flavored with cinnamon or orange, and made of ground pecans, walnuts, or pine nuts instead of almonds. While they are still warm from the oven, tradition has it that they are then liberally sprinkled with confectioners' sugar and, when cool, each one is wrapped in white tissue paper, which is bunched at each side, twisted, and the ends cut into shreds, making the cookies look like bonbons.

> ⅓ to ½ **cup unskinned almonds (about 2 ounces plus 10**
> **extra almonds)**
> 8 **ounces unbleached all-purpose flour**
> ⅛ **teaspoon salt**
> 1 **teaspoon baking powder**
> 2½ **tablespoons granulated sugar**
> 2 **ounces sweet butter plus 2 ounces vegetable**
> **shortening (in U.S.), 3 ounces sweet butter plus 2**
> **ounces vegetable shortening (in Mexico)**
> ⅓ **cup confectioners' sugar, approximately**

Preheat the oven to 350 degrees.

Spread the unskinned almonds and flour on separate cookie sheets and toast each on the top shelf of the oven until the nuts are crisp and the flour a deep creamy color—about 15 minutes. Set both ingredients aside to cool off completely.

Sift the cooled flour together with the salt and baking powder and put onto a marble slab or pastry board. Make a wide well in the center of the flour. Put the cooled nuts into the blender with the granulated sugar and blend until fine, then put, along with the butter and shortening, into the center of the well in the flour. Work together until smooth, then gradually gather in the flour and mix until the dough is crumbly, like pie crust. Put the dough onto a large square of thin polyethylene wrap and gather it into a ball, pressing the "crumbs" lightly together. Set the dough aside for a minimum of 2 hours (U.S.) in the refrigerator, and 1 hour (Mexico) out of the refrigerator but in a fairly cool place.

Butter a cookie sheet well. Unwrap the ball of dough, and leaving the dough on top of the wrap, put another square of the wrap over the surface of the dough. Press the dough out between the wrap with quick, short movements of your rolling pin until it is about ¼ inch thick; it will be very crumbly around the edges. Using a cookie cutter 2 inches in diameter, cut out as many cookies as you can. Gather up the remaining dough and roll out and cut more cookies. (Note: the cookies should be transferred to the cookie sheet on a spatula with very great care or they will break up.) Repeat until all the dough has been used up.

Bake the cookies on the top shelf of the 350-degree oven until they are a pale golden color—10 to 15 minutes. Sprinkle them well with the confectioners' sugar and set aside to cool before attempting to remove them from the sheet.

Polvorone wrapped in tissue paper

Carefully remove the *polvorones* to an airtight container or wrap in tissue paper, as follows: Cut 23 or 24 squares of tissue paper 8×8 inches. Place each cookie in the middle of a square and fold two sides over to cover it. Gently bunch the ends of the paper and twist them shut around the cookie. With scissors, cut the paper at each end into a fringe about 1½ inches deep.

23 to 24 cookies

Roscas "Ring" Cookies

I learned about *roscas* during my apprenticeship in the bakery. Practically any type of yeast dough or pastry, salted or sweet, was rolled out to a thin strand, doubled, then twisted and joined up at the ends, sprinkled with sugar or sesame seeds and baked until crisp. So, when some very sad *roscas* turned up at breakfast one morning, when I was on holiday, I thought I would find out exactly what the baker was doing wrong.

I got up at five the following morning and went into the kitchen as the baker was just beginning. Instead of measuring the flour—he said he was using about a kilo—he deftly sprinkled handfuls of it into a perfectly even ring with sloping sides. On the ridge he sprinkled the baking powder—evenly, neatly, not one grain out of place. He mixed butter, sugar, and canned milk in the center, but as he reached for the coloring and flavoring cans I stopped him. A little more butter this time, a little less liquid next, and fresh aniseed. The following day was better, the third day was perfect. All the kitchen help tried and approved, and he was very proud of the result.

> 8 *ounces unbleached all-purpose flour*
> ½ *teaspoon baking powder*
> ¼ *teaspoon ground cinnamon or* ½ *teaspoon aniseed*
> ¼ *teaspoon salt*
> 2 *ounces sweet butter, at room temperature*
> 2 *ounces vegetable shortening, at room temperature*
> 2 *ounces granulated sugar, plus sugar for dusting*
> ¼ *cup water*
> 2 *tablespoons cream or evaporated milk*

Sift the flour, baking powder, cinnamon, if you are using it, and salt onto a marble slab or pastry board. Make a well in the center, and into this put the butter, shortening, ¼ cup sugar, water, and cream. Work the ingredients in the center together with your fingers until they are completely incorporated and smooth.

Gradually work in the dry ingredients, and the aniseed, if used, and knead the mixture well. Work the dough *hard* for about 5 minutes, pressing it out with the palms of your hands, using them like pedals, against the working surface until it is smooth and pliable. (If you do not work it well enough, you will not be able to form the *roscas* as indicated.)

(continued)

Preheat the oven to 350 degrees and set an oven rack on the top shelf. Lightly grease two baking sheets.

Roll the dough into balls of about 1¼ inches in diameter. Take one of the balls and work it under your palms (on an unfloured surface, if possible) into a rounded, even strip of dough about ¼ inch in diameter. Double the strip, then press the ends together. Holding the ends firmly down onto the surface with one hand and starting from the other end, quickly and lightly twist the two strands together. (If you have trouble in rolling and twisting them, then make a simple ring with one strand of dough, rolling each ball out to a strip about ½ inch thick.) Join the ends to make a circle or "bracelet," about 2 inches in diameter, then place carefully onto the prepared baking sheet.

Proceed with the remaining balls of dough, and, when you have one baking sheet filled, bake until a deep golden color—about 15 to 20 minutes. As soon as you remove the cookies from the oven, sprinkle them liberally with the extra sugar. Let them cool off thoroughly before attempting to remove them from the baking sheet, then store in an airtight can or cookie jar.

20 to 22 cookies

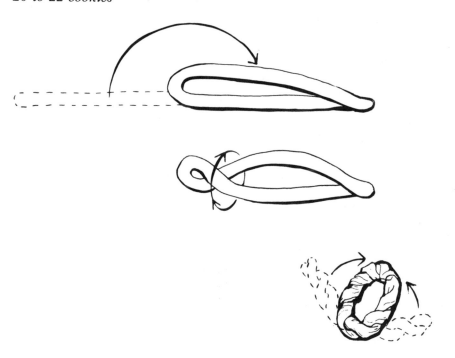

Drinks

Horchata de Melon Melon-Seed Drink

Horchata, a milky-looking drink originally made of almonds or a small white tuber called *chufa,* was brought from Spain to Mexico, where it became popular in Yucatán. There it is generally made by soaking and grinding raw rice, often with the addition of a few almonds, then strained and served over ice. It is considered delicious, healthy, and refreshing, but what drink wouldn't be refreshing in that heat? I personally had always thought it was just plain dull—but there are always surprises in Mexico.

   After lunch one day at a friend's house, I went back to the kitchen and saw that the maids were saving the seeds from the cantaloupes that we had been eating for lunch. They were going to make *horchata* from the seeds. Some cooks rinse, drain, and dry the seeds, but I think this is the most delicious version of all.

(continued)

Scrape the center fleshy part from 1 cantaloupe, seeds and juice included, into a measuring cup, and for every cup add:

1 cup cold water
1½ tablespoons granulated sugar, or to taste
1½ teaspoons lime juice, or to taste

Put all the ingredients together into a blender jar and blend until very smooth. Set aside in the refrigerator for a minimum of 5 hours, then strain through a fine strainer and serve over ice cubes.

1 serving

Rompope Mexican Eggnog

4 cups milk
1 cup granulated sugar
4-inch piece cinnamon bark or 1 vanilla bean
¼ teaspoon baking soda
12 egg yolks
¾ cup pure cane alcohol or rum or ½ cup brandy, or
to taste

Put the milk, sugar, cinnamon, and soda into a saucepan. Bring to a boil, then lower the flame and simmer for about 20 minutes, or until the sugar has melted completely and the mixture is reduced to about 3 cups. Set aside to cool off a little.

Meanwhile, beat the egg yolks until they form thick ribbons on the beater —about 10 minutes, depending on the efficiency of your beater.

Remove the cinnamon bark from the milk mixture. Gradually add the milk mixture to the egg yolks, still beating. Return to the pan and cook over a low flame, stirring and scraping the bottom and sides of the pan constantly, until the mixture thickens enough to coat the back of a wooden spoon. (Take care, as it can quickly turn to scrambled eggs. At the first sign of this tragedy, pour into the blender and blend until it is smooth.) Set aside to cool off completely.

Meanwhile, sterilize a 1-quart bottle in boiling water.

Gradually stir the alcohol into the "custard," pour into the bottle, and use immediately or store for future use.

1 quart

Tepache Fermented Pineapple Drink

One of the most refreshing drinks on a hot day is the slightly fermented infusion of pineapple called *tepache,* originating from the state of Jalisco. It should be made, if possible, in a large earthenware jug or pot and served ice cold or over ice cubes.

If you are using the *piloncillo,* soak it beforehand (see page 170).

> *1 very ripe pineapple (about 2 pounds)*
> *2 whole cloves*
> *2 whole allspice*
> *4-inch piece cinnamon bark*
> *9½ cups cold water*
> *1 pound piloncillo or dark brown sugar*
> *1 cup light beer*

Remove the stem and base of the pineapple and scrub the outside well. Cut into 1½-inch cubes, skin and flesh together. Crush the spices roughly and add them, together with the pineapple and 8 cups of the water, to a large earthenware jug. Cover and set in the sun or a warm place until the mixture begins to ferment and become bubbly on top—about 3 days, depending on the temperature.

Put 1½ cups of water and the sugar into a saucepan and bring to a simmer. Simmer, stirring from time to time, until the sugar has melted. Let it cool slightly, then add, along with the beer, to the pineapple infusion and stir well. Cover the jug and leave in a warm place for one or two days longer, until it has fermented. Strain and serve very cold.

About 2 quarts

Champurrado

It is rare to find little *merenderos* (cafés for breakfast and supper) like this one, the Café Melendez in Torréon, run by a middle-class family who still make delicious *tamales* and simple regional dishes in the tradition of the grand-mother who started the business in the early 1920s. I thought their *champur-rado* was particularly delicious, especially with the addition of the orange peel and, of course, the wonderfully rich milk of that area.

> *2 cups water*
> *Thin peel of 1 whole orange*
>
> *4-inch piece cinnamon bark, broken up*
> *2 tablespoons granulated sugar, or to taste, depending on*
> *   the chocolate*
> *4 cups milk*
> *3 ounces Mexican drinking chocolate*
> *2 tablespoons cornstarch*

Put the water, orange peel, cinnamon, and sugar into a pan and boil quickly for about 20 minutes, or until you have an infusion and the liquid has reduced by at least 1 cup. Add the milk, and just before it comes to a boil, the chocolate. Simmer the mixture until the particles of chocolate (Mexican drinking choco-late will take longer than others) have completely dissolved—about 10 min-utes.

Put the cornstarch into a small bowl. Stir in about 2 tablespoons of the milk mixture and smooth out the lumps with the back of a wooden spoon. Add about ½ cup more of the milk mixture to dilute the cornstarch thoroughly. Stir this into the saucepan and cook for about 10 minutes, or until the mixture thickens slightly, stirring almost constantly. Strain and serve hot.

About 4½ cups

Mexican Ingredients,
Cooking Equipment,
and Cooking Methods

INGREDIENTS

ACHIOTE

The small, hard red seeds of the annatto tree *(Bixa orellana)*, known as *achiote,* are used to give both color and flavor to the local dishes of the Yucatecan peninsula. They are ground with other spices, moistened with garlic, Seville orange juice or water, and formed into balls or cakes of varying sizes. I have included two recipes that use this *recado rojo* ("red seasoning")—Mondongo en Kabik (see page 73) and Lomitos (see page 47).

In Mexico *recado rojo* is packaged commercially and sold ready for use. While the majority of the cooks and housewives of Yucatán, Campeche, and

Quintana Roo buy this daily in the market as they need it, a very few of the more fastidious ones make their own.

I have not, so far, come across any of this commercially prepared *achiote* in markets in the United States, so you will have to prepare it from the seeds, which are widely available in Caribbean and Latin groceries as well as the specialist sections of ordinary supermarkets. But a word of warning about quality. The seeds should have a healthy, earthy-red color. I have come across seeds that were a dull brown and had lost all their color and flavor.

In Mexico, the whole seeds are ground and used, as opposed to other countries in the Caribbean. There they are soaked in oil, which extracts and takes on the color and flavor. Since the seeds are extremely hard, the best method is to grind them in a spice/coffee grinder, which will reduce them to a fine powder within seconds. If you don't have this useful little machine, then use a blender, but the result will not be as good.

If using the blender, put the seeds in a saucepan, cover with water, and let them simmer for about 5 minutes. Leave them to soak for an hour or so, by which time they will have swelled up and absorbed most of the water. Put into the blender jar and add a little more water, but only enough to release the blades of the blender. Blend as fine as possible—although it still won't be smooth enough.

Recado Rojo Red Achiote Seasoning

    1 tablespoon achiote *seeds*
10 *peppercorns*
¼ *teaspoon oregano*
½ *teaspoon salt*
  2 cloves garlic, peeled
  1 tablespoon vinegar

Grind the *achiote*, peppercorns, oregano, and salt to a powder in a spice/-coffee grinder.

Crush the garlic in a *molcajete* or mortar, add the ground spices, and gradually dilute with the vinegar. Form into small balls and store for future use; the seasoning will keep indefinitely in the refrigerator.

AVOCADO AND AVOCADO LEAVES

The beautiful avocado tree, *Persea americana,* a native of tropical America, is a member of the laurel family. It bears large, narrow, glossy, dark-green leaves and pear-shaped fruit, which used to be more generally known as "alligator pear." The name "avocado" is derived from the Nahuatl word *ahua-catl,* meaning "testicle," and their medicinal properties have been lauded for generations, since the Spanish conquest up until today.

The large, thick-fleshed fruit as we know it today is hybridized, but in central Mexico you can also buy the small native—*criollo,* as it is called. It has a thin layer of flesh around a large pit and a very thin skin, either dark green or black, which is often mashed with the flesh, to which it imparts a wonderful, anisey flavor.

When choosing an avocado, always feel it first. You will not be popular with your produce man, but remind him that for the prices he charges you are not going to buy a pig in a poke. A good, ripe one should be *just* soft to the touch at the stalk base—not too soft. The skin should firmly adhere to the flesh and the pit should not rattle around when you shake it. Avocados are always picked as they should be, unripe, and come to the markets unripened, so if you buy hard ones, allow them three or four days in a warm spot in the kitchen to ripen.

The flesh should be a deep yellow color, compact and creamy, with a rich, hazelnut-like flavor tinged with anise. Try to avoid the large, generally round avocados with thick, hard, bright green skins that come in from Florida and the Caribbean. The flesh tends to be watery and sweetish, fine for garnishing and salads but not good for *guacamole* or sauce. Don't think you will get the same result or texture if you use them.

The really good ones—with black, pebbly skins—come mostly from the West and are available most of the year. If you can't find them anywhere else, you can usually count on those health food stores that carry produce.

Avocado leaves, either fresh or dried, are also used for their flavor in Mexican cooking, in the states of Morelos, Puebla, and Oaxaca in particular. They are indispensable in the famous *barbacoas* of Oaxaca (see pages 122–33). Keep a supply and pop one into a stew to give it an exotic touch. If you do not live where they are grown, prevail upon friends in California or Florida to send some sprays of the leaves.

To store avocado leaves, dry them naturally; you'll find that they dry off quite quickly in the warmth of the kitchen alone. Keep them in an airtight

Avocado leaves

container away from the light, and in this way they will retain their flavor for some months.

The question always arises in regard to leaves of plants grown indoors from a pit. They are not very strong in flavor, so you would have to use about treble the quantity—and even then something would be lacking. (I would not have believed, in fact, how much difference there is in the flavor of leaves from different avocado trees. At a recent class in Rancho Santa Fe, one of the students brought along some leaves so that I could show those who were not already familiar with them. I toasted and ground them, but to my disappointment they had hardly any flavor. Another student volunteered to bring the leaf of the *fuerte* tree, a type of avocado. She did, and it had a strong, rich flavor.)

BANANA LEAVES

Just the mention of banana leaves brings to my mind a lovely old man in the Medellín Market in Mexico City. He sells nothing but the banana leaves that are stacked seven feet high behind him. With a deft slash of his machete he cuts out the very tough stalk and center vein, and then, after folding the tender green leaves with much care, ties them into a neat bundle and presents them to you.

I have often wondered just how much he makes from his day's labor with his modest merchandise, but that doesn't seem to be so important to him. What does seem to be is the constant stream of men and women who stop by often just to gossip, a Yucatecan singsong cadence in their voices. He appears to be the living neighborhood newspaper and his stand a center of information for the local Yucatecan community. I have never seen him anything but smiling and happy, and I cannot help but compare him to his snarling, tough counterpart whom one too often finds on Ninth Avenue in New York.

I suppose it is commonly believed that banana leaves are used only as a wrapping for *tamales,* while in fact all over the southern part of Mexico they are used as a wrapping, one that imparts its flavor, for a number of different foods. In Yucatan, for example, they are used for *cochinita pibil* and *muk-bil pollo* (*The Cuisines of Mexico,* pages 169 and 103). In this book they are used for Asado de Puerco a la Veracruzana (see page 44).

If you don't have a banana tree at your back door, or can't find one in your neighbor's garden, plant one, if the climate is right. Apart from adding something rather special to your Mexican food, you'll find it a very decorative plant. If that doesn't work, then ask in your local Caribbean markets. You will often find banana leaves stashed away awaiting a Puerto Rican cook who wants to make some *pasteles* (a type of *tamal* made in Puerto Rico for Christmas and Easter). (Casa Moneo, in New York, for instance, is now carrying them the year round; see Sources for Ingredients, page 273.) They have been cured for storing and look decrepit and unsavory, with a dark color and strong smell, but they are perfectly adequate. They should be stored in a polyethylene bag in a cool, dry place, or at the bottom of the refrigerator, and will last some months. They might be covered with a white mold. Just rinse it off and use as instructed in the recipe.

BAY LEAVES *See* **Herbs, dried.**

CHAYOTE

The *chayote,* or vegetable pear, is a native of Mexico, and its name is derived from the Nahuatl word *chayutli.* In the markets in Mexico you will find three types: the large, green ones covered with spines like a porcupine; the small, cream-colored ones; and finally the light green ones that are also available in Latin and Caribbean markets throughout the United States. Unfortunately, the latter are picked before they are really ripe and take a lot of cooking before they are tender.

An average-sized *chayote* measures about 5 inches long and 3 inches at its widest, and weighs about 1 pound. It has a thin, tough, smooth, undulating skin. The surface is softly ridged, forming natural vertical sections, and the flesh is pale green toward the outside, changing to a creamy white around the center core. The core encases a delicious "almond"—a delicacy to which the cook is entitled.

The *chayote* is a favorite vegetable in Mexico, but it is also cooked with sugar and almonds and served as a dessert.

A *chayote* vine is not difficult to grow in a fairly warm climate. It is as decorative as a grapevine, and you will be rewarded by ripe, tender fruit with a delicate flavor.

CHEESES

The Mexican cheeses used for the recipes in this book, with suggested substitutes, are:

CHIHUAHUA   This is a mild, spongy, pale-yellow cheese originally made in great wheels in the Mennonite farming communities in the state of Chihuahua; there are many copies now. Having a high fat content, it melts easily and is rather like a mild Cheddar, which would be a suitable substitute, as would Monterey jack, or a mild, domestic Muenster.

ASADERO   The literal translation of this cheese's name is "broiler," or "roaster"; the cheese itself is made by the same method as the braided Oaxaca cheese and, presumably, mozzarella. Rennet is stirred into warmed raw milk to which a certain proportion of soured milk has been added (nobody will say just how much; it seems to be a regional secret). As soon as the curd is firmly set, it is cooked and stirred—always in the same direction—over a fairly high flame until tough, skeinlike curds have formed. The "skeins" are broken off into lengths, wound into small balls, and cooled. The very best *asadero* that I have tried came from the state of Coahuila, where the milk is particularly rich in butterfat. The cheese melts easily when heated and strings appropriately—a Mexican requirement. Substitute jack, *teleme*, or a mild, domestic Muenster.

AÑEJO   This "aged" cheese is white and crumbly, often very dry and salty, rather resembling a dry feta. The latter could be substituted where small quantities are called for.

RANCHERO SECO   This "farmhouse" cheese is a dry, cream-colored cheese with a rather strong flavor. Use either the Parmesan-type cheese from the Argentine called Sardo or Romano as a substitute.

PANELA   This white, spongy, salty, semisoft cheese is rather bland but delicious when freshly made in Mexico. I remember when spending a few days relaxing at San Patricio on the Jalisco coast I would buy it daily to accompany a simple supper of fresh rolls and mangoes. Many of the families there make it daily from raw milk and rennet tablets. It is ridged on the outside, marks made by the baskets in which it is set to drip overnight. Copies are made in the United States—I have seen them in Texas and California—and I have even made them myself, but the result is insipid, owing no doubt to the pasteurized milk. Substitute *queso fresco* (see below) or feta in small quantities.

QUESO FRESCO This is a pale cream-colored, moist, crumbly, soft cheese made in round cakes of different sizes, but usually about 1½ inches in depth. At its best—eaten fresh at a ranch in the country where it is made—it is slightly acidy but with a creamy flavor. It is sometimes called *queso de metate,* because the curds are pressed out on the *metate* (grinding stone) until they are compact enough to be packed into the small wooden hoops that give them their shape.

There are a few excellent commercial brands with a limited distribution in Mexico, but for the most part they are inferior to the homemade ones. There are some acceptable copies, which I have found in Los Angeles and San Francisco, being made in the United States. It is quite possible that their production is small and distribution limited, but Casa Moneo in New York is now selling and distributing them (see Sources for Ingredients, page 273). There are some unacceptable substitutes, like the brick *queso blanco* sold in many Latin American markets in the East. They have no flavor and go rubbery when heated. An acceptable substitute would be a good-quality farmer cheese that is sold loose in delicatessens; but you will have to add salt and perhaps a touch of sour cream to liven it up.

CHICHARRÓN

Chicharrón is the name given to the crisp sheets of pork skin that are an indispensable part of Mexican food; see further description and preparation in the recipe for Chicharrón en Escabeche (page 14). It is readily available in Mexican markets in the Southwest, and very recently *chicharrón* of very good quality has become available in the East. Packed well in New Jersey, it is sold and distributed by Casa Moneo (see Sources for Ingredients, page 273).

CHICKEN BROTH

For cooking many of the soups and rice dishes, you will need a good chicken broth. In an emergency you could use canned broth, which is very wishy-washy, or bouillon cubes, which even at their best are powerfully strong with artificial flavoring salts and coloring. I much prefer, as you can see, to make my own. I make it in quantity, freeze it, and then degrease before using.

If you can find a good fat hen, so much the better. It takes a long time to cook and often the meat is too stringy to use, but it does make a wonderful broth. If you cannot find a hen, then use a chicken with a lot of extra giblets and backs. When the flesh of the chicken is cooked, take it off the bone and shred it for tacos or whatever you like. Crack the leg bones and return them, with the rest of the carcass, to the pot to cook for another hour. Food regulations in the United States have taken all the fun out of making a good chicken broth. In Mexico I buy the whole hen or chicken. Not only the chicken and giblets go into the pot but the feet, neck, and head, and quite often the intestines as well—although they are time-consuming to clean. For an authentic chicken broth, then—and note that this is not for the squeamish—cut the claws off the feet and discard them. Singe the legs over a hot flame—they will blister and char—and then peel off the outer skin. Cut the beak from the head, pluck out the larger feathers, and singe off the finer downy ones. Turn the intestines inside out or cut them open and wash very well under running water. Put everything into the stock pot, including any unlaid eggs that may be inside the hen, and proceed as described below.

Many of the older Mexican cooks make a broth entirely of chicken legs. It has a delicate flavor and sets to a milky-colored thin jelly. I prefer a more robust broth, but I avoid using any strong root vegetables or herbs—the flavor has to be chickeny.

> *A large boiling fowl or 1 chicken with extra giblets and*
> *backs (see note above), cut into serving pieces*
> *1 medium carrot, scraped and sliced*
> *1 small white onion, peeled and roughly sliced*
> *2 cloves garlic, unpeeled and left whole*
> *6 peppercorns*
> *1 tablespoon salt, or to taste*

Put all the ingredients into a large saucepan, cover them well with cold water, and bring to a simmer. Cook over a low flame until the meat is tender—about 3½ hours for a hen, 40 minutes for a chicken.

If you are cooking a chicken, remove the meat from the bones and set aside for your intended purpose. Crack the largest bones and return the carcass to the pan to cook for 1 hour longer. Adjust the seasoning, then strain the broth, discarding the vegetables and chicken debris. Store the broth in the freezer until ready to use and then skim off the fat before defrosting.

About 3½ quarts

CHILIES, CANNED

Some of the recipes in this book call for *chiles serranos* or *jalapeños en escabeche*, which means that they are canned in a souse, or pickle. Traditionally this includes vinegar, a little oil, some herbs, garlic, onion, and slices of carrot. Many Mexicans wouldn't think of sitting down to a meal without having a bowl of pickled chilies on the table to season their food. These chilies are very widely distributed under different labels and appear in the Mexican food section of most larger supermarkets. Of course, if you have fresh chilies available and can spare the time, you can pickle your own (see page 164).

Canned *chiles chipotles en vinagre* or *adobo* are very popular. They are imported and are available in all the specialty stores that carry Mexican foods. They may not, of course, be substituted for regular *chiles chipotles* (see pages 226–27) unless specified in the recipe.

Some of the recipes in this book call for "canned, peeled green chilies." These are not pickled chilies, but are packed in brine; Ortega is the best brand because they are flame peeled and then packed in a brine that is mild, not overpowering, as many are.

Clemente Jacques have a new canned product on the market which is very good. Labeled "whole green chilies, fire roasted and peeled," they are in fact, as you can see by the drawing on the label, *chilacas* (*chiles pasillas* when fresh). Although they have lost their lovely color, they have retained their flavor and can be used for any recipes using *rajas*, instead of *chiles poblanos*. They are not suitable for *chiles rellenos*.

CHILIES, DRIED

BUYING When you are buying dried chilies, note the following:

1. Never rely on the name labeling in the stores. Become familiar with how they look, taking special notice of the descriptions in this book.

2. If you are ordering by mail, send a sample.

3. If you need a certain chili and it is not in the store, don't give up—ask them to order for you. If one store won't do it, then another will, so keep trying.

4. Where there is a choice, buy loose rather than packaged chilies so you can see the quality.

STORING When you buy dried chilies, make sure they are in good condition before storing them away. Occasionally you may be sold some that have been attacked by moths, which eat away the flesh, leaving the tough outside skin and a deposit of very small, but visible, eggs. Others have been packed too damp and will be covered with a whitish mildew. The defective ones should be taken out and, preferably, burned.

If the chilies are in good condition and stored in a cool, dry place, they will last for a year or two, just drying out more and more.

USE   Each chili has its own flavor and quality, and cannot be interchanged with another unless the recipe indicates it. Use the standard size as a guide to quantity in each case. Where, for example, a recipe states "5 *chiles pasillas,*" go by the standard average size in this section and make up for any of less than average size.

CHILE ANCHO   This chili is the one most commonly used throughout Mexico. It is curious that in Morelia it is often called *pasilla*—which is very confusing because there is a *chile pasilla* (see page 228)—and that name has followed it to California. It is, in fact, the *chile poblano* (see pages 230–31), ripened and dried. It has a deep, reddish-brown color—brick red when soaked in water—and a wrinkled, fairly shiny skin. It is triangular in shape, and a good-quality one will measure about 3 inches at its widest point and 5 inches long. It has a pleasant, sharp flavor and ranges from mild to hot.

It is never used in a table sauce—that is, as a condiment—and while it is sometimes stuffed, it is mostly soaked and ground for cooked sauces.

It is now widely available in the United States, often labeled "chili pods."

CHILE DE ÁRBOL   The name means "tree chili." It is long and skinny, 2½ × ½ inches average size, and has a brilliant red, thin, smooth, shiny skin. It has a vicious bite, so treat it with caution. It is generally used for table sauces —see pages 153 and 154. The *chile de árbol* is available in Mexican markets in California. Where not available, use any small, very hot chili.

CHILE CASCABEL   This small, round chili is so named because it sounds like a rattle when it is shaken. It has a smooth, brownish-red skin, and usually measures 1 inch in diameter. Its flavor when toasted and ground for both table and cooked sauces is very pleasant indeed, and it is not as *picante* as the *guajillo,* which in some areas carries its name (see page 227). Because of this confusion, it would be well to send a sample when ordering by mail (which is how you will probably have to shop for it; the *chile cascabel* is not always easy to find).

CHILE CHIPOTLE, CHILE CHIPOCLE, CHILE CHILPOTLE   This is the *chile jalapeño,* ripened, dried, and then smoked. Its light brown, wrinkled skin smells distinctly of smoke, and its name, in fact, means "smoked chili." Its average size is 2¼ inches long and somewhat under ¾ inch wide. It is used in rather an unusual and interesting way in the recipe for Albóndigas en Chipotle Quemado (see page 58).

They are sometimes rather difficult to find but if necessary you could mail order. Don't substitute canned *chipotles* (see page 225) unless the recipe says you can.

CHILE GUAJILLO   A long, slender, pointed chili whose brownish-red skin is smooth, shiny, and tough, the *guajillo* is often referred to as *chile travieso,* or "naughty" chili, because of its fierce bite. The size of an average guajillo of good quality is 4½ inches in length and 1¼ inches in width. Because of its resemblance to the tail of a rattlesnake, it is often called *cascabel,* especially in Mexico's Bajío area, and that name has carried over into the United States as well. For this reason, you have to specify which *cascabel* you want, this one or the round one (see page 226). The *guajillo* is used in table and cooked sauces. The skin is extra tough, so it will need longer time for soaking.

It is quite widely distributed and shouldn't be difficult to find. However, there is a lot of mislabeling, and you may find yourself with a package of so-called *guajillos*—see the description of *chile de la tierra* on page 228— which do not have the same flavor or bite.

CHILE MORA   In markets in Puebla and Veracruz, the *chile mora* is often called *chipotle,* and the *chipotle* described on pages 226–27 is called *chipotle meco* (*meco* means "blackish red"), but they are readily distinguishable. The *mora,* unlike the *chipotle,* oddly enough, *is* blackish red in color, has a wrinkled, tough skin, and its tip is rounded. A typical size would be 2 inches long by ¾ inch wide. Like the *chipotle,* it has a smoky flavor and is very *picante.*

Although none of the recipes here specifically call for it it is a suggested substitute for *morita* (see below). I have seen it occasionally in Mexican markets on the West Coast and in Casa Moneo in New York City (see Sources for Ingredients, page 273).

CHILE MORITA   This is a small, mulberry-red chili, triangular in shape and about 1 inch long and ½ inch wide. It has a slightly smoky flavor and is very *picante.* The recipes Chamberete de Res en Chile Morita, (see page 66), Salsa de Muchos Chiles (see page 152), Asado de Puerco a la Veracruzana (see page 44) call for it, and substitutions are suggested if it is not available. It is mostly used in recipes from the area east of Mexico City, including the high areas of the state of Veracruz.

A greater variety of chilies is being sold in Mexican markets these days, and you may very well find it if you look carefully.

CHILE MULATO   The *chile mulato* is the same shape as the *ancho,* but a first-quality sample will be slightly larger. The skin is tougher and smoother than the *ancho* and of a brownish-black hue. Sometimes it is difficult to tell the difference between the two chilies. Open them up and hold them against the light—the *ancho* will have a reddish tone and the *mulato* a dark, rich brown. When soaked in water it has a sweetish, almost chocolaty flavor.

This chili is generally used soaked and ground in cooked sauces, the classic example being *mole poblano* (*The Cuisines of Mexico,* page 199), and in this book it is used for Consomé de Camarón Seco (see page 20).

The *chile mulato* is not always available, but you can always order by mail where indicated in Sources for Ingredients (pages 271–77).

CHILE PASILLA   This is a long, slender chili with a rounded tip. The skin is wrinkled and of a blackish tone. When fresh—but not available in the United States—it is a blackish-green color and is known as *chilaca.* An average size would be 6 inches long and ¾ to 1 inch wide. The seeds and veins clustered at the top by the stem are very hot indeed, but the flesh itself is generally mild and has a slight, "tobaccoish" flavor. It is toasted and ground for table sauces, soaked and ground for cooked sauces—there are many examples of that in this book—and fried and crumbled as a condiment (see page 260).

It is distributed fairly widely. In California I have seen it called *chile negro.*

CHILE DE LA TIERRA, CHILE COLORADO   This is the *chile verde,* or *Anaheim,* ripened and dried. When dried, it has a tough, dark, reddish-brown, matte skin. It is full at the top with a rounded tip, and an average one would measure 4½ to 5 inches long and 1 inch wide. It is quite mild and does not have much flavor. It is the same as the *chilacate* used around Guadalajara. I have seen it in many Mexican markets in the United States packaged and sold as *guajillo,* so beware!

It is used here in Carne de Puerco en Chile Colorado (see page 60). Since it is easily available, I won't suggest a substitute.

CHILIES, FRESH

The interest in Mexican food in the United States is enormous and growing fast, and because of it more and more fresh chilies—not to mention other ingredients—are becoming available in places other than just the Southwest. The principal chilies used—*serranos, jalapeños,* and *poblanos*—are, I understand, now being grown in the United States, along with New Mexican and Anaheims, which have always been available (see Sources for Ingredients, pages 261–67).

If you are allowed to pick them out yourself, select those chilies that are still green and have a smooth, unwrinkled skin and a sharp, fresh smell. Fresh chilies will keep for some time—depending, of course, on their condition when you bought them and good storage. They should be rolled in paper toweling and stored in a paper bag in the refrigerator. Don't put them into polyethylene bags, which tend to create moisture and hasten ripening and spoiling.

CHILE SERRANO   The *chile serrano* is a small, smooth, mid-green chili, mostly rounded but sometimes pointed at the end. An average-sized chili would measure 1½ inches long and just under ½ inch wide. The flesh has a strong, fresh flavor, and the seeds and veins are very *picante*. They are generally used while they are still green, and in various ways: raw for Salsa Mexicana Cruda (see page 161) and Guacamole (see page 7), toasted for Salsa Arriera (see page 156); they can also be boiled for some sauces. I have included one example of *chiles serranos* used ripe and red: Salsa de Chile Serrano Rojo (see page 157).

They should keep for ten days to two weeks if wrapped in paper and refrigerated, but as soon as they become wrinkled they lose their sharp flavor and crisp texture. I do not recommend freezing them; they lose their texture, flavor, and some of their heat.

If a recipe calls for fresh *chiles serranos,* do not used canned. The pickle in which *serranos en escabeche* are canned will change the character of the sauce. Substitute instead fresh *cayennes* or *jalapeños.*

CHILE JALAPEÑO   The *chile jalapeño* is a mid- to dark-green chili with a smooth surface and more often rounded at the tip than pointed: an average one measures 2½ inches long and ¾ inch at its widest part. It has a unique, fresh flavor and is *picante*. It is also known as *chile cuaresmeño* ("Lenten" chili). *Jalapeños,* like *serranos,* are used in various ways: fresh in a relish, as in Rajas de Chiles Jalapeños Frescos (see page 164); cut into strips and cooked with *nopales,* as in Nopales al Vapor (see page 147); and boiled and blended, as for Puerco con Verdolagas, (see page 54).

The same rules apply about storage as for *chiles serranos* (see page 229).

Do not substitute canned chilies if fresh are called for; instead use *cayennes* or *serranos.*

CHILE CAYENNE   This is a mid-green, long, thin, pointed chili that is widely available. An average size would be 3 inches long and ⅜ inch wide. It is not a Mexican chili, but could be substituted when fresh *serranos* and *jalapeños* are not available. I suggest, however, that you remove some of the seeds and veins, as they are fearsomely hot. You will find them wherever there is a mixed population, since they are used by Chinese, Indians, and Koreans.

CHILE GÜERO   As its name implies, *chile güero* is fair—a pale yellow chili that can vary very much in size, but an average one would be 4 to 5 inches long and 1 inch wide. Pointed at the end, with a smooth, small-ridged, undulating surface, it can vary from quite hot to hot and has a delicious and distinctive flavor. In Yucatán, where it is called *x-cat-ik,* it is larger and more pale green than yellow. There are two examples of its use in this book: typically, in Yucatecan cooking, it is charred and put into a sauce whole, as in Pollo Tekantó (see page 90); fresh and whole, it is used in Lentejas Guisadas (see page 142). I often feel tempted to throw it fresh and whole into stews, even if it doesn't say so in the recipe.

Confusingly, in central Mexico there is another yellow, triangular, pointed chili, about 1 inch at its widest part and about 1½ inches long, that is also called *güero,* but in other parts of the country I have heard it called *cera* ("wax"), *huachinango,* and *caribe.* It is given the latter name in Durango and Jalisco, where it is canned extensively (both commercially and at home), often with other vegetables—sliced *jícamas,* raw quinces and so forth—for their well-known relish called *frutas en vinagre.* I have seen it in Californian markets, and although it does not have the same flavor as the first *güero* mentioned, it could easily be substituted for it.

If you can't get any of these, go for appearance and use a large, yellow-green Italian pepper.

CHILE HABANERO   This "Havana" chili is shaped like a small lantern, about 1 inch across at its widest part and a little over 1 inch long. It is a light green color and turns, as it ripens, to a bright orange. It should not, however, be confused with the smaller lantern-shaped sweet chili, called *aji,* which is often given away free when you buy coriander in Puerto Rican and Dominican groceries.

The *chile habanero* has the reputation of being the hottest of the lot—if anyone can really judge—but it does have a distinctive and delicious flavor. It is used in various ways in recipes in this book: chopped raw and fried for Frijoles a la Huacha (see page 38), charred and added whole to Sikil-P'ak (see page 5), raw and whole in Frijoles Colados Yucatecos (see page 40), to impart flavor but not heat.

You will find *habaneros* in markets wherever there is a mixed Caribbean community, as they are used quite extensively in Jamaica and Haiti.

Store them as you do the other fresh chilies (see page 229). There is no real substitute, of course, but you could add any fresh, hot green chili that is available, rather than nothing.

CHILE POBLANO   This chili may at one time have been grown principally around Puebla, as its name infers, but in fact it is now harvested in many parts of Mexico. In Durango they will have none of that name, and were shocked when I even suggested it. They simply call it *chile para rellenar,* or "chili for stuffing." Confusingly, in California—and even in Baja California—they call it both *chile ancho* and *pasilla* (see the dried chilies of those names on pages 226 and 228). (Another curiosity, picked up when I was traveling and wandering through markets. In late October the markets of Tehuacán, in the state of Puebla, are flooded with very large "*poblano*-type" chilies that very soon turn to a deep red. They are called *miahuatecos,* for the name of the village where they are planted. Nobody in the market, for reasons of regional chauvinism, would have it that they were a type of *poblano.* They have a rich, delicious flavor and are very *picante.*)

The *poblano* can vary in shape, color, size, and flavor, depending on where it was grown, the time of year, and so forth. To my mind—and palate—this chili is at its peak in summer and early fall, when it has a shiny, black-green skin and a rich aroma. The shape of the *poblano* is triangular, about 3 inches wide at the top and tapering to the apex, and they are about 5 inches long. Their surface is undulating, and they are distinguishable by a deep ridge at the base of the stem. They can be fairly mild to hot. With minor exceptions, they are always charred and peeled and then stuffed whole for recipes like Chiles Rellenos de Elote con Crema (see page 136) and Chiles Rellenos con Calabacitas (see page 138), or cut into strips *(rajas)* or small squares for dishes like Sopa Ranchera (see page 23).

In Durango, and nowhere else that I have come across, they char and peel the chilies while still green and then dry them in the sun—another version of *chiles pasados* (see page 232). They are tough and almost black when you buy them in this state, but have a wonderfully concentrated flavor after they have been soaked briefly and then stuffed in the usual way.

Poblanos should be stored like any other fresh chilies (see page 229). You can, in a pinch, peel and freeze them for a short period. If left in the freezer for any length of time, however, the flesh becomes too soft and watery and they lose their flavor.

There is no really satisfactory substitute for these chilies. For some of the recipes—Rajas de Chile Oaxaqueñas (see page 137), for example—you could use canned, peeled green chilies (Ortega has the best), but the flavor will suffer and there can certainly be no substitute in *chile relleno* recipes.

You will find them easily in Mexican markets and the main supermarkets in California, Texas, and the Southwest generally; Mexican markets in Chicago and surrounding areas; Denver; Casa Moneo in New York (see Sources for Ingredients, pages 271–77). If you don't live in any of these areas, perhaps a friend who does would send you a package of *poblanos* by special handling. Or, better still, go to Mexico. You must try them at least once.

CHILE VERDE, CHILE ANAHEIM   This is a light green chili with a rounded tip and an average size of 1 inch wide and 6 inches long. It can range from mild to hot and does not have a predominant flavor. It is used extensively in the local dishes of Chihuahua and Sonora.

These chilies are always charred and peeled, then stuffed or cut into strips for the classic Chihuahua version of *chile con queso* (*The Cuisines of Mexico*, page 262), or diced for Carne con Chile Verde (see page 65). In the state of Chihuahua (and possibly elsewhere, though I have yet to come across it), they are charred, peeled, and dried in the sun for winter use. In this state they are called *chiles pasados*. When they are needed, they are soaked in hot water for a brief period and then used just as if they were fresh.

They are readily available in markets in the Southwest, and now Casa Moneo carries them fresh the year round in New York (see Sources for Ingredients, page 273).

If you cannot buy them fresh, then buy the canned, peeled green chilies (see page 225).

CHORIZOS

I suppose it is perverse of me, but when I get set to describe ingredients the best and the worst examples always seem to come to my mind. How can you compare those atrocious so-called *chorizos* available on the West Coast—the ones made of ground meat packed into plastic casings that turn to a chili stew when heated—and the delicious, rich sausage made in and around Toluca in the state of Mexico?

Chorizo is, in fact, made all over Mexico, and each region has its own balance of spices, chilies, and herbs. In Yucatán, for instance, the sausages are predominantly seasoned with *chile seco* and *achiote,* and in parts of northern Mexico with *chile colorado* and cumin. But the original, and still important, center of *chorizo* making is Toluca, which lies west of Mexico City. Indeed, some gastronomic wit has propounded that Hernán Cortés was the first *choricero* (chorizo maker) in Mexico, for it was he who introduced porciculture to the valley of Toluca.

It is said that the diet of the pigs in Toluca, of the tough, fibrous local corn, produces the best, leanest pork. In fact, the leading *chorizo* maker there today says that lean pork is the important factor, and that for centuries it has been the custom in Toluca to make the pigs run about and burn off any excess fat.

In the "creation" of this same *chorizo* maker there are only coriander seeds, paprika, various herbs and chilies, and of course the pork; but—as with other families who have dedicated themselves to *chorizo* making for centuries—the exact ingredients and quantities of his are a closely kept secret.

In a recent article it was reported that there are at least 124 varieties of *chorizos* in Mexico, which is hardly surprising when you see what is offered to you in the markets there. Apart from the standard, commercially made ones there are *almendrados* (with almonds), *envinados* (with wine), the *verdes* (very *picante* green ones to eat with rice), the dried *chorizon* (which can be eaten raw), and the *longaniza* (made in one long length). *Chorizos* came to Mexico via northern Spain, which had Roman influences in its cooking. Spain is famous for its *chorizos*—which are made of a high proportion of roughly chopped smoked pork and are much tougher in consistency than the Mexican —so it is ironic that ever-growing quantities of the Mexican product are shipped to Spain each year. The pork for the Mexican *chorizos* is chopped (not ground), seasoned, and stuffed into casings made from pig's small intestine. Some of it is sold fresh, the rest is dried for later use.

Next time you go on a picnic, take some *chorizos* along and broil them slowly until crisp on the outside and cooked through, then wrap them in some tortillas that you have also heated over the hot charcoal. They are delicious just as they are or with a good helping of Salsa de Tomate Verde (see page 161).

When you are cooking *chorizo* for recipes in this book, remove the skin, crumble the meat, and cook over a low heat until the fat renders out. Raise the flame and cook for a while longer over medium heat, but remove before the chilies and spices burn.

There is a recipe for homemade *chorizos* on page 194 of *The Cuisines of Mexico*. The best I have come across in the United States are those made in Supermercado Maria Cardenas in Chicago (see page 272).

CINNAMON

The light-brown cinnamon bark from Ceylon is used a great deal in Mexican cooking. It is softer and has a more delicate flavor than the very hard, dark reddish-brown, strong-flavored bark from Malabar.

COOKING OILS AND FATS

SHORTENING. See Ingredients for Mexican Baking (page 185).

OIL   For general cooking purposes I have suggested peanut or safflower oil. When I first went to live in Mexico, everybody was using sesame oil (not the heavy brown sesame oil used by the Chinese, by the way), which has now given way to safflower. I happen not to like the flavor of corn oil, which always seems rather heavier than the other two.

A few of the recipes call for olive oil. I prefer a heavy, fruity one, such as Amastra from Sicily, which can be purchased in the Greek or Italian stores on Ninth Avenue in New York; in California I have seen one rather like it that is sold in bulk and has a lovely flavor.

LARD   Some dishes really do require a good pork lard, Frijoles Refritos (see page 37), for instance. There are a few exceptions in the Midwest and the Southwest, but generally the commercial brands are dead white and tasteless and filled with preservatives. You may be lucky enough to have small Italian or Hungarian butchers in your neighborhood, who make their own, but if not try your hand at it.

Home-Rendered Pork Lard

2 pounds pork fat
1 cup cold water

Have ready 3 eight-ounce sterilized jars. Cut the fat into small pieces and pass it though the coarse disk of a meat grinder. (You can also process the fat in the food processor by turning the blade on and off until the fat reaches the proper consistency.) Put the fat in a bowl, pour the water over, and set aside in a cool place to soak for a minimum of 6 hours.

Preheat the oven to 350 degrees.

Transfer the soaked fat—it should have absorbed most of the water—to a heavy pan and place on the top shelf of the oven. Cook until the fat starts to render out—about 15 minutes—then reduce the oven heat to 225 degrees and continue cooking for 2 to 2½ hours, straining off the fat from time to time into the sterilized jars. If the fat starts to color too much, then reduce the heat again.

Set the jars aside for about 36 hours and then seal and store in a cool, dry place or in the refrigerator, where the lard will keep for several weeks.

Note that when you strain the lard into the jars, the water in which you soaked the fat will collect at the bottom. Siphon this off with a bulb baster or you will shorten the storage life of the lard, since the water increases the danger of spoilage.

About 1½ pounds

CORIANDER *See* Herbs, fresh.

CREAM

Some recipes from central and northern Mexico call for cream. The best quality available there is thick and rich and sometimes slightly soured, like the *crème fraîche* of France. There is one very good *crème fraîche* in the United States with the brand name of Santé, but it does have limited distribution. If you cannot find it, then make your own—although I must warn you that the homemade variety will not thicken a cooked sauce in the same way as the real thing.

Thick Sour Cream

> *2 tablespoons buttermilk or 1 tablespoon plain yogurt*
> *½ pint heavy cream*

Mix the buttermilk or yogurt well with the heavy cream in a bowl or jar. Cover with polyethylene wrap and set aside in a warm place until it is set—5 to 8 hours, depending on the quality of the cream, heat, and so forth. Put the thickened cream into the refrigerator, preferably overnight, to thicken.

About 1 cup

A note of warning: If the cream doesn't set, don't blame the recipe. We are inundated with milk and cream that is doctored to last forever; this will never sour properly. Note also that some creams will sour more quickly and become thicker than others. An expert on the subject told me that souring and thickening are uncontrollable factors that depend on the culture of the buttermilk, the amount of light and heat to which the cream has been exposed before it was used, and even the bacteria in one's own kitchen.

Why can't you use commercial sour cream? You can, in recipes where the cream is not cooked. When heat is applied to commercial sour cream, it doesn't melt nicely but shrinks up and becomes rather rubbery. If you dilute it with milk first and then put it into a sauce, it acquires a curdled appearance, which does nothing for the sauce. Where it can be used perfectly well is in those recipes calling for uncooked sour cream topping.

EPAZOTE *See* **Herbs, fresh.**

FLOUR *See page 185.*

GREEN TOMATOES *See* **Tomates verdes.**

HERBS, DRIED

The use of herbs in Mexican food is so diverse and fascinating a subject that it could fill one, if not several, books. I shall only touch briefly here on the herbs, both dried (see below) and fresh (see pages 237–39) used in the recipes in this book.

Many vegetable stands in Mexican markets will sell small bundles of dried herbs—*hierbas de olor* or "fragrant herbs"—which are generally, although not always, used together as a *bouquet garni* is used in French cooking: they consist of bay leaves, thyme, and marjoram.

BAY LEAVES   The bay leaves in Mexico are thin, elongated, and pointed at the tip. They have a much more delicate flavor than their European counterpart, and an average-sized one would be 1½ inches long and just under ½ inch wide. Since the European bay is much more widely available, I have given quantities in the recipes bearing that in mind. But I suggest that you double or treble the quantity when using the Mexican variety, depending on how fresh and fragrant they are.

OREGANO   Dried oregano is used very widely in Mexican cooking. It would be confusing to go into all the varieties used in different regions, and my advice is to buy whole leaf—never the powdered—oregano from Mexican markets wherever possible.

HERBS, FRESH

CORIANDER   The fresh, green leaves of coriander or Chinese parsley (*Coriandrum sativum*)—*cilantro* in Spanish—are used a great deal in Mexican food. The dried seed is occasionally used, but the two are not interchangeable, as so many people think.

There is a long-leafed herb used in Tabasco, where it is confusingly called *perejil* (parsley), and in the northern part of Veracruz State, where it is known as *cilantrón*. Although it tastes very much like coriander, it has a tougher,

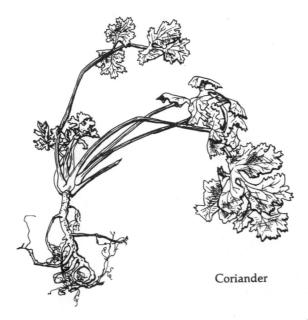

Coriander

dark-green, serrated leaf. Its botanical name is *Geringium foedidum*. This is also used in some Caribbean countries, so you have to remember when buying coriander in Puerto Rican and Dominican markets that you will get the long-leafed variety if you ask for *cilantro* and the normal coriander if you ask for *cilantrillo*.

Coriander is widely available in Far Eastern, Indian, Caribbean, and Mexican markets. Try and buy it with the roots on. Remove any leaves that might be yellowing and practice Julia Child's method of keeping parsley fresh and in good condition: store in a tall, narrow container with water in the bottom for the roots; cover the leaves with a plastic bag and keep in the refrigerator. Coriander can last about ten days, providing, of course, that it was fresh when you bought it and the weather not too hot and humid. There is no substitute

Epazote

for this wonderfully crisp and pungent herb. If you don't have it, leave it out. The commercially dried coriander is only useful when you really can't get the fresh, and then it should be used only in recipes where it is to be cooked, not used fresh.

EPAZOTE   This herb *(Chenopodium ambrosioides)* is one of the pungent herbs used extensively in the cooking of central and southern Mexico; in the north you are more likely to find it among the dried, medicinal herbs. A tea made of it is said to soothe the nerves and dispel intestinal parasites, while to cook a pot of black beans without it is unthinkable.

Although indigenous to tropical America, *epazote* has traveled north, and I have found it in Central and Riverside Parks in New York; on the sidewalks of Richmond, Virginia; in woods in Georgia; and in the parking lots of downtown Houston. It is known in the south of the United States as "wormseed" or "Mexican tea," and somebody from Tennessee told me—after I had been extolling its virtues to an audience in Mexico City—that her mother made cakes of the small, hard green seed mixed with molasses, which were fed to the children as a vermifuge.

If you cannot find *epazote* growing wild, then plant seeds. At my urging, Horticultural Enterprises in Dallas have developed them commercially (see Sources for Ingredients, page 272), and because of the demand created by students of mine around the San Diego area, Taylor Farms there have seedlings. The plants will reseed themselves and grow like weeds—which, of course, they are. Once firmly established, you should be able to keep some healthy plants growing indoors throughout the winter months.

Epazote grown in the United States does not have such a strong flavor, especially during the damp spring weather, and the leaves are broader and lusher compared with their Mexican counterparts. In fact, in Mexico there are two main types of plants, those with reddish-purple stems and very dark green leaves, and those with broader, lighter green leaves. It is a matter of taste which you use, and Mexican cooks have their strong preferences.

Leaves of the *epazote* plant are long and serrated. The plants very quickly run up spiky flowers formed by clusters of small, hard green seeds.

Use dried *epazote* only if you really have to.

MINT   Mint is used in Mexican cooking, but rather sparingly, in meatballs, soups, and (surprisingly) in beans—see Frijoles a la Huacha (page 38).

PARSLEY   Where parsley is called for in Mexican cooking, Italian parsley should be used if available.

HUITLACOCHE

Huitlacoche, or *cuiclacoche (Ustilago maydis),* is *the* most exotic of fungi; it forms on ears of corn. The kernels are swollen and deformed, black and juicy inside and covered with a crisp, silvery-grey skin. The texture and inky flavor bear no resemblance to any other fungus that I have tasted.

You can find small quantities of *huitlacoche* in Mexican markets—only, unfortunately, those in and around Mexico City where it is much esteemed— the year round, but it tends to be rather starchy and dry until well into and just after the rainy season, say from July to October. Then it is readily available and at its best.

There is a limited production of canned *huitlacoche,* which I find rather dry and tasteless, although it is all right as an exotic novelty—but then I always much prefer to eat fresh foods that are in season.

MASA, MASA HARINA *See* Tortillas.

MEXICAN GREEN TOMATOES *See* Tomates verdes.

MINT *See* Herbs, fresh.

NOPALES

The fleshy green leaves, sometimes called "joints" or "paddles," of the nopal cactus are edible, indeed, they are eaten in great quantities in the central and more arid parts of Mexico. In markets there you will find them already cleaned, or they will be cleaned while you wait; all the prickly spines will be deftly scraped off, leaving as much as possible of the outer green layer. I understand that they are being grown commercially in the Southwest United States and are more readily available fresh, but if you cannot find them, then in a pinch you could use the Clemente Jacques brand that are packed in brine. On no account use those that are *en escabeche,* or pickled.

If you do buy fresh *nopales,* be sure to choose the smallest, thinnest leaves, which are much more tender than the big, thick, fleshier ones. Cut them into ½-inch, or even smaller, squares and they'll be ready to cook.

I am afraid I have been guilty of going along with practically everyone else and cooking *nopales* to death by boiling them in water and then rinsing them

—by which time all the color and food value has been lost. Now I cook them for all my recipes as I do in Nopales al Vapor (see page 147). If you do them this way for your salads and eggs and other dishes that call for them, you will find that they have a better color, are crisper, and have a higher nutritional value.

ONIONS

Large, sharp white onions are generally used throughout Mexico. They are widely available in the United States and should be used wherever possible instead of the more commonly grown yellow onions, which nearly always tend to be sugary sweet, spoiling the balance of flavors in any dish in which they are used. Do not use Spanish onions.

In Yucatán, the regional dishes are adorned with chopped purple onion, while in the central part of the country peasant dishes are cooked with the large, green onion called *cebolla de rabo*. This is the size of the U.S. boiling onion, and most of the green as well as the white part is used. I have seen them in markets in New York, especially on Ninth Avenue, where they are called "Texas scallions" (in Chicago they are called "nob onions"). In Mexico City it is common to see them being broiled over charcoal, with green leaves intact, and then eaten with broiled meats and tacos.

OREGANO *See* **Herbs, dried.**

PARSLEY *See* **Herbs, fresh.**

PLANTAINS

I suppose one could call plantains (*plátano macho* in Mexico) "vegetable bananas." They are, in fact, long, curved, thick-skinned bananas, pointed at the end and almost triangular in form. They can be found in any Caribbean, Latin American, or Mexican market, but care should be taken in choosing them. In the Caribbean they are used when they are almost green and starchy, but for Mexican cooking they must be very ripe, almost juicy, and sweet.

PUMPKIN BLOSSOMS *See* **Squash blossoms.**

PUMPKIN SEEDS

Pumpkin seeds have been used since pre-Columbian times as an important ingredient in Mexican food. Toasted in their hulls, they are eaten as a snack or ground for such dishes as Legumbres en Pipián Oaxequeño (page 148) or Sikil-P'ak (page 5); hulled but unroasted and unsalted, they are used in *moles*, the sauce for *papa-dzules* (*The Cuisines of Mexico,* page 70), or Camarones en Pipián (see page 95).

In different regions of Mexico the seeds of different squashes are used, but I think it would be confusing here to list them all. You will probably not have a choice anyway, so buy whatever is available in health food stores or Mexican markets—the taste does not vary that much. The hulled seeds do tend to become rancid unless stored in a cool place, and they can become so old that there is no oil left in them—as I learned to my shame during a demonstration of *papa-dzules,* when I couldn't squeeze more than a few teaspoons of oil from them.

RICE

For all the recipes in this book use a long-grain, white, *unconverted* rice. I have found an enormous difference in rice in different parts of the United States and again in Mexico, so it would be as well to do a trial batch with any new brand to make sure how much liquid it will absorb and how much bulk it will give. I say this from experience. Recently I was demonstrating a rice dish with stuffed chilies. It hardly expanded at all, and I was left with a rather rich—and "thin"—casserole; there was not enough bulk to absorb the richness of the other ingredients.

SALT

I always use a good rock or sea salt for cooking as well as on the table, and my recipe quantities are for those types of salt. It is rather awkward when cooking to add salt from a salt mill, so I grind some ahead in the blender.

SESAME SEEDS

Sesame seeds are used a great deal in Mexican food, as a topping for breads and pastries or as a thickener for sauces. It makes no difference whether you use the creamy-colored ones that have been highly refined or the greyish-colored ones that are available in most Mexican markets. If you are using the latter, do be sure to pour them from one hand to the other to separate the loose chaff that invariably accompanies them.

SEVILLE OR SOUR ORANGES

There are various strains of sour oranges, *naranjas agrias,* one of them being the Seville orange, which is always used in making the bitter British marmalade. They are small, with a brilliantly orange, thinnish skin. Those generally available in the United States are imported from the Caribbean. They are almost misshapen, with their thick, pitted skin, which is yellowy green rather than orange in color, and slightly sharper in flavor than the genuine Seville.

It is a pity that these oranges are not more generally available, as they grow easily and in some places the trees bear fruit the year round—I have, for example, seen them lining the streets and college campus in Claremont, California. Caribbean markets often carry them, and on New York's Upper West Side I have seen them on Korean fruit stands in all seasons. Try ordering some; they are around.

If you see them and want to buy in quantity, while they will keep wrapped in paper and stored in the bottom of the refrigerator for some weeks, you could squeeze out the juice and freeze it with a little of the grated rind to ensure a supply for your Yucatecan dishes the year round. There is no real substitute for that wonderful, sharp, and fragrant juice, but in a pinch you could mix up the following concoction as a slightly inadequate substitute.

Mock Seville Orange Juice

> *1 teaspoon finely grated grapefruit rind*
> *3 tablespoons orange juice*
> *3 tablespoons grapefruit juice*
> *2 tablespoons lemon juice*

Combine all the ingredients.

½ cup

SHRIMPS, DRIED

See the note before the recipe Consomé de Camarón Seco on page 20.

SQUASH BLOSSOMS

Squash and pumpkin flowers, *flores de calabaza,* are used in the cooking of central Mexico. As the rainy season progresses, well into July, the flowers become larger and more fragrant, and I cannot pass the lovely sight of a peasant woman sitting on the sidewalk, surrounded by her merchandise of small, tender squash and piles of fresh, deep-yellow flowers, without stopping to buy some, whether I need them or not.

In Mexican markets they are sold—like any other flowers—in bunches of about thirty with their stems tied together. They are actually available the year round, but out of the rainy season the flowers tend to be tightly closed and rather dry, and will not have a delicate flavor and texture. You can, of course, use blossoms from your garden; and remember that they taste best when absolutely fresh. Unfortunately, they are tasteless when cooked and then frozen.

No two cooks agree about cleaning them. Some remove the stems, some don't; others remove the whole stalk, while the rest leave part of it on. This is the way I clean them in order to preserve flavor and texture to the utmost:

Pull off the tough leaves of the green calyx, and with each sectional leaf should come a tough, stringy strip from the outside of the stem. Leave only about 2 inches of stem to each flower. Rinse the flowers in cold water and chop them or cut them roughly with a pair of scissors.

They are now ready to cook.

SUGAR

For the recipes in this book, granulated sugar is called for, except where *piloncillo* is mentioned. This is the name given in central Mexico—in Oaxaca it is *panela*—to the dark-brown, unrefined sugar, with a strong flavor of molasses, that comes in cones that weigh about ½ pound each. Any dark-brown sugar can be substituted.

In Mexico they are now producing a coarse granulated sugar that is not very highly refined or very white—and while I certainly don't mind that, I do mind the fact that it does not caramelize well; it should not be used for flans.

TOMATES VERDES, MEXICAN GREEN TOMATOES

The Mexican green tomato is a pale green fruit that, enclosed in a green, papery husk, ripens to yellow. It is not an ordinary unripe tomato but a variety of *Physalis,* the same family as the Cape gooseberry and ground cherry. In the center of Mexico it is called *tomate verde,* and in the northeast *fresadilla;* elsewhere it is either *tomatillo, tomate de cáscara,* or *tomate de bolsa*—so you have your choice of names.

Tomate verde

The tiniest *miltomate* that grows wild in the cornfields is about ½ inch in diameter; the largest cultivated and irrigated fruit can reach almost 2 inches in diameter. Generally used when they are green rather than yellow, *tomates verdes* vary in acidity. Some give a slight sweetness to a sauce, while others are so acidy that one has to add a touch of sugar. They are now grown in the United States, and there is a much wider distribution of the fresh ones than previously, but if you don't have a continuous supply, then I suggest that you clean, cook, and freeze them whole in the water in which they were cooked (see below). If you cannot buy them fresh, and cannot grow them in the garden (although they are easy to grow, and seeds can be obtained from Horticultural Enterprises; see Sources for Ingredients, page 272), then buy canned ones. I find the imported Clemente Jacques brand preferable, as the canning liquid is not as harsh as the other brands. But always drain the canned ones and use plain water for blending.

Fresh, raw *tomates verdes* can, if stored in a paper (not polyethylene), bag, last for about two weeks—providing, of course, that they were in good condition when you bought them.

To prepare** tomates verdes **for sauces Strip off the papery husks and rinse in cold water. Put into a saucepan, cover with water, and simmer over a low flame until the fruits are soft and the skins tender. (Depending on size, they can take from 20 to 30 minutes to cook thoroughly.) You will need to turn them over during the cooking time, as the top layer seems to float with the uncooked side up. Do not let them boil, or they will split open and lose their seeds and pulp in the cooking water.

TOMATOES

Tomatoes are indigenous to Mexico and South America, and they are grown in Mexico throughout the year. They must be among the best in the world; they are vine ripened and come to the markets large, juicy, and sweet.

The Italian plum tomato—called *jitomate guaje* ("gourd" tomato) or *guajillo,* like the chili—is also grown extensively. The skin is much tougher than that of the ordinary tomato, and unless your blender blades are very sharp you may have to skin the tomato (see page 262) before blending, pass the sauce through the fine disk of a food mill, or sieve it.

TORTILLAS

Tortillas are, of course, indispensable as far as Mexican food is concerned. And while they are now widely available, both fresh and frozen (see Sources for Ingredients, pages 271–77), I do suggest that you try making your own, using either prepared *masa,* if you can get it, or *masa harina.* If you persist, you will soon get the knack, and I promise you that the result will be worth the extra effort. Besides a recipe for corn tortillas, I'm including one for wheat-flour tortillas and for *totopos* or *tostaditas,* those popular little crisp-fried tortilla "scoops" that go with so much.

Prepared *masa* is sold in many of the places that sell fresh tortillas. Failing that, Quaker *masa harina,* which is parched corn that has been treated with lime and then ground, will, when mixed with water, do almost as well. You will need a tortilla press (see page 256), two small polyethylene bags, and one or two heavy griddles or frying pans.

>   *2 cups Quaker* masa harina *or ½ to ¾ pound prepared*
>   masa
>   *1⅓ cups water, approximately (optional)*

If you are using prepared *masa,* you will not of course need the water. If using the *masa harina,* put it in a mixing bowl, add the water all at once (this will keep lumps from forming) and mix together quickly, just until the ingredients are combined. Set the dough aside for 20 minutes. While the dough is resting, place your heavy griddle or griddles (using two will speed up the process) over a medium flame and let heat up thoroughly; you should be able to hear the dough sizzle faintly when a tortilla is placed in it if the griddle has been heated to the proper temperature.

After the resting period, make your first tortilla, to test the consistency of the dough. (If you are using prepared *masa,* start following the directions at this point.)

Open up the tortilla press and place one of the polyethylene bags on the lower part. Roll a piece of the tortilla dough into a ball 1½ inches in diameter and place on the bag, slightly more toward the hinge than the handle of the press. Put the second polyethylene bag carefully on top. Close the press and push the handle firmly down, then open it up and carefully peel off the bag

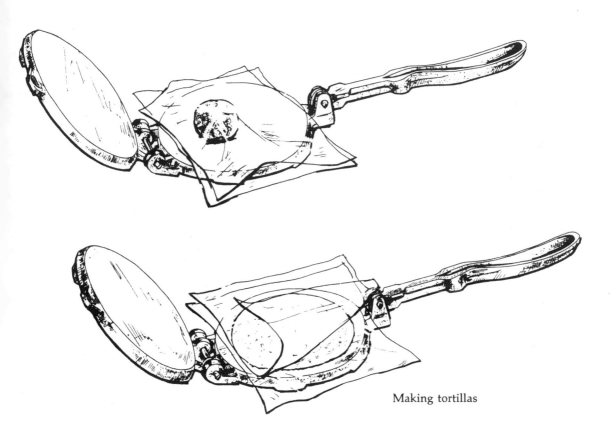

Making tortillas

(continued)

on top. Remove the second bag, with the tortilla on it, and invert it, so the dough side is down, on your other, upturned hand, on the fingers rather than the palm as much as possible. Very carefully peel the bag from the dough (*not* the other way around) and lay the tortilla on the hot griddle. Do this slowly and evenly; if you just drop the tortilla on the griddle, you will get air bubbles and the dough will not cook properly.

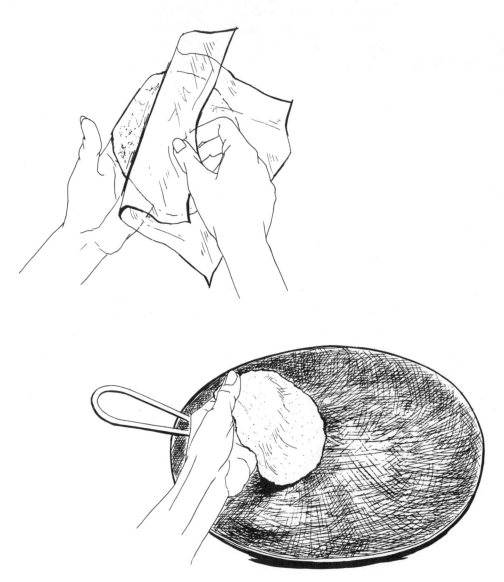

A puffed-up tortilla

Look at the tortilla on the griddle. If it looks thick, with a grainy, uneven edge, the dough is too dry. Work a little—only a *little*—more water into the dough in the bowl; you don't want to make the dough sodden and unmanageable. (If you had trouble peeling the bag off the tortilla in your hand, it may be too damp; sprinkle a very small amount of *masa* into the bowl, mix it in briefly, and try again.)

If your tortilla seems right, or when your dough reaches the right consistency, cook the tortilla on the hot griddle until it *just* begins to dry out around the edges. At that point, flip it over and cook it on the second side for a slightly longer time, until it just begins to color. Flip it back onto the first side and finish cooking it through (the whole process, if the heat is right, should take about 2 minutes). You will be able to tell if your dough is really the right consistency and cooking at the proper temperature if the tortilla puffs up when you flip it back onto the first side. Remove it from the griddle and wrap it in a thick towel or napkin.

Proceed with the rest of dough, checking it from time to time to see if it is drying out and adding a little water if it is. As each tortilla is finished, stack it with the previous ones, and keep well wrapped in the towel, so they stay warm and flexible.

About 16 five-inch tortillas

Wheat-Flour Tortillas

Wheat-flour tortillas are northern Mexican in origin. They are most commonly served wrapped around a meat or other filling as *burritos,* but they can also be served as regular tortillas are, hot and freshly made, to accompany various dishes. In this book, I suggest they be served with Queso Flameado (see page 10) Carne con Chile Verde (see page 65), and Caldillo de Puerco Duranguense (see page 56). You may purchase them (see Sources for Ingredients, pages 271–77), or you can make them according to the directions below.

> *1 pound all-purpose flour, sifted*
> *2 ounces (¼ cup) solid vegetable shortening or pork lard*
> *2 teaspoons salt*
> *1 cup warm water*

Put the flour in a bowl and rub the shortening into it well, using your fingers.

Dissolve the salt in the water and add to the flour/shortening mixture. Mix it in thoroughly, then knead the dough for about 3 minutes. Set aside, covered, for at least 2 hours, unrefrigerated.

Heat a heavy griddle or frying pan over a medium flame.

Knead the dough again briefly, then take a piece of it and roll it into a ball about 1½ inches in diameter. With a rolling pin on a floured board, press the dough out into a circle, then roll it out, turning it to keep it circular, into a paper-thin circle about 7 inches in diameter. Place the circle of dough on the heated griddle; it should sizzle lightly if the griddle is the proper heat. Let the tortilla cook for about 20 seconds, or until bubbles appear on the surface and the underside begins to brown. It may puff up; if so, simply press it back down on the griddle. Turn the tortilla over and let cook for somewhat less time on the second side. After the tortilla has been removed from the griddle, place it in a polyethylene bag.

Proceed with the remainder of the dough, stacking the tortillas in the polyethylene bag as they are finished.

Wheat-flour tortillas will keep for several days in the refrigerator, and they may be frozen. To reheat, simply warm them through in a hot pan.

2 dozen 6- or 7-inch tortillas

Totopos or Tostaditas

Totopos or *tostaditas* are small, triangular tortilla crisps using for scooping up foods such as Guacamole (see page 7) Sikil-P'ak (see page 5), or Frijoles Refritos (see page 37). The more usual way is to fry them crisp, as described below, but I personally prefer them toasted crisp in a 300° oven (for about 40 minutes, turning once or twice) or on a griddle or *comal* on top of the stove.

You can prepare them ahead of time and, in fact, store them in an airtight container (in a cool place, however, or they will become soft and rancid). You can then "refresh" them a little in the oven before serving.

A word of warning: As you fry the *totopos,* put them in an inconspicuous place. They are considered fair game for anyone wandering through the kitchen, and as likely as not you will not have enough to go around when you are ready to serve.

Totopos can be made with fresh tortillas rather than stale, but they will absorb more fat and take longer to cook.

> *6 tortillas (see page 246), preferably stale*
> *Peanut or safflower oil for frying*
> *Salt, if desired*

Before they dry out too much, cut the tortillas into six triangular pieces Heat the oil to the smoking point and fry some of the tortilla pieces—a small quantity at a time so they do not overlap in the pan—turning them over from time to time so that they cook evenly. When they are a deep golden color and crisp right through, they are done.

Remove them with a perforated spoon, draining them well over the pan and then on paper toweling.

Note that since this is a way of using up stale tortillas, and salt is never put into everyday tortilla dough, if you want them salted, either sprinkle them with salt after they come out of the pan or salt them beforehand, as follows: Put a bowl of very salty water by the frying pan. Quickly dip a small handful of the tortilla pieces into the water, then throw them into the pan (watch out —they will splatter) and fry them crisp as described above.

3 dozen totopos

See also the ingredients for baking on page 185.

COOKING EQUIPMENT

BEAN MASHER

Once in a while, if I am in a great hurry and want to cook some *frijoles refritos,* I'll put them into the blender, but I really enjoy mashing and frying them in the traditional way—you can work out some problems while doing it—with a wooden Mexican bean masher. It isn't essential, of course, but nice to have. In the United States you should find one in Mexican markets that also sell cooking equipment (see Sources for Ingredients, pages 271–77) and sometimes in shops selling Mexican arts and crafts. If you can't find one, then an ordinary wooden potato masher will do; the metal ones do not mash beans effectively.

BLENDER

You simply have to have a blender for Mexican cooking; the food processor is not a substitute. Choose a heavy one—it has a lot of heavy work to do—as opposed to the light, countertop fixture. It is important to be able to dismantle the cutting blades from the jar. Pieces of dried chilies, for example, tend to stick underneath the blades, and cleaning is much more difficult when they cannot be taken out. It helps enormously to have two jars, each with a set of cutting blades, when preparing a Mexican meal, since it is quite often necessary to blend more than one sauce at a time.

COFFEE/SPICE GRINDER

A small coffee/spice or nut grinder is a necessity for many Mexican dishes that call for ground *achiote,* pumpkin or sesame seeds, or spices, since even the sturdiest blender cannot do such an efficient job. Of the brands I have tried, I find the Moulinex to be the best designed and most efficient. It can be found in most of the specialist cookware stores.

COMAL

A *comal* or Mexican griddle is indispensable; it is used for cooking tortillas, for toasting chilies, garlic, and so forth. If you are using a charcoal fire for cooking, the very best is a *comal* of unglazed earthenware, about ½ inch thick; it can be obtained from 9 inches to 3 feet in diameter.

You must cure a new earthenware *comal* before using it. Smear it on both sides with a thick paste of powdered lime and water. Put it onto the hot fire until the lime paste is gradually cooked dry and falls off.

The most practical *comal* of all—and sometimes available in Mexican grocery stores in the Southwest—is a very thin sheet of metal with a small looped piece of metal as a handle. It always looks rather battered; as soon as the hot flame hits, it warps up and down unevenly. But it does make good tortillas, which always seem lighter when the flame is as near as possible to the dough. Most readily available is a cast-iron *comal* or griddle, either round or elongated so that you can cook about three tortillas on it at a time. It is sold in Mexican groceries and supermarkets. Gourmet and kitchen specialist stores now carry a rather elegant *comal* made of heavy stainless metal with a wooden handle—mine always get burned. As a last resort, use a heavy frying pan, but the high heat is liable to warp or crack it, and the high sides can burn your hands.

COOKWARE

In Mexico I use the attractive glazed, earthenware *cazuelas* in which food can be cooked and served—but because of FDA objections and the possibility that nontraditional or inappropriate ware will be chosen, I won't elaborate on it. It is necessary, however, to have heavy dishes and pans that can be put straight onto the flame and serve the dual purpose of cooking and serving—such as LeCreuset ware. I have found that the most useful sizes are an oval casserole large enough for one or one and a half chickens; a heavy Dutch oven with tightly fitting lid to cook dishes like Cochito al Horno (see page 41) and Asado de Puerco a la Veracruzana (see page 44); casseroles about 7½ in diameter at the bottom, 10 inches at the top, and at least 3½ inches deep for rice and stews and similar dishes; a wider, shallower casserole about 12 inches in diameter for *moles* and dishes like Pollo Enchilado (see page 83) or Conejo en Chile (see page 77); an ovenproof dish of a standard size about 8½ × 13 × 1½ inches for Sopa de Pan (see page 21) or Chiles Rellenos de Elote con Crema (see page 136).

FLAN MOLD

In Mexico they make a compact, one-quart flan mold that comes in three parts: the water bath, mold, and lid. Inexpensively made of light tin, it looks quite primitive and flimsy, but it works well. Always make sure you dry it well after use or it will rust.

It will probably leak at first, so before using it to cook a flan, put some water into both water bath and mold and set it in a 300-degree oven for about 2 hours. Then test again for leaks. If it continues to leak in places, you will have to have it soldered.

I don't believe anyone is importing them, which is a pity, but when in Mexico City you can buy them in the annex outside the Merced Market (passage 6, stand 82, telephone 768-48-39).

FOOD MILL

A food mill is indispensable for Mexican cooking if you don't want to spend hours pressing the cooked ingredients through a strainer. I have always found the French Mouli food mill with its three graded disks to be the most efficient.

FRYING PANS

You will need some very heavy frying pans, and I suggest three sizes—6, 8, and 10 inches. I am personally devoted to the cast-iron ones.

LIME SQUEEZER

The Mexican lime squeezer looks rather rough and ready, but it is the most efficient one I know. The large limes in the United States (key limes excepted) tend to have tough skin, and there is nothing more frustrating than having to make *margaritas* or *cebiche* and squeezing limes with those fancy contraptions that you find in most bars. You usually have very little juice and very sore hands at the end of it all.

MOLCAJETE AND TEJOLOTE (Mexican Mortar and Pestle)

No self-respecting cook in this hemisphere should be without this classic piece of kitchen equipment. The *molcajete*, the mortar, is in the form of a thick bowl supported by three short legs, and is made of porous volcanic rock. The *tejolote,* the pestle, is cylindrical, or triangular in shape. They are used mostly for grinding spices or making table sauces. A word of advice about choosing one. There are more bad than good ones on the market, especially in the United States. The very best, made of heavy, black basalt with fine pores, are hard to come by. The next quality will be a dark greyish color, and the worst will be a light grey, coarsely grained rock that, as you work it with the *tejolote,* grinds quickly to a fine dust. Throw *that* one away.

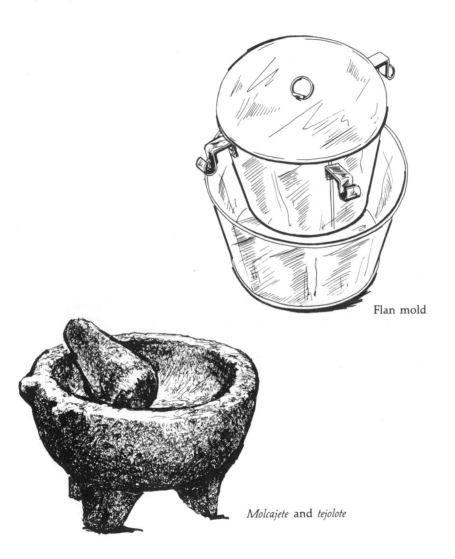

Flan mold

Molcajete and *tejolote*

The *molcajete* has to be cured before using. Take a handful of dry, uncooked rice or corn and grind it with the *tejolote* until it is reduced to a powder. Wash the *molcajete* out and start again. If it is of a good quality, then three grindings should be sufficient, but you may have to repeat the process six times before it has been cured sufficiently (i.e, when you make a sauce or *guacamole*, it isn't gritty).

In some areas of Mexico ceramic *molcajetes* are used. While the clay is still wet the bottom of the bowl is deeply scored, crisscross fashion. When it has been fired in the kiln the rough surface is suitable for grating such things as onion and chilies. I don't find them as durable or efficient as the basalt ones.

One further test to see if your *molcajete* is worth buying: insist that you be allowed to put some water into it; if it drains out rapidly it is too porous. Pass on to the next one.

SCALE

I find it irritating and time consuming to be constantly pressing ingredients into measuring cups when it is so quick and accurate to weigh them. I would choose a scale that is easy to read and gives the weights in both pounds and kilograms. It is particularly important to weigh rather than measure flour for baking.

TORTILLA PRESS

Unless you intend to spend your life patting out tortillas by hand, you should buy a tortilla press. They are carried in most Mexican and Chinese markets and in specialty kitchen stores (see Sources for Ingredients, pages 271–77). I recommend the 6-inch size.

TWELVE-INCH RULER

Always keep a ruler handy. It does help so much when you cook things that are new to you, such as tortillas (see page 246), Sopaipillas (see page 180) or Buñuelos (see pages 175–79).

See also the special equipment for baking listed on pages 183–84.

COOKING METHODS

FRYING ONION AND GARLIC

As the Mexicans would say, *acitronar* onion and garlic. That means they should be cooked gently in oil, without browning, until they are translucent and fairly soft. Don't hurry this procedure. It is essential to have them cooked before the rest of the ingredients are added—unless, of course, it is otherwise stated.

COOKING AND SHREDDING MEAT OR POULTRY

Traditionally throughout Mexico—although I can think of a few exceptions— meat or poultry for filling tacos, for stuffing chilies, or for *picadillo* (shredded meat filling) is shredded and not ground. The basic method for preparing meat or poultry in this way follows:

> *1 pound meat, cut into 1½-inch cubes, or 1½ pounds*
> *   chicken*
> *Water or broth to cover*
> *¼ small onion, roughly chopped*
> *1 clove garlic, peeled and chopped*
> *1 teaspoon salt, or to taste*

Trim the meat of excess fat but leave some on for flavor. Put it or the poultry into a saucepan with the rest of the ingredients, the water or broth barely to cover, and bring to the simmering point. Continue cooking slowly until the meat or poultry is tender. Remove from the flame and let cool off in the broth. As soon as it is cool enough to handle, shred the meat or poultry (first skimmed or boned) as fine as you can be bothered to do it—but not shredded to hairs, as one sees so often in California. In the case of meat, remove any tough gristle or tendons but leave the fat. I personally prefer to cook the meat—particularly the chicken—in a light broth to give added flavor.

This should yield 1¼ to 1⅓ cups shredded meat.

TOASTING AND CHARRING

In the instructions for many Yucatecan dishes you will see the word "toasted" after these ingredients: onions, garlic, chilies, and some herbs. The toasting of these ingredients gives a distinctive flavor to the dish in which they are cooked. Occasionally in central Mexico ingredients for a particular dish have to be *asado,* which means either "roasted" or "broiled"; this can be achieved by cooking either directly on hot charcoal or on a hot bakestone or *comal.*

GARLIC OR ONION   Place the unpeeled onion or head of garlic on a hot, ungreased griddle or *comal* and cook over a medium flame, turning it from time to time until the outside skin is charred and the flesh inside is transparent but still a little crisp. Depending on the instructions in the recipe, the onion or garlic will be used just like that or peeled.

FRESH CHILIES   Put them onto a hot, ungreased griddle or *comal* and cook over a medium flame, turning them over from time to time until the skin is blistered and charred and the flesh is half cooked. Do not peel them; follow the instructions in the recipe.

DRIED CHILIES   See pages 259–60.

HERBS   Put the herb (oregano, bay leaf, etc.) into a small, ungreased frying pan. Shake the pan over a medium flame until the leaves begin to change color and send off a lovely musky smell.

SEEDS   Sesame or pumpkin seeds should always be toasted before grinding. Put them into an ungreased frying pan and stir them over a medium flame until they begin to change color. The sesame seeds turn very quickly to a good golden color; take care they do not burn.

Shelled pumpkin seeds will swell up as they begin to change color, and they are done when they are very slightly browned. Keep turning them over so that they warm through evenly, and take care, as they pop about explosively.

Unhulled pumpkin seeds for Legumbres en Pipián Oaxaqueño (see page 148) and Sikil-P'ak (see page 5) should be well browned on the outside; many will pop open, exposing the green seed inside. Both hulls and seeds are used.

Always let seeds cool off before attempting to grind them or they will clog the blades of the grinder.

CHILIES, DRIED

CLEANING   Dried chilies may appear dusty or have some earth on them. If you are going to use them without soaking—as, for example, in Salsa de Muchos Chiles (see page 152) or Aguayón Estilo Leonor (see page 76), then just wipe them with a damp cloth before toasting. Do not immerse them in water.

REMOVING THE STEMS, SEEDS, AND VEINS Some of the dried chilies come with their stems intact. There is certainly no use for them, although, some recipes, such as Chiles de la Sierra (see page 162), indicate that they be left on for appearance's sake.

If the chilies are from the newest crop, they will be pliable, though dried, and easily slit open and the seeds and veins removed. If they are dry or brittle, then heat them through slowly on a warm griddle or *comal,* turning them over from time to time, and they will gradually soften up enough so they can at least be opened and the seeds and veins removed without being broken into a hundred pieces.

TOASTING As you will see from the recipes in this book alone, there are substantial differences in preparing chilies for a sauce, differences that are quite often regional. For instance, in the recipe for Manchamantel (page 81), the chilies are cleaned and then fried, as they would be for *mole poblano (Cuisines of Mexico,* page 199); for Pollo en Ajo-Comino (see page 87) and Cochito al Horno (see page 41), the chilies are cleaned and boiled, while in Caldillo de Puerco Duranguense (see page 56), the chilies are boiled without being cleaned of seeds and veins; and so on. The preparation of dried chilies is indicated, then, in each recipe.

Lightly toasting For some dishes, such as Pollo Enchilado (see page 83), the sauce for Tortillas Dobladas (see page 117), and Lolitos (see page 116), the chilies have to be lightly toasted, which brings out the flavor. After removing the seeds and veins, flatten the chilies out as much as possible and put them onto a warm griddle or *comal.* Leave for a minute or so, then turn them over. When the inside flesh turns an opaque pale brown and they begin to emit a pleasant aroma, they are sufficiently toasted. (Craig Claiborne, from all his practical experience, gave me this Mexican cooking hint: he presses the opened chili down onto the hot *comal* with a flat lid.) The chilies are then usually soaked in hot water.

Toasting well For some table sauces, like Salsa de Muchos Chiles (see page 152), and cooked sauces, like that for Aguayón Estilo Leonor (see page 76), the chilies have to be well toasted. After removing the seeds and veins from the chilies (although occasionally for table sauces the veins and seeds are not removed before being well toasted), flatten them out as much as possible and toast on a warm griddle or *comal,* turning them from time to time so they do not burn; if they do, the sauce will have an acrid flavor. As the inside becomes opaque and the outside begins to blister slightly, remove the chilies and let them cool off. There should be a strong, earthy aroma to them, and if they have been toasted sufficiently, when cool they should be brittle and crumble easily. (If the chilies are very fresh and pliable, it could take 8 to 10 minutes for them to reach this point.)

COOKING DRIED CHILI SAUCES   When cooking any sauce of blended chilies, make sure that the fat is not too hot or the sauce will scorch immediately and the taste will be impaired.

FRYING AND CRUMBLING   *Chiles pasillas* are often fried and crumbled to season a soup, *sopa de tortilla* (*The Cuisines of Mexico,* page 143) being the classic example. They are used here for Caldo de Habas (see page 19) and Aguayón Estilo Leonor (page 76), not only adding piquancy but lending a delightful smoky flavor to the dishes.

> *2 tablespoons peanut or safflower oil, approximately*
> *3 chiles pasillas*

Heat the oil to smoking in a small frying pan and fry the chilies over a medium flame, turning them around occasionally—if not punctured, they will inflate —until the outside skin is crisp to the touch. This should take about 5 minutes, depending, of course, on how dry the chilies were in the first place.

When they are cool enough to handle, crumble them roughly, together with the seeds and veins. (If you do not like your food *picante,* then remove some or all of the seeds and veins clustered at the top just before crumbling them.)

CHILIES, FRESH

CHARRING, PEELING, AND CLEANING   You will see that the instructions for using *chiles poblanos, chilacas,* or *Anaheim* call for them to be peeled and cleaned. In Mexican peasant cooking this is done by charring them right on the charcoal or wood fire, which enhances the flavor.

If you are cooking with gas—which is, of course, much easier and better for this process—place the whole chilies, with stalk intact if possible, onto the flame of an open burner and let the skin blister and char very slightly. Turn them over and repeat the process until they are evenly blistered and charred. Be careful: if you do not char them enough, they will not peel easily; if you char them too much, then the flesh will be dried and perhaps burned through. (After all my years in Mexico, I am still learning: a friend in California had her maid come in and help us with a class. She set about cleaning *chiles poblanos,* first coating them lightly with oil before charring them over the flame. Her grandmother taught her to do it in this way. It certainly helps when the chilies have very irregular surfaces; this way every part gets charred evenly.) Place them immediately into a polyethylene bag, or wrap in a damp cloth, and let them "sweat" for about 15 to 20 minutes. (While the skin could be removed almost immediately after they are placed in the bag, more time is required so that the steam generated from the heat will cook the flesh slightly.) At the end of the "sweating" time, remove the skin.

If you cook with electricity, then use a preheated, *hot* broiler and place the chilies about 2 inches from the source of heat. Do not attempt to cook them in a very hot oven; the flesh will become too soggy and they will have none of that required "burnt" flavor.

If you are preparing the chilies to stuff, make a slit down one side of the chili. Carefully cut out the core—which is covered with seeds—under the base of the stem. Remove as much as you can of the veins without tearing the flesh of the chili. Rinse to remove the rest of the seeds. (If you do not have a waste disposal unit in your sink, then I find it helpful to carry out this cleaning process under the cold faucet, with a strainer underneath to catch all the pieces.) If the chili is of good quality and you have worked carefully, you should have a complete "shell," with stalk, stalk base around the top, and flesh intact, ready to stuff. If the flesh is a bit ragged, don't worry—you can always cover it with sauce after stuffing. If it is terribly ragged, and past redemption, then cut it into strips and reserve for *rajas,* or chili strips.

PREPARING RAJAS   The preparation of chilies for *rajas* is the same as above except that the stalk is discarded and one need not be so meticulous about keeping the top whole, since the flesh is cut from it and into strips about ½ inch wide and 2½ inches long. I don't waste anything: the thick flesh around the base can also be used, ground up in a sauce or for rice, or for any similar purpose.

HANDLING CHILIES   Remember that when you are cleaning either fresh or dried chilies, the veins and seeds are the hottest parts; the flesh inside is hot by association. Even if you have a tough skin, but are not used to handling chilies, it is advisable to wear a pair of thin rubber gloves (surgical ones are best for this). If you don't wear gloves, remember, after you handle chilies, to scrub your fingertips, especially under the nails, with plenty of soapy water and then soak them for a few minutes in strongly salted water. This will help to avert the alternative, fiercely stinging fingertips for some hours and the resulting agony you will experience if you forget and rub your eyes. (If you do rub your eyes, rinse them immediately and well with cold water.)

REGULATING THE "HEAT"   As you open up the chili, your nose should tell you how *picante* it is—these types of chilies can vary from mild to very hot. If you think that they are going to be too hot for your taste, then soak them either in a mild solution of eight parts of vinegar to one of water or in 1 tablespoon salt to 1 quart of water for about 30 minutes and then rinse well.

TOMATOES

SKINNING AND SEEDING Plunge raw tomatoes into boiling water to cover and leave them while you count up to fifteen, then remove and put into cold water to stop the cooking process. Slip the skin off, which should be very easy unless the tomatoes are not very ripe—in which case you shouldn't be using them for these recipes at all. Cut out the core, then cut the tomatoes in half, and squeeze the seeds out into a strainer. Press the seeds down to extract all the juice, and reserve.

BOILING For some of the recipes in this book the tomatoes have to be boiled, or rather simmered, in hot water until they are cooked through but not too mushy. A medium-sized one will take about 15 to 20 minutes, depending, of course, on ripeness.

If you have an efficient blender with sharp blades, you need not skin the tomatoes after cooking, the exception being Italian plum tomatoes, which tend to have a much tougher skin.

BROILING It is traditional in Mexican peasant cooking to cook tomatoes for sauces right on the *comal*, over a charcoal fire. While cooking, they are turned from time to time until the skin is blistered, with dark brown patches, and the flesh inside is very soft. They are then ground, without peeling or coring. This method gives a wonderfully robust, earthy flavor to the sauces, but it is time consuming and makes an awful mess of your *comal* as well. I suggest that you compromise in the following way.

Preheat the broiler to medium. Choose a shallow, flameproof dish into which the tomatoes to be broiled will fit comfortably and can be turned easily (if the pan is too large, then the sweet juice that they exude in the cooking will dry up) and line it with foil. Place the tomatoes on the foil and broil about 2 inches from the flame. As they blister and brown on one side—try not to char them too much—turn them over, repeating this process from time to time during the cooking period until they are evenly browned and soft inside— about 20 minutes for a medium tomato. If any part of the skin has become blackened and rather hard, then peel it off; otherwise blend the whole tomatoes—skin, seeds, core, and all.

Guide to Vocabulary and Pronunciation

Included in the following lists of words, definitions, and pronunciations are the most important words and terms in the book, as well as a few terms not used here but equally important to the world of Mexican cooking.

achiote	*seeds of the annatto tree*	ah-chee-OH-teh
acitrón	*candied biznaga cactus*	ah-see-TRON
agua, aguado	*water, watery*	AH-gwah,
		ah-GWAH-thoh
aguacate	*avocado*	ah-gwah-CAH-teh
albóndigas	*meatballs*	ahl-BON-thee-gahs
al gusto	*to taste*	ahl-GOO-stoh
almendra,	*almond, with almonds*	ahl-MEHN-drah,
almendrado		

almuerzo	*midmorning breakfast*	ahl-MWER-soh
ancho	*name for a variety of chili (lit., "wide")*	AHN-choh
añejo	*aged*	ah-NYEH-hoh
antojito	*appetizer*	ahn-toh-HEE-toh
arroz	*rice*	ah-RROS
asadero	*type of cheese made in the Mexican states Chihuahua and Michoacán*	ah-sah-THEH-roh
asar, asado	*to roast or broil; roasted or broiled*	ah-SAHR, ah-SAH-thoh
ayocote	*a large bean found in central Mexico, often a mauve-tinged chocolate color*	ah-yoh-COH-teh
barbacoa	*barbecued meat*	bahr-bah-KOH-ah
blanco	*white*	BLAHN-koh
bolillo	*small, elongated yeast roll*	boh-LEE-yoh
borracho	*drunk*	boh-RRAH-choh
botana	*name given to an appetizer served with drinks*	boh-TAH-nah
buñuelo	*fritter*	boo-nyoo-WEH-loh
cabrito	*kid*	kah-BREE-toh
cacahuazintle	*corn with very large, white kernels, hominy*	kah-kah-wah-SEEN-tleh
calabacita	*zucchini*	kah-lah-bah-SEE-tah
calabaza	*pumpkin*	kah-lah-BAH-sah
caldo	*broth*	KAHL-thoh
camarones	*shrimps*	kah-mah-ROH-nehs
campechana	*an oval-shaped puff of pastry with a shiny, caramelized top*	kahm-peh-CHAH-nah
campo	*the country*	KAHM-poh
carne	*meat*	KAHR-neh
carnitas	*name given to a dish of little pieces of browned pork*	kahr-NEE-tahs
cascabel	*name for a round chili (lit., "rattle")*	kahs-kah-BEL
cazón	*dogfish or small shark*	kah-SOHN

cazuela	*earthenware casserole*	kah-SWEH-lah
cebiche	*fish marinated in lime juice*	seh-BEE-cheh
cebolla	*onion*	seh-BOH-yah
cebollin,	*chive; chivelike plant in*	seh-BOH-leen,
cebollina	*southeastern Mexico*	seh-boh-LEEN-ah
cecina	*name given to thin strips of*	seh-SEE-nah
	dried meat or jerky	
cena	*supper*	SEH-nah
chamberete	*shin, generally of beef*	chahm-beh-REH-teh
chayote	*vegetable pear*	chah-YOH-teh
chicharrón	*crisp-fried pork rind*	chee-chah-RROHN
chilaca	*name given to a long, thin,*	chee-LAH-kah
	dark-green chili	
chile	*chili, hot pepper*	CHEE-leh
chipotle,	*name for a smoked chili*	chee-POH-tleh,
chilpocle		cheel-POH-kleh
chirmole	*a black seasoning paste of*	cheer-MOH-leh
	burnt chilies and other	
	spices, found in	
	Southeastern Mexico	
chorizo	*a spicy pork sausage*	choh-REE-soh
cilantro	*coriander*	see-LAHN-troh
cochinita	*a small pig*	koh-chee-NEE-tah
cocido	*cooked*	koh-SEE-thoh
cocina	*kitchen*	koh-SEE-nah
colado	*strained*	ko-LAH-thoh
colorado	*colored, often applying to*	koh-loh-RAH-thoh
	red-colored dishes	
comal	*thin plate of earthenware or*	ko-MAHL
	metal for cooking tortillas	
	or toasting other foods	
comida	*the main meal of the day*	koh-MEE-thah
comino	*cumin*	koh-MEE-noh
concha	*name given to a sweet roll*	KOHN-cha
	with a sugar decoration in	
	the form of a shell	
costillas,	*ribs; little ribs*	koh-STEE-yahs,
costillitas		koh-stee-YEE-tas

crema	cream	KREH-mah
crudo	raw	KROO-thoh
cuerno	croissant	KWEHR-noh
doblada	regional name (Hidalgo) given to a tortilla spread with chili sauce and doubled over (lit., "doubled f")	doh-BLAH-thah
dulce	sweet	DOOL-seh
elote	ear of fresh corn	eh-LOH-teh
enchilada	a tortilla dipped in chili sauce and filled, generally with cheese, meat, or other filling	ehn-chee-LAH-thah
enchilado	covered with chili sauce	ehn-chee-LAH-thoh
encurtido	pickled, preserved	ehn-koor-TEE-thoh
ensalada	salad	ehn-sah-LAH-thah
epazote	the herb Chenopodium ambrosioides	eh-pah-SOH-teh
escabeche	pickle or souse	ehs-kah-BEH-cheh
estilo	in the style of	ehs-TEE-loh
estofado	stew	ehs-toh-FAH-thoh
flameado	flambé	flah-meh-AH-thoh
flan	caramel custard	flahn
flor	flower	flohr
fonda	inn	FOHN-dah
fresco	fresh	FREHS-koh
frijoles	beans	free-HOH-lehs
frito	fried	FREE-toh
fruta	fruit	FROO-tah
gordita	a thick cake of maize dough and lard	gohr-THEE-tah
guacamole	a "concoction" of crushed avocado	gwah-kah-MOH-leh
guajillo	name for a long, dried chili	gwah-HEE-yoh
guajolote	turkey, orig. wild turkey	gwa-hoh-LOH-teh
guavina	a small fish found in the Papaloapan river	gwah-VEE-nah
guiso, guisado	stew, stewed	GHEE-soh, ghee-SAH-thoh

haba	*fava bean*	AH-bah
habanero	*name for a fiery chili used in Campeche and Yucatán*	ah-bah-NEH-roh
harina	*flour*	ah-REE-nah
hoja santa	*Piper sanctum, a large leaf used in Southern Mexican cooking*	OH-hah-SAHN-tah
hongo	*mushroom*	HOHN-goh
huevo	*egg*	WEH-voh
huitlacoche	*a fungus that grows on corn*	wee-tlah-KOH-cheh
jaiba	*small, hard-shelled crab*	HAHY-bah
jalapeño	*name for a small fat green chili*	hah-lah-PEH-nyoh
jitomate	*tomato*	hee-toh-MAH-teh
[en]kabik	*from the Mayan, meaning "spicy broth"*	ehn KAH-beek
leche	*milk*	LEH-cheh
limón	*lime*	lee-MOHN
lolito	*small cake of tortilla dough, filled and then baked on a griddle, from Hidalgo*	loh-LEE-toh
maguey	*century plant, agave*	mah-GAY
maíz	*dried corn*	mah-EES
manitas	*pig's feet (lit., "small hands")*	mah-NEE-tahs
mano	*the muller for the grinding stone*	MAH-noh
masa	*dough of ground dried corn and water*	MAH-sah
metate	*flat, rectangular tripod of basalt used for grinding such things as corn and chilies*	meh-TAH-teh
mixiote	*parchmentlike skin stripped from the outside of the maguey leaf; also, name given to packages of meat cooked in the maguey "parchment"*	mee-see-OH-teh

molcajete	*mortar of basalt for grinding chilies and sauces*	mohl-kah-HEH-teh
mole	*concoction or mixture*	MOH-leh
mulato	*name given to a dark black-brown dried chili*	moo-LAH-toh
Náhuatl	*the* lingua franca *of the peoples of the central highlands of Mexico*	NAH-wahtl
naranja	*orange*	nah-RAHN-hah
negro	*black*	NEH-groh
nopal	*fleshy oval joint of the* Opuntia *cactus*	noh-PAHL
ojo	*name given to a circular Mexican pastry: flaky pastry around the outside and spongecake in the middle (lit., "eye")*	OH-hoh
olla	*round earthenware pot*	OH-yah
pan	*bread*	pahn
pan dulce	*sweet roll*	pahn DOOL-seh
panadería	*baking; bakery*	pah-nah-deh-REE-ah
papa-dzul	*a Yucatecan specialty*	pah-pah-DZOOL
pasilla	*name given to the dried* chilaca	pah-SEE-yah
pepita	*pumpkin seed*	peh-PEE-tah
perejil	*parsley*	peh-reh-HEEL
pescado	*fish*	pehs-KAH-thoh
pib, pibil	*Yucatecan pit barbecue; barbecued*	peeb, pee-BEEL
picadillo	*ground or shredded meat mixed with other ingredients and usually used as a stuffing*	pee-kah-DEE-yoh
picante	*hot, meaning "spicy"*	pee-CAHN-teh
piloncillo	*dark brown unrefined sugar, in the shape of a cone*	pee-lohn-SEE-yoh
pim	*round cake of tortilla dough and lard baked on a griddle*	peem

piña	pineapple	PEE-nyah
pipián	a sauce of ground nuts or seeds and spices	pee-PYAHN
plátano	banana	PLAH-tah-noh
plaza	market or central square	PLAH-sah
poblano	name for a large green chili (lit., "from Puebla")	poh-BLAH-noh
pollo	chicken	POH-yoh
porro	leek	POHR-roh
puerco	pork	PWEHR-koh
puesto	a stand in the market or on the street	PWEHS-toh
pulque	the fermented milky sap from the century plant	POOL-keh
quemar, quemado	to burn; burned	keh-MAHR, keh-MAH-thoh
queso	cheese	KEH-soh
rabo	tail or stalk	RAH-boh
raja	name given to a strip, usually of chili	RAH-jah
ranchero	country-style (lit., "of the ranch")	rahn-CHEH-roh
recado	seasoning (Yucatecan)	reh-KAH-thoh
refrito	well fried (lit., "refried")	reh-FREE-toh
relleno	stuffing	reh-YEH-noh
res	beef	rehs
rojo	red	ROH-hoh
rosca	cookie baked in the shape of a ring (lit., "ring")	ROHS-kah
sacahuil	large tamal wrapped in banana and palm leaves from the Sierra Huasteca	sah-cah-WEEL
sal	salt	sahl
salpicón	shredded or finely cut	sahl-pee-KOHN
salsa	sauce	SAHL-sah
saragalla	shredded seafood cooked with almonds, raisins, etc.	sah-rah-GAH-yah
seco	dry	SEH-koh

serrano	*name for a small green chili*	seh-RRAH-noh
sopa	*soup*	SOH-pah
sopes	*name given to little round antojitos of tortilla dough*	SOH-pehs
taco	*name given to a tortilla wrapped around a filling and sometimes fried*	TAH-koh
tamal	*a piece of dough (ground corn beaten with lard) steamed in a corn husk or banana leaf*	tah-MAHL
tejolote	*pestle for the molcajete*	teh-hoh-LOH-teh
tierra	*land or earth*	TYEH-rrah
tomate verde	*Mexican green tomato*	toh-MAH-teh BEHR-theh
torta	*a sandwich made with a round roll*	TOHR-tah
tortilla	*a thin, unleavened pancake of ground, dried maize*	tohr-TEE-yah
tostada	*a tortilla, fried crisp and garnished*	tohs-TAH-thah
totopos, tostaditas	*small, triangular pieces of crisp-fried tortilla*	toh-TOH-pohs, tohs-tah-THEE-tahs
trigo	*wheat*	TREE-goh
tuna	*the prickly pear, fruit of the nopal cactus*	TOO-nah
vapor, al vapor	*steam; steamed*	vah-POHR, ahl vah-POHR
verde	*green*	BEHR-theh
verdolagas	*purslane*	behr-thoh-LOH-gahs
vinagre	*vinegar*	bee-NAH-greh
Yucateco	*of the state of Yucatán*	yoo-kah-TEH-koh

Sources for Ingredients

The list that follows, which is in alphabetical order according to metropolitan area in the United States, followed by a listing for Canada, is not meant to be all inclusive. Supermarkets and specialty shops in all areas of the country are sure to have many of the ingredients necessary for Mexican cooking.

Albuquerque

Valley Distributing Co.
2819 2nd Street N.W.
Albuquerque, New Mexico 87107
A wide variety of dried chilies and Mexican ingredients; mail orders.

Atlanta

Rinconcito Latino
Ansley Square Mall
1492B Piedmont Avenue N.E.

Atlanta, Georgia 30309
(Tel: 912 874-3724)
Masa harina, dried chilies (limited variety), canned chilies, etc.

Boston area

Garcia Superette
367 Centre Avenue
Jamaica Plain
Boston, Massachusetts 02130
(Tel: 617 524-1521)
A wide selection of Mexican produce,

canned goods, dried chilies, and other ingredients; mail orders.

Stop and Shop
390 D Street
East Boston, Massachusetts 02228
(Tel: 617 463-7000)
A limited number of Mexican canned goods and some tropical produce.

India Tea & Spice Inc.
9-B Cushing Avenue
Cushing Square
Belmont, Massachusetts 02178
(Tel: 617 484–3737)
Some spices, dried chilies, fresh chilies, coriander, etc.; mail orders.

Star Market
625 Mt. Auburn Street
Cambridge, Massachusetts 02238
(Tel: 617 491–3000)
Some Mexican canned goods, some tropical produce.

Chicago

La Casa del Pueblo
1810 Blue Island
Chicago, Illinois 60608
A large Mexican supermarket stocking fresh and dried chilies among other ingredients.

Casa Esteiro
2719 West Division
Chicago, Illinois 60622
Dried and fresh chilies and many other Mexican ingredients.

Supermercado Maria Cárdenas
1714 West 18th Street
Chicago, Illinois 60608
(Tel: 312 666–2532)

There are many Mexican markets in this area, and it would be impossible to list them all. However, this is perhaps the most complete, carrying a large range of ingredients and fresh produce, tortillas, dried and fresh chilies, *nopales,* pumpkin seeds, peeled fava beans—and the *chicharrón* comes sizzling hot from the back of the store where it is prepared daily.

Claremont (California)

Many of the large supermarkets in this area carry a variety of Mexican ingredients, including corn and wheat-flour tortillas and fresh produce. Seville orange and banana trees are abundant for those interested in Yucatecan cooking.

Dallas

Horticultural Enterprises
P.O. Box 34082
Dallas, Texas, 75234
Seeds for chilies, *tomates verdes, epazote.*

Denver

Safeway Supermarket
2660 Federal Boulevard
Denver, Colorado 80219
A limited range of Mexican ingredients, including fresh green chilies (*serranos, jalapeños,* and *poblanos*), and *tomates verdes.*

The three stores below carry a variety of dried chilies, cooking equipment, dry and canned Mexican ingredients, and fresh produce.

Casa Herrera
2049 Larimer Street
Denver, Colorado 80205

Johnnie's Market
2030 Larimer Street
Denver, Colorado 80205
(Tel: 303 255–7085)

El Progreso
2282 Broadway (near corner Larimer)
Denver, Colorado 80205
(Tel: 303 623–0576)

Western Beef Co.
2048 Larimer Street
Denver, Colorado 80205
(Tel: 303 534–3880)
A limited range of Mexican ingredients,
dried chilies, and fresh produce.

Detroit

There are a number of Mexican supermarkets just over the Windsor Bridge
around Bagley Avenue.

Fresno (California)

Chihuahua Tortilleria
718 F Street
Fresno, California 93706

Houston

Rice Food Market
3700 Navigation Boulevard
Houston, Texas 77003
Fresh chilies and Mexican produce of all
types, some dried chilies (ancho, guajillo, mulato), Mexican dry and canned
goods.
   Most of the larger markets on Rice and
Weingarten carry fresh produce and
some Mexican ingredients. There are
many small Mexican groceries in the
Navigation Boulevard area, and these
carry a small selection.

Antone's Import Co.
807 Taft, 8111 South Main, 1639 South
Voss Road
Houston, Texas
Some dried chilies, canned goods, corn

husks, whole spices, etc., at all three
branches.

Los Angeles

El Mercado
First Avenue and Lorena
Los Angeles, California 90063
Many of the stands in this Mexican-like
open market sell Mexican canned goods,
fresh and dried chilies, and cooking utensils.

Central Market
Broadway (downtown)
Los Angeles, California
Large selection of very fresh Mexican
produce, cheeses, dried chilies, spices,
tortillas, etc.

Milwaukee

Casa Martinez
605 South 5th Street
Milwaukee, Wisconsin 53204
Chorizos, masa harina, añejo cheese,
dried chilies, some fresh chilies, Mexican
chocolate, etc.

Modesto (California)

Don Juan Foods
1715 Crows Landing Road
Modesto, California 95351

New York City and Vicinity

DOWNTOWN

Casa Moneo
210 West 14th Street
New York, New York 10014
(Tel: 212 929-1644)
Large variety of Mexican ingredients, in-
cluding canned goods, dried chilies,

chorizos, spices, and cooking equipment; mail orders. Casa Moneo now carries, year round, fresh *chiles serranos, jalapeños,* and *poblanos; tomates verdes;* coriander and banana leaves; *queso fresco; panela; chicharrón.*

MIDTOWN

Trinacria Importing Company
415 Third Avenue
New York, New York 10016
(Tel: 212 LE2-5567)
Mexican canned goods, fresh chilies on occasion, fresh coriander, spices.

H. Roth and Son
968 Second Avenue,
New York, New York 10022
(Tel: 212 RE4-1110)
Mexican canned chilies and *tomates verdes,* spices, etc. (For mail orders write H. Roth and Sons, 1577 First Avenue, New York, New York 10028.)

International Groceries and Meat Market (Tel: 212 BR9-5514)
529 Ninth Avenue (between 39th and 40th Streets)
New York, New York 10018
Apart from a very large range of Greek foods, they carry beans of many types, split dried fava beans, whole spices (including *achiote* seeds), various nuts, oils, etc.

UPTOWN (East)

La Marqueta
Park Avenue between 112th and 116th

Stand 499, at 114th Street. Almost always fresh green chilies from Mexico *(serranos* or *jalapeños).*

Stands 461 and 462 (between 114th and 115th Streets) Coriander and *chiles habaneros* all year round.

Stand 387½. Banana leaves, Seville oranges, coriander, tropical products.

Stand 372. Seville oranges.

UPTOWN (West)

Latin American Grocery
2585 Broadway
New York, New York 10025
(Tel: 212 MO6-0901)
Masa harina, canned chilies, fresh coriander.

Hummingbird Foods and Spices
2520 Broadway
New York, New York 10025
A large variety of spices from India, the Caribbean, etc. Fresh *chiles habaneros* (called Congo), *flor de Jamaica.*

BAY SHORE (LONG ISLAND)

Baja Tortilla Factory Ltd.
245 North Fehr Way
Bay Shore, New York 11734
(Tel: 516 242-0524)
Fresh tortillas and fresh *masa.*

Oakland

Mi Rancho
464 Seventh Street
Oakland, California 94607
A large selection of Mexican ingredients, fresh produce, tortillas, fresh *masa,* etc.

Oklahoma City

Mayphe's International Foods
7519 North May Avenue
Oklahoma City, Oklahoma 73116
(Tel: 405 848-2002)
A few Mexican ingredients. Will order.

Portland (Oregon)

Corno & Son
711 Southeast Union Avenue
Portland, Oregon 97214
Masa harina, some dried chilies, fresh
chilies, spices, etc.

Saint Louis

Soulard Market
Some fresh chilies and coriander, whole
spices.

900 Geyer Street
(Sr. Jesús Lagunas)
(Tel: 314 231-3036)
Masa harina, chiles anchos, tortilla
presses, canned Mexican goods, etc.

Saint Paul

Morgan's Mexican and Lebanese Foods
736 South Robert Street
St. Paul, Minnesota 55107
(Tel: 612 222-9124)
Fresh Mexican produce, including chilies, *nopales, tomates verdes, chayotes,*
and all basic ingredients, mail order.

Joseph's Food Market
736 Oakdale Avenue
St. Paul, Minnesota 55107
Various Mexican ingredients, homemade
chorizos, etc.

Salinas (California)

Sal-Rex Foods
258 Griffin Street
Salinas, California 93901

San Antonio

Frank Pizzini
202 Produce Row
San Antonio, Texas 78207
(Tel: 512 CA7-2082)

Dried chilies, spices, dried herbs; mail orders. The open market and the small produce stands on Produce Row can supply
fresh Mexican produce year round. The
larger supermarkets in the area carry
some produce and other Mexican ingredients, such as tortillas.

San Diego area

Several of the larger supermarkets and
some small markets, especially in the National Avenue area of San Diego, carry a
variety of Mexican canned goods, tortillas, fresh produce, etc., but it is across the
border in Tijuana where everything of
quality is available, especially around the
area of the main market (see below).

Woo Chee Chong
633 16th Street
San Diego, California 91001
(Tel: 714 233-6311)
This is one of the largest and most completely stocked supermarkets for Far
Eastern foods that I have come across.
They also carry some Mexican ingredients and produce, including *masa
harina,* spices, *achiote* seeds, *jícamas,*
coriander, *chicharrón, chiles serranos,
jalapeños,* and *caribes,* etc., etc.

El Indio Shop
3695 India Street
San Diego, California 92103
(Tel: 714 299-0333)
A limited range of Mexican ingredients,
dried chilies, tortillas, *masa* for tortillas,
cheeses, etc.

El Nopalito Tortilla Factory
560 Santa Fe Drive
Encinitas, California 92024
(Tel: 714 436-5775)

Main market (Revolución) Tiajuana, B.
C., Mexico for all Mexican ingredients
and produce.

Casa Magui, S.A.
Av. Constitución 932
Tijuana, B.C., Mexico
(Tel: 5-7086)
Yucatecan ingredients: fresh *chiles habaneros*, and *güeros (x-cat-ik)*, Seville oranges, *lima agria, achiote*, seasoning pastes, dried *epazote*.

Fruteria Jacaranda
Stand 90
Interior Mercado
Tijuana, B.C., Mexico
The widest selection of dried chilies, spices, *achiote*, dried seeds, *flor de Jamaica*, etc.

San Francisco

La Palma
2884 24th Street
San Francisco, California 94110
(Tel: 415 MI8-5500)
Fresh and dried chilies, fresh *tomates verdes*, canned goods, spices.

Mi Rancho Market
3365 20th Street
San Francisco, California 94110

Casa Lucas Market
2934 24th Street
San Francisco, California 94110
(Tel: 415 826-4334)
A large selection of Mexican ingredients, dried chilies, fresh produce, fresh *epazote* in season. Mail order.

Guatemala Imports
3403 Mission Avenue
San Francisco, California 94110
Banana leaves.

Santa Barbara

Villareal Market
728 East Haley Street
Santa Barbara, California 93101
(Tel: 904 963-2613)

An excellent selection of canned goods, *chorizos*, fresh and dried chilies, fresh tortillas, cooking utensils.

Santa Cruz Market
605 North Milpas Street
Santa Barbara, California 93101
An extensive variety of dried chilies, Mexican cheeses, and many other ingredients.

La Tolteca
614 East Haley Street
Santa Barbara, California 93101
Fresh *masa* and tortillas.

Santa Fe

Theo. Roybal Store
Rear 212, 214, 216 Galisteo Street
Santa Fe, New Mexico 87501
Herbs, cooking utensils, spices, many Mexican ingredients; mail orders.

Washington, D.C. area

Casa Peña
1636 17th Street N.W.
Washington, D.C. 20009
(Tel: 202 462-2222)
Achiote, canned *chiles chipotles* and *jalapeños*, dried chilies (*mulatos, anchos, pasillas*), *flor de Jamaica*, tortillas (including wheat-flour), sesame seeds, dried herbs, corn husks, *masa harina*, beans, fresh coriander, plantains, occasionally *chiles poblanos*.

Americana Grocery
1813 Columbia Road NW
Washington, D.C. 20009
(Tel: 202 265-7455)
Canned chilies (*chipotles, jalapeños, largos, güeros*), dried chilies (*anchos, guajillos, pasillas*), *nopales, masa harina*, beans, white hominy, plantains, *chayotes*, coriander. Occasionally fresh *jalapeños*.

Casa Lebrato
1729 Columbia Road 1731 N.W.
Washington, D.C.
(Tel: 202 234-0099)
Corn husks, *masa harina,* fresh plantains, coriander, canned chilies, and occasionally a limited supply of dried chilies.

Safeway
1747 Columbia Road N.W.
Washington, D.C. 20009
(Tel: 202 667-0774)
Fresh *tomates verdes, nopales,* tamarind pods, *chiles serranos, jalapeños,* and occasionally *poblanos.*

Arlington Bodega
6017 North Wilson Boulevard
Arlington, Virginia 22205
(Tel: 703 532-6849)
Masa harina, corn husks, Mexican *chorizos,* canned chilies, occasionally fresh *chiles jalapeños,* dried chilies *(guajillos, mulatos, anchos, pasillas),* spices, etc.

Bethesda Avenue Co-op
4937 Bethesda Avenue
Bethesda, Maryland 20014
(Tel: 301 986-0796)
Fresh coriander, plantains, *chayotes, masa harina,* corn husks, occasionally fresh chilies. Will be getting some Mexican cheeses, will order special ingredients.

Canada

TORONTO

El Capricho Español
312 College Street
Toronto, Canada
(Tel: 967-6582)
Masa harina, chorizos.

El Sol de España
College Street at Ossington
Toronto, Canada
Masa harina, chorizos.

Sanci Fruit Company
66 Kensington Avenue
Toronto, Canada
(Tel: 368-6541)
Masa harina, fresh chilies.

Home of the Gourmet
550 Yonge Street
Toronto, Canada
(Tel: 921-2823)
Frozen tortillas, miscellaneous chilies, *salsas, moles.*

New Portuguese Fish Store
Augusta Street
Toronto, Canada
Huachinango, pompano.

Dinah's Cupboard
9 Yorkville Avenue
Toronto, Canada
(Tel: 921-8112)
Mexican chocolate, spices.

Wong Yung's
187 Dundas Street West
Toronto, Canada
(Tel: 368-3555)
Fresh coriander.

OTTAWA

El Mexicano Food Products Ltd.
285-A St. Patrick Street
Ottawa, Ont. KIN 5K4, Canada
(Tel: 613 238-2391, 613 224-9870)
A large selection of dried and canned chilies, Mexican cheeses, and other basic ingredients. They also make and distribute tortillas.

Index

Codex Borbonicus, plate 23. Symbol of corn, represented as an offering in a fiesta of the first fruits.

Codex Borgia, plate 9. Ilama Tecutli, "the Old Goddess," seen here grinding corn on a *metate;* the symbolism of the *mano* exuding blood is complicated.

Codex Borgia, plate 63. Fertility symbol of corn, topped with a representation of pulque.

Codex Borgia, plate 52. Cinteotle, god of corn.

The decorations at the beginning of each chapter are bark-paper representations of plant spirits made by the Otomi Indians. These Indians, who inhabit the northern part of the state of Puebla, believe that the spirits protect the newly sown seeds and will produce good crops.

The illustration on the title page is a scene from the sixteenth-century *Florentine Codex,* which is part of Fray Bernardino de Sahagún's *Historia General de las Cosas de Nueva España.*